T0354796

The Path
of
The Three Great Quests

authorHOUSE®

AuthorHouse™
1663 Liberty Drive
Bloomington, IN 47403
www.authorhouse.com
Phone: 1 (800) 839-8640

Published by AuthorHouse   01/28/2016

ISBN: 978-1-5049-1105-4 (sc)
ISBN: 978-1-5049-1570-0 (e)
ISBN: 978-1-5049-1958-6 (hc)

Library of Congress Control Number: 2015908708

Print information available on the last page.

This book is printed on acid-free paper.

Liberty and justice for all

Chapters

Introduction

A Banquet of Vastness
The Journey of a Thousand Horizons
A Taste of The Fruit of Light

The Way of The Path

The Three Great Quests

The Chamber of Initiation

(The devotee' knelt to be initiated into discipleship.

The Guru whispered the sacred Mantra into his ear warning him not to reveal it to anyone.

"What will happen if I do?" Asked the devotee'.

The Guru responded, "Anyone you reveal the mantra to will be liberated from the bondage of ignorance and darkness of suffering, but you, you yourself will be excluded from discipleship and suffer damnation."

No sooner had he heard those words than the devotee' rushed to the marketplace, collected a large crowd around him, and repeated the sacred mantra for all to hear.

The other disciples later reported this to the Guru, and demanded that the student be expelled from the monastery for his disobedience.

But the Guru smiled and said, "He has no need of anything I can teach. His action has shown him to be a Guru in his own right.")

"Multiply The Light"

This is The Way of The Path

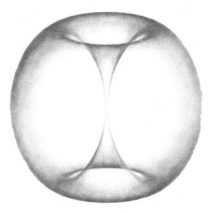

Architect of Truth

"I stand before the masters who witnessed the creation, who were with Ra that morning the Sun rolled into being, who were with Osiris in the grave as he gathered himself together and burst from the Tomb white with heat, a light and shining God. Hail Thoth, Architect of Truth. Give me words of Power that I may recall all my years and weave together my history. Hail Thoth, Architect of Truth. Give me words of Power that I may form the characters of my own evolution. I stand before the masters who witnessed the generations, who were the authors of their own forms, who rolled into being, who walked the dark circuitous passageways of their own becoming, who saw with their own eyes their destinies, and the shapes of things to come. I stand before the masters who witnessed the working of magic, who were with Isis the evening she became the swallow, and her lamentations filled the air, who were with her as she shook down her black hair and veiled the God's transformation in secret, who witnessed the conception of The Divine Child though his coming was yet unrevealed. Hail Thoth, Architect of Truth. Give me words of Power that when I speak the life of a man I may give his story meaning. I stand before the masters who know the histories of the dead, who decide what tails to hear again, who judge the books of lives as either full or empty. Who are themselves Authors of Truth.

And they are Isis and Osiris The Divine Intelligences. And when the story is written, and the end is good, and the soul of a man is perfected, with a shout they lift him into heaven. Hail Thoth! Architect of Truth! Give me words of Power that I may complete my story and begin life anew. I stand before the masters who witnessed the transformation of the body of a man into the body and spirit, who were witnesses to the resurrection when the corpse of Osiris entered the mountain, and the soul of Osiris walked out shining. He gathered his heel and his leg; he gathered his arms and his backbones. He gathered his dreams crackling inside the dark cave of his skull. He knitted himself together in secret. He came forth from death a shining thing, his face white with heat. (Material excerpted from the book "Awakening Osiris" © 1998 by Normandi Ellis, with permission from Red Wheel/Weiser LLC Newburryport Ma, and San Francisco Ca, www.redwheelweiser.com)

Introduction

A Banquet of Vastness

(Life is comprised of tastes. Books are like food, and while some folks prefer spicy books full of action and adventure, others favor more bland stories with safe and solemn endings. No antacids hidden in the bedside drawer required. But remember, some people buy the antacids because they prefer spicy foods, and that so much so they're willing to go to great lengths to enjoy their personal preferences.

If you try to convince someone who prefers bland foods that spicy foods taste better, not only will you will struggle mightily, but also you'll most likely be unsuccessful. Independent of how resiliently we cling onto our tastes and preferences they don't prove which flavor is better or worse, or even which book might be right or wrong. A person's pallet reveals who they are, and what they prefer. Like self-expression, personal preferences are insight to the flavors of our inner world more than they are insight to the value of the outer world.

As you sample this banquet of many disciplines, remember not to forget, there will be many aromas you'll like, while there will be other flavors you might think need a bit more--- or a lot less, spice. And this is wonderful! Because this book is a spice rack full of black pepper adventures and sweet cinnamon dreams that you get to pick and choose from to spice up your own banquets.

One day you'll find that you've taken a dash of wisdom from this section, a pinch of knowledge from that topic, and used it with the skill of a gourmet chef to make the banquet of your own ideas unique to your personal palate. You'll smile at how the mixture of these spices enhances the taste of the subjects you're already familiar with, and gives them that tang of zest that only adds to the flavor of what you already like. You might even come to wish that you had found this new and unique flavor quite a bit sooner.

Therein lays the true nature and wonder of verity, the intrinsic value of diversity, and the rapturous revelries of personal preference that cause us to cling to them so dearly. The multiplicity of the outer world does not take away from the preferences of our inner world. The Vastness of Variety enhances both the inner and outer world, by satisfying our preferences, and then adding a new gusto of flavor to all pallets. Vastness is what causes life, this book, and the never-ending choices of variety to be so magnificent.)

The Journey of a Thousand Horizons

(The Path of The Three Great Quests is a journey of a thousand horizons, a journey of vast perspectives. The student stands on the precipice of vastness staring teary eyed into the magnificence of a sparkling universe as it challenges their youth and inexperience to comprehend the immensities of such an eternal splendor. Having valiantly dove off the precipice of vastness, plunged headlong into the abyss below, and gleefully swam in the eternities of an ever diverse oceanic universe--- The master embraces seeing life with new eyes, he understands the wisdom of tranquility within the throes of a violent storm, and he realizes the illusive vastness that yet goes unseen. The difference in perspectives that lies between the student and master are not as important as the journey that lies between them.

A gulf of terminology, a barrier of experience, and an altitude of enlightenment separate the student and master's mutual knowledge. Therein lays The Journey of The Path and The Three Great Quests, which the master and the student must walk and achieve together. The greater meaning of the journey is to cultivate and polish The Way of The Path with sincerity and watchful care at every step along the way. In this way, the master and the student will be like a cloud that keeps absorbing water. Their bodies, minds, and spirits will billow and must eventually burst forth over a New Horizon of Truth and Greater Understanding. In these magnificent moments, when The Thunderbolt of Enlightenment flashes forth from the darkness of ignorance to illuminate The Light of Knowledge, their cups overflow with a euphoric serenity. Their mutual shift into a new paradigm becomes the gift of a vast banquet with new flavors yet to be savored. Their sweet cinnamon dreams have a new spice to sprinkle over their warm bread, their black pepper adventures have a new sauce to dip their freshly cooked meat in, and the student and the master have a common flavor that carries a mutual understanding.)

A Taste of The Fruit of Light

(The student is the garden of the master. The student's heart is full of fertile seeds just waiting to sprout. The lessons of the teacher are the soil in which the student's new awareness takes root. However, even the best Masters can impart only a fraction of the teaching. Thus, even though the teacher sits calmly with patience, shares The Light of Compassion with joy, and attends wisely their loan of an apprentice with the fidelity of honor--- It is only through the devotion, practice, and virtue of the student, that the dormant glory of their blossom springs valiantly from the mire, and the disciple comes to bear The Fruit of Light in this world.

The Fruit of Light is declared and decreed when individuals separated by a thousand years, ten thousand miles, or having never met one another have sought The Path from within, and yet they speak as One. They may describe it in different languages, they may use different labels, or they might express it with different disciplines. Yet, their different flavors of personal preference will carry the same efficacious spirit and aromatic zest. This spirit will be declared and decreed when others observe The Fire of Compassion sparkling in your eyes, before they know the light of insight that your eyes can see. When others recognize a New Horizon of Truth fused within your words, before they understand the vast meaning of your message. And, when others observe The Light of Virtue in The Path you walk, before they are wise to The Path you're following.)

(The Path of The Three Great Quests is to taste that which cannot be tasted, to touch that which cannot be felt, to hear that which cannot be heard, and catch a fleeting glimpse of that which cannot be seen. This is The Light of Knowledge and The Fruit of Awareness, which have a delicate but fleeting taste to them, which moves over the horizon of awareness very quickly. Like a rare and precious flower, which only blooms for a brief time under extraordinary conditions, it must be savored in the moment, and recorded for tomorrow---

"And it came to pass that a rich man paid a monk a large sum of money to paint the most exquisite portrait of a tiger ever. "Come back in six months," the monk requested. The rich man returned, but was politely turned away by another monk who said, "The Tiger is not yet finished." Again, many moons later, the rich man returned, but was politely told, "The Tiger is not done, please return again." A few months hence, the rich man was welcomed in, taken into a large hall full of meditating monks, and asked to sit on the large pillow and enjoy some warm tea while the others slowly fell into silence. The monk entered, bowed, and began an intricate dance. Spinning and pivoting, leaping and bounding, the monk painted the picture of the tiger in a dizzying array of dynamic flips, highflying kicks, and rapid blurry punches that appeared as if he was a tiger battling another tiger rather than an artist painting a tiger. Amazed at the display of such skill, talent, and so caught up in the rapturous revelries of the moment, the rich man never realized nearly 12 hours had passed before the monk concluded his dazzling dance in a sudden moment of stillness, solemnity, and a polite bow of silence.

The rich man immediately spoke up, "If you could do this all the while, why did I have to wait so long?" The monk smiled graciously and opened a nearby closet where hundreds of drawings of tigers fell out and scattered aimlessly across the floor. "The Tiger is Within," the monk calmly declared and decreed with the hint of a smile, "I had to learn how to see him inside of me before I could bring him out on my canvas."

---The Fruit of Awareness is The Illumination of The Fruit of Light, which reveals both The One Within, and The Journey of a Thousand Horizons. This has been a brief taste of that which cannot be tasted, a fleeting feeling of that which cannot be felt, a distant echo of that which cannot be heard, and a memorable glimpse of that which cannot be seen. You must savor its flavor in this moment, and remember how to share it with your students tomorrow.)

The Way of The Path

The Path is not far off
The One who seeks it
Has already found it

Dominion

If knowledge speaks and understanding listens
Then wisdom knows when to speak and when to listen

(As I look around our world today, it has become painfully apparent that our technology has surpassed our humanity, and we are unwittingly leaving our humanity behind in favor of that technology. But then I think of The Source Field and The Source from which it emanates, and my reasoning is rejuvenated with the hope that there will once again come an epoch for mankind when our humanity will catch up with our technology, and our technology will only be used humanely. This will be an era when The Source will once again be the origin of our humanity, and The Source Field will once again be the root of our technology. The Journey of The Path is a pilgrimage to reconnect with The Source, a banquet of ten thousand horizons, which molds our perspectives toward vastness. The Three Great Quests are the swinging hammer and sparking anvil of technology, which forges the new paradigms of tomorrow in the refining fires of The Chamber of Initiation. Three as One, they're a movement into a condition where the condition itself is the point, the reward, and transformative elixir of endless possibilities all rolled into one glorious package. They reincarnate us out of the ashes of yesterday, transform us in The Egg of Life of today, and vault us over a New Horizon into the full potential of The Phoenix of Tomorrow.)

The Dominion of Relativity

(In our day, the idea of relativity is considered a "methodology of thought": a manner of thinking which seeks to make individual points of view ambiguous, indefinite, or unclear, and thereby validate any point of view just by claiming, "It's all relative." with the dismissive wave of an apathetic hand. In this manner, the idea of relativity is used to cloud the knowledge between true and false, to skew the line between right and wrong, and turn a foundational observation into a foggy haze of corrupted knowledge that dilutes direction, confuses comprehension, and prevents perception. This modern day corruption of Relativity allows any point to be considered just as valid as another based on any fabricated point of view, no matter how outlandish its postulations may be. Moreover, it allows a sickness to infect our methods of reasoning, and brings us to a terminal illness where we can no longer decipher right from wrong, up from down, or north from south. Inevitably, individuals who follow this method of madness find themselves walking right into a snare, which they proclaim, "Doesn't exist! Because, I don't believe in 'that'." Yet, cliffs do not discriminate against the sighted or the blind.

Genuine Relativity is the recognition that information greatly affects our opinions, decisions, and therefore determines the personal perspective that we take on any subject. We recognize, when we take on a new point of view, we're modifying our reasoning. Not because the thing we're observing is changing, but because looking at something from multiple points of view creates a more complete picture. Altering perspectives provides us with preexisting information, which we didn't have before, and it's that more complete understanding that modifies our reasoning.

An example of Relativity: The first man is standing in a Berlin train station asking, "When will the train arrive?" The second man is standing in outer space looking down. The second man notes that the universe is inflating. The Milky Way is revolving with three other galaxies, and rotating on its axis. The sun is moving within the galaxy, and in relation to other nearby stars. The earth is revolving around the sun, and rotating on its axis. Thus, because the second man can see Berlin moving at an unbelievable rate of speed, while the train is merely creeping along the surface of the earth at a galactic snail's pace, he asks--- "What time will Berlin arrive at the train?"

In view of both men, a third person can see how both questions are equally valid. Whether looked at from the first or second person's point of view, both sound pertinent, because they remain physically congruent and intellectually cohesive. However, ambiguous relativity cannot exist for the third party, who possesses The Vastness of the more complete picture. Nor would the blind idiocracy of erroneous relativity exist for the first two men, if they exchanged points of view with the third person.

This example reveals great value in looking at something from many perspectives. This isn't because it implies the virtue of an open mind. Nor is it because this method satisfies the three principals of knowledge--- a justified, true, belief. And, it's most certainly not because it eliminates radical skepticism. It's because multiple perspectives tend to give us a more complete comprehension of what's really happening: the big picture. Moreover, when we use multiple perspectives to overlap *common points of data* from each storyline, we always attain a better foothold from which to reason with. Genuine Relativity is revelatory, not the creation of ambiguity. Genuine Relativity is that which unveils the unknown, but reveals that which has always been. Genuine Relativity dispels myopic points of view, and validates Vast points of view. Paramount to this, Vast Perspectives shift paradigms, and new paradigms shift realities.)

(Claiming pontifical proof via one's own methodology will never withstand the oppositional differences of others who possess the liberty to express different perspectives or unique ideas. While a scientist desires to measure the universe, an artist waxes philosophical, and marvels in the poetry of its beauty. While theologians kneel and pay homage to the higher power that created the universe, a warlord sets his sights on conquest. All boast their claim to the proof of correctness, the throne of righteousness, or the supreme authority of verification. Yet, no matter whose lens of perspective we look through, they equally bear the weight of ostracism by those who are not only absent the perspective of their discipline, but also by those who sing and dance, or pound and prance to the beat of their own drum.

If something is true in one discipline, it will be verifiable in another discipline, via the common doorways between each, or by ubiquitous expressions that are found in all disciplines. For instance, if geometry is "number in space", and music is "number in time", then the common validation between geometry and music is the doorway that "number" gives in the form of mathematical disciplines. Secondly, the concepts of "light and dark" and "opposing polarities" transcend disciplines, and don't require a "common doorway". It's just as easy to understand that a string on a violin that's too loose or too taunt is no different from a lover who's too passionate or too apathetic.

Like many rooms in the same house, common doorways between disciplines erase the illusion of their separateness. Ubiquitous expressions transcend the foreign tongue of each perspective. Both, join "that which is not seen as common" as One, and create a synergy greater than the sum of its parts. Thus, a clear case to prove any issue withstands the test of oppositional perspectives in those realms where the scientist, the artist, and the theologian embrace a common language and mutual understanding. This Realm lies in The Dominion of Relativity, its common doorways, ubiquitous expressions, and the paradigm shifting perspective of "The Paintbrush of Vastness".)

We don't observe the world as it is but as we are.
Everyone paints life with the paintbrush
of their own perspective.
The One who paints with The Paintbrush of Vastness
Is rewarded with the wonderment of its grandeur.

The Dominion of Light

(It's said "The only constant is change", but this just isn't so. A single molecule of oxygen may bond itself with earth, fire, wind, water, or wood to make it appear to transform into something else. Yet, no matter in what condition the molecule resides, or in what product it bonds to, the molecule that we label oxygen is still the same root element it has always been. Even if it should turn from solid, to liquid, or gas these alterations don't change what it is. The constant change we perceive is an illusory dance of the elemental world, which makes us perceive constant change, while it's actually functioning quite repetitively.

There's another illusion that's quite consistent, despite our perspective of its transformative nature. The swift movement of photons compels us to reason that light has transformed into darkness when the lights go out. However, there's a distinctive difference between how the light and darkness behave, as compared to the recombining elements. The light doesn't transform its root element with the darkness of the void in the same manner that the recombining elements alter their geometrical nesting orders to create new forms of the same product. True darkness, is absolute absence, and possesses nothing to mix with the light. On the other hand, light begins as a field of potential, collapses into a wave of emergence, and nests into an expression of photonic substance. It then reverses its flow, moves back into a wave, and expresses itself as a field once again. Unlike absolute absence, even when light moves out of our ability to perceive it, it still has a form of substance, even if that substance is spread out in a field of potentialities.

Because of these simple properties, one may take on the vast perspective that, one may never possess a flashlight that shines or emits darkness, and thereby block the light of day, in the same manner that a flashlight divides the darkness of the night. One true constant, the light determines cause and effect. As a field, wave, or photon, light possesses a universal dominion over the dark emptiness of the void. The void can never overshadow light, and darkness has no say in the issue. The darkness of the void is subservient to, and its dominion is determined by the presence or absence of light.)

(Dr. Moon's model of the elements relates the number of protons in a given element with a three dimensional Platonic Solid. These shapes can be placed inside of one another; or "nested", to equate the number of protons in an element with the number of corners of each nested Platonic shape. Oxygen has eight protons; this corresponds to the cube, which has eight points. Silicon has 14 protons; this quantity corresponds to the number of points of an octahedron nested in a cube, or a cube nested in an octahedron (« »). The entire periodic table of elements can be expressed in this manner, so as to relate all elements to geometrical mathematics, and thereby be translated into other disciplines.)

The Dominion of Intelligence

(In the same manner that physical constants cause the illusion of constant change while maintaining a circular consistency, so too there are nonphysical constants that seem to change, but are very consistent. From our perspective, time appears to be a constant, but time slows down in locations of greater mass, and accelerates where there's less mass. As the mass of an object increases it is said to deform the fabric of space to a greater degree. This distortion of space, in a spherical movement of increasing densities toward a central singularity, causes the object to collect mass at a greater rate of speed.

However, there is an inverse function to this cause and effect. As an object increases in size and mass its temperature increases as well. Both, agitate molecules, cause incoherence, and reduce quantum viscosity, which slows the speed $\{(R) = Rate\}$ at which time travels through or around a given object. The variable fluidity of time becomes a (function) of {density and degree of turbulence} that defines a localized condition of the continuum. This dual action between accelerating accretion and decelerating time coherence creates a balancing act between the elements of matter, the forces of time, and the manner in which our universe expresses itself.)

(One of the first laws of physics and thermodynamics is entropy. Entropy is the cause of chaos. Entropy is, "That which disassembles". The forward movement of time increases the amount of entropy within forces or elements. Our common doorway between science and other disciplines becomes a mathematical expression of the sentence below. However, unlike photons or time, entropy is not a particle, energy, force, or field. Entropy is more akin to the void of darkness caused by the absence of substance.

{Entropy + Rate of Time = Increasing Chaos}
{Entropy = Void}

Intelligence is, "That which assembles". Initially, Intelligence begins assembling by duplicating itself within forces, photons, energies, or elements. It always begins with a self-similar relationship building a 1 to 1 ratio. In other words, whatever Intelligence is building with, it constructs it again in the exact same manner as it did before, and it typically uses the same building blocks it was working with. This initial stage of intelligence expresses itself within the spin of torsion fields. Torsion fields may be thought of as {(eddies) = (spinning energy nested in water)}, {(tornados) = (spinning energy nested in air)}, or the repeating ladder of a {(double helix) = (the energy of intelligence (expressed in a photonic or wave condition), and imbued into the matter of amino acids that spins and replicates)}. In the same manner that an eddy of water or tornado of air are formed by the energy field that's moving them, so too DNA is shaped by the energy of the torsion field nested within the elements. The torsion field does not form around the DNA, the DNA forms around the torsion field.

Intelligence moves from the self-duplication of the 1 to 1 ratio to a 1 to 1.618 relationship known as Phi = (Φ). Once it has reached this stage, Intelligence assembles forces, photons, energies, and elements into peculiar geometries, which allow us to measure its presence, determine its degree of presence, or recognize an event of its absence. In the same manner that we reduced Entropy to an equation to find common doorways with other disciplines, and a common understanding with others who possess different perspectives, so too we can reduce Intelligence into a similar equation, as it relates to its function with the common variable of time.

{Intelligence + Rate of Time = Increasing Order}
{Intelligence = Light}

If we sat on a beach all afternoon we could watch the absence of entropy pull a sand castle apart. However, we wouldn't observe any effect of entropy on a plant sitting right next to that same sand castle. In the same manner that darkness takes over in the absence of light, so too entropy takes over in the absence of intelligence. Once The Light of Intelligence within our plant leaves, the void of entropy will step in, and the progression of time will pull apart its components.

In the same manner that light is the antithesis to the darkness of the void, so too The Light of Intelligence is the antithesis the emptiness of entropy. In the same manner that light is greater than the emptiness of the void, so too Intelligence is greater than the absence of entropy. In the same manner that light has dominion over the void, so too Intelligence has dominion over entropy. The knowledge of these ideas become quantifiable observations, whose vast perspectives simultaneously amplify both our scientific knowledge, and theological understanding of what constitutes the difference between life and death. Under the dominion of vastness of this new perspective, death is not so much the ending of a life, as much as it's the movement of intelligence out of that which it was nesting within, and over the horizon of our present perspective.

When we comprehend something from the paradigm of many disciplines, perspectives of vastness become quantifiable observations that amplify the meaning and significance of each point of knowledge.

This singular act renders an altogether new perspective of each discipline. The methodology of reasoning through the doorways of disciplines incontrovertibly demonstrates they are all spokes in the same wheel of greater understanding, all gears of the same machine with a common function, and all parts of a larger device that possess a greater purpose and more marvelous meaning.

{Light > Void} = {Intelligence > Entropy} = {Life > Death}
{Entropy + Rate of Time = Increasing Chaos}
{Intelligence + Rate of Time = Increasing Order}

)

The Two-Way Door of Dominion

(Dominion is that thing which we consider as having power, one thing over another. When we say that something has dominion, we're saying there's always something that causes one thing to possess some kind of power, authority, or root cause of effect, which gives it strength or control over something else. If something has dominion, it is that thing which influences, not that which is influenced.

As a scientific principal dominion is typically thought of in the elemental manner, such as the dominion of diamonds cutting softer elements. However, dominion speaks the language of theology and philosophy, just as easily as it pontificates esoterically and artistically. Therefore, dominion can be thought of in a non-substantive manner as well.

The dominion of {Light verses dark}, {time verses matter}, or {entropy verses Intelligence} can be expanded into greater vastness, and contemplated in a more intellectual manner. Such as, the dominion of "The Light of Knowledge" over the darkness of ignorance, or the dominion of the, "Ah Ha!" moment of inspiration over a stupor of thought. In the same manner that the presence of light has dominion over darkness, so too the presence of knowledge possesses dominion over ignorance. In the same manner that Intelligence has dominion over entropy, so too inspiration dispels the disparity of a stupor of thought. Not all of this is something that is substantive in mass, observable in force, or provable with energy after the scientific method, yet it is something that is philosophically repeatable, and scholastically verifiable. Moreover, like raw math, dominion retains the unique value of being transitive through all disciplines. Adopting this perspective moves the student's understanding of dominion toward vastness, and a greater meaning of each spoke in the wheel of the larger machine.

Dominion can be thought of in reverse, as in the dominion that occurs in the *absence* of that thing which possesses dominion. In the same manner that the absence of light gives dominion to darkness, so too the absence of knowledge surrenders dominion to ignorance, and the absence of Intelligence surrenders dominion to entropy. In the absence of light and knowledge, both darkness and ignorance possess their own form of dominion over everything within their realm.

{Knowledge > Ignorance}
{Knowledge has dominion over ignorance}
{Darkness = Entropy = Absence = Ignorance = Suffering}

As Euclid would stipulate, two things that are equal to a third thing, are also equal to one another. Ignorance is the most loathsome of all diseases, for it's the absence of entropy of the mind, and the root of all suffering.

What does life look like in the absence of the dominion of electricity? There would be no computers, no televisions, no radios, no telephones, no telegraphs, and certainly no lights as we think of them in the form of light bulbs. Without the current of electricity, not only would we lose many of the benefits that our technologies provide, but we would also suffer greatly due to their absence. Many time saving labors would be laid squarely on our couch potato backs. People who are the keepers of knowledge will perish in greater numbers, because of the inability to manufacture and distribute goods and services, which create favorable living conditions, and provide basic common needs. We immediately lose a hundred years of advancement; which has really been the crutch that the dominion of electricity and petroleum products has held us up with, and we go back to a way of life well before the 19th century.

What does life look like in the absence of fire? There are no combustion engines of any kind. There's no way to cook the bugs out of our food or water. There's no way to forge metals, and create larger contraptions, which would allow us to forage for greater resources. Suddenly, we're back to scavenging for what we can see with our eyes, throwing spears at large beasts that carry off little children, and subsisting off aquatic resources with all the nightmares of a vast uncharted ocean.

Even an agrarian society, which has been the backbone of humanity for the last 5,000 years, is no longer possible in the absence of fire. Those who would be the keepers of The Light of Knowledge, can no longer spend their time creating repositories of information, whose Light can be called upon to improve everyone's daily situations. Under the dominion of the absence of electricity and fire these Gnostics live rough and tumble lives, they die young, and they take most of their education with them. Moreover, humanity is left in a kind of ignorant darkness that is unable to move beyond the dim light of a few basic lessons provided by a brief life of subsistence.

In the same manner that the presence of these powers possesses the dominion to take us from the Proverbial Stone Age to what we call the modern world, so too we recognize the dominion of their absence to force even the best of us back into the darkness of ignorance and the bondage of suffering. We also recognize that with the addition of each of these powers, there comes a different appearance to what our societies look like, what values they embrace, and what ethics they live by. Moreover, it governs what they are, or are not capable of conceiving of, or giving birth to.

As Euclid would stipulate, two things that are equal to a third thing, are also equal to one another. The Two Way Door of Dominion would stipulate that if one direction is True the inverse property must be equally True; wherein we subtract something from one item, which in turn carries a domino effect that affects the balance and harmony of the other two related items. "In the same manner that the addition of one thing to another inevitably leads to the addition of a third thing to both, so too the absence of one thing from another inevitably leads to the absence of a third thing to all." While this specific thought is not among Euclid's Common Notions; we can see how this Common Notion is a transitive notion through all disciplines.)

A New Horizon of Dominion

(The Minoans designed a vast empire that circumnavigated the globe almost 5,000 years before the birth of The British Empire, which accomplished an equivalent task. We now know that the Minoan Empire brought silk from the orient to Egypt, and that they brought dog-sized mammoths from the isolated southern islands of Kamchatka to the Pharos of Egypt. Because of the vastness of their oceanic travels, and the lack of seamanship accredited to the Sumerians, we can theorize with a high degree of confidence that it was the Minoans, or Sumerians aboard Minoan vessels, who brought the Sexagesimal based cuneiform Sumerian Fuente Magna Bowl from what is modern day Turkey/Iraq, all the way to Mezzo America where archeologists recently unearthed it.

Found at the bottom of The Aegean Sea in 1900-1901 A.D., The Antikythera Mechanism is thought to be an astronomical and distance calculator that was built with the acute specifications of a Swiss watch of the 19th century. Based on the coral structures growing on it, the Antikythera Mechanism is believed to have been constructed sometime between the age of Alexander The Great (325 B.C.) and the first century B.C. However, this method of dating doesn't account for how long it might have been around before it was deposited in the sea. Nor does this dating account for the advanced knowledge and understanding it took to construct such a device, especially during a time when historians say that Europeans were little more than equestrian goat herders.

{195,955,200,000,000}

Sumerian texts say the Nineveh Number; The Master Number that governs all galactic cycles, was given to them by the Annunaki. According to our current historical records, the Sumerian civilization was supposed to be humanity's first real civilization. So, how would they know anything about an astronomical number that governs all galactic cycles? Annunaki means, "Those who came from the sky". This begs the question as to who these life forms were, or if they were the builders of the "Astronomical and distance calculator".

Like the gulf of terminology, barrier of experience, and altitude of enlightenment that separate the student and master's mutual knowledge, the divide between the question and the answer is not more important than the journey of discovery that happens between them. According to our current interpretation of history, finding the Antikythera Mechanism and thinking that the Nineveh Number made its first appearance during man's first culture, are the equivalents of a caveman finding the yardstick of the universe and a modern computer outside the opening of his cave one random morning. The dominion of this Light of Knowledge poses some paradigm changing questions that must be asked, it points the direction to a journey that must be taken, and a maturity into the condition of a Vast Understanding that must be achieved.

The Sexagesimal rhythms of the three corresponding rings of The Mayan Calendar calculating labeling systems correlate to the I-Ching patters of 64, as well as the sprocket numerology of the Antikythera Mechanism, as well as the numerology for The Great Year embedded in The Great Pyramid of Egypt, which is also interrelated to the Nineveh Number. However, the I-Ching is supposed to be from Asia, the Antikythera Mechanism is thought to be Hellenistic, The Mayan Calendar is considered South and Central American, and The Great Pyramid is thought to be Egyptian (R1b1). These are cultures, who until recently, were thought of as not having been in communication with one another whatsoever. Yet, all of these designs function off the same inter-related numerical mechanisms, and their designs reveal a common emergent numerology, which were held as theologically sacred, and scientifically imbedded into what each culture fabricated. Here we see science and theology, each discipline moving through the maturity of their own storylines, and each storyline unique to a culture, but all possessing transitive common denominators, common notions, and a two-way door of dominion.

The Dominion of this new information *"of that which has always been"* is causing us to take on new perspectives, and shift into new paradigms as to what constitutes the genuine origins of our deep past. One perspective it's creating is that humanity is far older than we think we are, and the universe is far more divine than we think it is. Another perspective is the undeniable knowledge that mankind has attained to worldwide empires, and been in possession of great technologies even in our deepest past. We see correlations emerge from the darkness of what has failed to be passed down, staring back at us with some very complex and interrelated disciplines, which allowed the ancients to do things that we just cannot seem to replicate today.

So, "Why are we 'just now' uncovering all of these correlations in the last 30 to 40 years?" "Why do societies continue to give birth to great intellect, and why does that intellect continue to die back out?" "Why do we move from scratching a living out of the dirt, to great empires, only to fall back into scratching a living out of the dirt?" To answer those questions we only need to accept the perspectives revealed by our initial premise. In the same manner that the presence of something can create dominion, so too the absence of something can create another kind of dominion. In the same manner that the addition of one thing to another inevitably leads to the addition of a third thing to both, so too the absence of one thing from another inevitably leads to the absence of a third thing to all. Just as the light possesses dominion over darkness, so too the lack of light can create a dominion of darkness. Just as the use of fire and electricity can move us to city life, so too the ignorance of their use can put us back in the fields, forests, or caves. Just as the presence of knowledge can divide the darkness of ignorance, so too the void of ignorance can compel one into entirely different lifestyles with vastly divergent ethics, values, and focus of daily tasks. Even going so far as to cause us to forget ourselves entirely, and return us to a form of savagery we currently think ourselves to be incapable of; a savagery we're slowly emerging from--- again. In the absence of The Light of Knowledge, the darkness of ignorance possesses the dominion to breed the angst of anger, to fund the ferment of fear, and expand the agitation of aggression, such that it dominates and controls everything.

These patterns of dirt to empire, and empire to dirt... These patterns of The Two-Way Door of Dominion... They all reveal that humanity has, not so much moved into the dominion of the void of ignorance, but have moved in and out of the dominion of The Light of Knowledge... These "two-way" patterns also reveal that we're still emerging from a kind of psychological and physiological darkness, which we're becoming more and more conscious of as the light of ancient knowledge continues to illuminate the perspective of our modern awareness, and transform it into a new paradigm of Vastness Understanding.)

(Now that we can see dominion through the perspective of the two-way door of the presence or absence of powers that affect the physical, the ethereal, and or the intellectual realms in a beneficial or detrimental direction, let us ask ourselves a very important question.

"Is there yet another power, greater than fire and electricity, which we're not presently harnessing?" Are we living in the dark ages of fire, and the squalor of electricity, because of the absence of another form of energy that we're failing to recognize, and efficiently harness? Is there another Force, which possesses the dominion to advance us as far as fire took us from the caves, and as far as electricity took us from Rome?

In the simplest terms and the most convenient definitions, the answer is an emphatic and euphoric, Yes! There exists an energy, a condition of being, a "Field of Power" that the ancients were well aware of. The Quest to attain and harness such a thing would be "A Pearl of Great Price"; something so intrinsically valuable that its worth would exceed every other lifelong endeavor. Like The Quest for The Holy Grail, "Only the worthy will find it." For it's not an item that greed's lust can pilfer. It's The Way of The Path that must be walked. It's a Trivium and Quadrivium of Polymath Disciplines that must be earned. It's The Quest that must be understood, a choice that must be embraced, and an absent Chamber that must be entered. It is about a journey that refines every ounce of our being, and transforms us from top to bottom. It illuminates us with The Light of Virtue, it invigorates us with The Intelligence of Truth, and it warms us with The Fire of Compassion. It gives meaning to the meaningless, reveals the invisible, makes tangible the ethereal, and bestows value to the useless.)

Virtue

I have been all things unholy
If God can work through me
He can work through anyone
Saint Francis

The Light of Compassion

(Although the prophets, gurus, and masters call it by many names, and think of it in many manners, Virtue is One Light, Virtue is One Power... In the same manner that there are Three Virtues embraced in Christianity--- "Faith, Love, and Charity", so too there are Three Virtues embraced in Japan--- "Truth, Courage, and Compassion". The Three Jewels of The Tao are "Compassion, Moderation, and Humility"; while in the Hindu traditions Daya (Compassion) is coupled with the two central Virtues of Charity and Self-Control. For Buddhism and Jainism, Karunā (Sanskrit; Pāli) is Compassion or Pity. The Three Virtues of Islam can best be expressed in their description of Allah (سبحانه و تعالى), in the declaration of The Basmala, "In the name of God, the most Gracious, and Merciful". While the Hebrew tradition speaks of Virtue as the 13 attributes of God's Compassion. God is "The Compassionate One", and is invoked as "The Father of Compassion" in His 13 forms of Compassionate work. Hence, Rah'mana, or "Compassionate One", becomes the designation for His revealed word, and the reason behind all of His thoughts and actions.

Derived from the notion that everyone counts, Compassion or Charity; also known as Mercy or Benevolence, is foundational to the highest principles of judicial, philosophical, and theological ideologies. Everyone counts, because every intelligence possesses the intrinsic value of The Self (The Spirit, Atman, or Life Force). Compassion is central to Virtue, in which the emotional capacity of empathy for the suffering of others is regarded as a part of The Transformative Energy of The Universal Love of Altruism. Compassion is considered a cornerstone to all beginnings, as well as a keystone to all completions, for a greater Collective Interconnection of Oneness of all things (∞).)

(Do you remember the story about the Prophet and the Jew? Every day the Jew would pass the Prophet's house and throw garbage. One day, the Jew didn't come, and the Prophet wondered where he was. When the Prophet learned the Jew was sick he went to make sure he was ok--- This is The Virtue of a Muslim.

Do you remember the story about the Dali Lama's mother and the invading Chinese? The Chinese killed many Tibetans. The Chinese sacked their country claiming its land and wealth for themselves. One day, a famine stricken Chinese family showed up on the mother's doorstep, and she gave the entire contents of her pantry to them to make sure they were ok--- This is The Virtue of a Tibetan.

Do you remember the story about The Child of Light and The Child of Darkness? Every day The Child of Darkness did something to harm The Child of Light. One day, something bad happened to The Child of Darkness, and The Child of Light went to illuminate The Child of Darkness to make sure they were ok--- This is The Virtue of The Children of The Light.)

(Genuine Virtue is that nourishment, which fills the emptiness of our hearts... Virtue is that fire, which evaporates the oceans of our tears... Virtue is that water that extinguishes the fire of venom in our veins...

Genuine Virtue is that Power, which ignites our motivations... Virtue is that light, which illuminates the darkness of the abyss... Virtue is that beacon of hope that shines a light in the dark storm of an uncertain night...

Genuine Virtue is that healing elixir, which cures the sickness... Virtue is the inoculation, which thwarts the poison... Virtue is the band-aid that allows injuries to heal, and the scars of tribulation to fade...

This is The Way of The Path...)

A New Horizon of Virtue

(In the Christian understanding, the vice of jealousy is the emotional desire to possess what others have. In the Islamic or Semitic understanding, jealousy is the desire to destroy what others have, not so you'll have more and suffer less, but so they'll possess less and suffer more. In the Christian since, if one were to steal "The Light of Compassion", in the same manner that one steals a car, at least someone could still have that thing which possessed value, and both the thief and others could yet potentially benefit from its use. However, this second form--- Extinguishing The Light of Compassion, rather than just taking it--- is far more detrimental than the first. In the same manner that blowing out the last candle in a room puts everyone in total darkness, so too this second form of greed becomes a greater social betrayal, because it leaves everyone subject to the dominion of darkness.

Those who reside in the darkness of ignorance reason that by taking or destroying what others possess, that they will alleviate or remove their personal suffering. To one degree of understanding, this is true. By taking or demolishing what others possess the emotion of jealousy does appear to subside. At least until they see someone else who has what they want, or possesses that thing which they don't want them to have. Then, as reliable as the sunset brings darkness, the emotion resurfaces, and the dark vice of jealousy swells to midnight proportions. If the dominion of this path attained a universal expression, it would produce a world where everyone suffered equally in the bondage of vice, the prison of ignorance, and would be equal subjects of the dominion of the void.

Eventually, one must step out of the darkness of ignorance, and into the dominion of The Light of Knowledge. One must eventually learn that one can never become poor enough to help the poorest souls, without becoming a liability to their loved ones. One must understand that one cannot become sick enough to heal the afflicted, without becoming a casualty. In addition, one must attain the wisdom that one cannot sow the seeds of greed and jealousy, and yet bring the abundance of light and wealth of knowledge where there exists the famine of darkness, the poverty of empty hands, and the foolishness of hollow minds.

The Mullah does not extinguish one Light in order to ignite another Light. The Path of The Mullah ignites The Fire of Knowledge within those who reside in the darkness of ignorance. The Guru does not struggle against one individual to liberate the captive from their oppression. The Path of The Guru brings The Light of Virtue where there is the darkness of vice; this liberates both the captive and captor. The Prophet does not destroy one Child in order to Enlighten another Child. The Path of The Prophet brings The Message of God: The Light of Compassion, to awaken all who slumber in the bondage of ignorance, the suffering of vice, and the irrational reasoning of affliction.

One does not attain Virtue by surrendering to others what one possesses. Neither does one destroy what one possesses, so others will not feel jealousy or greed. Rather, one cultivates The Flame of Virtue within, they nurture and mature that flame into a fire that can be seen from afar. Then they share that Light in the same manner that one candle multiplies its flame with another.

---This is The Path of The Masters.

In the same manner that light and knowledge have dominion over darkness and ignorance, so too The Light of Virtue possess dominion over the darkness of anger, fear, and aggression. Just as darkness and ignorance possess dominion in the absence of light and knowledge, so too anger, fear, and aggression possess their own dominion in the absence of Virtue. To do away with darkness, we must pick up, and embrace the light. To do away with ignorance, we must pick up, and multiply knowledge. To do away with anger, fear, and aggression, we must pick up the light, multiply knowledge, and proliferate The Virtue of Compassion.

The Paths of Virtue, Truth, and Compassion are more about the miracle of multiplying bread and fish, than the moral code of surrendering a coat because you have two. When one realizes, there is no limit to multiplying knowledge… When one understands, there is no ending to the resource of Virtue… Moreover, when one awakens to the wisdom that there is no personal loss when multiplying Light, Virtue, or Knowledge… Then one realizes that the answers to our dilemmas have less to do with the allocation of limited resources, and more to do with multiplying things that cause the two-way door of dominion to swing in a favorable direction for one and all (Page 16, Common Notions).

In the same manner that one doesn't so much as remove darkness, as turn on the lights, so too one doesn't so much as remove *anger*, as practice Virtue. One doesn't so much as remove fear, as exercise Truth. One doesn't so much as remove *aggression, as* demonstrate Love. One doesn't so much as begin The Path out of the dark side, as much begin The Path toward The Light. To practice The Way of The Path, calm your body, mind, and spirit. Cleanse yourself of malice and evil desires by replacing them with The Light of Compassion, warm feelings of Virtuous behaviors, and by speaking great, noble, and eternal Truths. Your spirit will be free when you declare The New Horizon of Truth, with The Fire of Compassion sparkling in your eyes, and The Light of Virtue cultivated in your heart. Remember not to forget, even the smallest flicker of Light is enough to show you the way out of a dark room.)

The Way of Virtue

Villainy wears many masks
But none more deceptive than virtue
Johnny Depp

(While it's not the writer's job to give into hopelessness, no one can tell writers not to discuss despair. For, the paintbrush of creativity requires the darkness of despair to be so black, to make the light of hope shine so brightly. In the same manner that the righteous hero requires a villainous scoundrel, so he may reveal his valiance, so too the despair of yesterday needs to be so wrong, so the golden path into tomorrow can be made so right.

It's the writer's job to find greater meaning in suffering, greater light in darkness, to locate that last ounce of hope in the wasteland of absolute hopelessness. It's the writer's job to be patient, to come up with the right words, and prove beyond the shadow of a doubt that--- truth persists in the midst of lies, compassion persists in the midst of rage, life persists in the midst of death, and light persists in the midst of darkness.

It is the writer's job to find a better way. Not just transcend their audience into the panacea of a new world, but to lay out a golden path, which guides both the hero and villain alike into that bright new tomorrow. The writer's job is to use their paintbrush of creativity to prove beyond the shadow of a doubt that light, hope, and that magical "something", which allows us to overcome all odds, was always with us from beginning to end. On this Path, that special quality is Virtue.)

(At the beginning of any journey, The Path we should take isn't always so clear. Unlike something more obvious or blatantly wrong, which could be easily spotted for what it is, the use of that which appears to be genuine is oft employed to beguile others into following the wrong path. The mirrored illusion of virtue is a treacherous path, because it's a reflection of the original, a facsimile, a copy. Like counterfeit money, it's commonly mistaken for the genuine article, and is either willfully or mistakenly circulated about posing as the original.

For instance, in any given story, men tend to lie to make themselves the victor, while women tend to lie to make themselves the victim. Thus, we take each person's narrative of an event with a measure of indecision, especially wherein heroism for men, or victimization for women are concerned. We hesitate, not so much because their story may be an outright lie or contain exaggerations, but because it's masculine heroism and feminine victimization that yanks at our moral compass. A man loves to rescue a damsel in distress, because it makes him feel strong and powerful; a masculine imperative. In the same emotionally charged manner, women love to hear about a man's heroism, because it makes them feel safe and secure; a feminine imperative. If either of these fibs are counterfeits, the man might be rescuing a manipulative Jezebel, and the woman might be falling asleep in the arms of a predator.

These false virtues wreak havoc on our logic; they manipulate our compassions, and pluck on our heartstrings to get us to support something that's erroneous, or worse; something that's self-inducing. They make us think there's an empty space, to get us to follow their ways, and fill a vacuum that's nonexistent. They tell us we're inadequate, so we might do what they say to become adequate, and repair something that isn't broken. These kinds of counterfeit paths can initially seem to be virtuous, but they lead into other paths whose karma is linked to anger, fear, and aggression.

This kind of virtue is like looking at something in a mirror. It may appear as the genuine article at first, it might even strike one as "The thing to do at the time". Moreover, it will play havoc on your reasoning and draw you in like bait on a hook. However, as time passes, one will be forced to take a closer look to observe the subtle inconsistencies that makes one question its authenticity. Should the student not heed the warning signs, and elect to continue to follow this path, they will come to observe unnecessary aggression getting the better of otherwise good and decent people, because "things" don't seem to be going as expected. As events progress further, one will come to observe the dominion of anger, fear, and aggression multiplying into atrocities. They will be committed in the name of personal survival, or in the name of restoring the original cause. When the facsimile of virtue is subjected to the test of fire, and the trials of time judge its power, it will always be seen to warp into the vice that it truly originated as.)

(Opposing those who practice the dark dominion of vice with replies of righteous anger, justified fear, or defensive aggression in response to their wrongdoing, multiplies the vice of antagonism, it doesn't attain, nor multiply The Light of Virtue. This isn't because it moves against someone who needs to be quarantined, so as not to poison others with their affliction of irrational reasoning, or the destructive poison of their ego-induced aggression. One shouldn't follow these other paths, because an Anti course of action tends to diminish or extinguish one's own Flame of Virtue. Thus, it is by removing one's own force and power of dominion over darkness, that one prevents it's Power from being multiplied.

After all, when one hates Mr. Scrooge for being a "scrooge", one's own anger, fear, and aggression only serves to reinforce, and even justify, their heartless actions toward the suffering of those who will not Love, or even care about them anyway. It's very difficult to harm someone who genuinely loves you. Moreover, it is near impossible to harm someone that you genuinely love. This is why, in the story "A Christmas Carol", Mr. Scrooge's nephew shows Mr. Scrooge undeserved kindness, longsuffering patience, and generous understanding no matter how hateful or scornful Mr. Scrooge is. The nephew maintains his own Light of Virtue by maintaining Compassion for all, deserving or not, and shining it wherever he goes.

By the end of the story, it is the cumulative contrasts of Compassion and hate of many souls in his past, present, and future (Δ) that sparks The Light of Compassion in Mr. Scrooge's heart. He then goes about nurturing the flame of this new fire with loving thoughts, kind words, and good deeds in the name of his, and everyone else's, welfare. Like living in a room where everyone's candle of Compassion is lit, one cannot help but want to join in, and light their candle of Compassion as well.)

(In the same manner that The Light is multiplied by those who elect to embrace and practice The Light, so too anger, fear, and aggression is multiplied by those who elect to embrace anger, spread fear, and extinguish other's Light of Compassion with unchecked aggression. We must learn to interrupt that cycle within ourselves, by cultivating Virtue and Compassion in our meditations and prayers. Then, we'll have plenty of it on tap, so we might multiply it with others when we see they are--- Not so much under the dominion of darkness, or sick with irrational reasoning, ---but living without The Dominion of Light... After all, The Way of The Path is about illuminating hearts and awakening minds, not condemning others for weaknesses we all possess.

Our choice to embrace The Path of Virtue will give us the patience to come up with the words that will transform minds. Our Truths will reveal the irrational reasoning, by showing The Light of a better Path. In addition, our Compassion will demonstrate that life persists in the midst of death, truth persists in the midst of lies, and light persists in the midst of darkness. For none are more enslaved to ignorance, than those bound with a knowledge, which possesses no Virtue. None are more ensnared by the darkness of vice, than those who follow an understanding that possesses no Truth. And, none are more plagued by suffering, than those who are confounded by a wisdom, which possesses no Compassion. If King Solomon asked God for wisdom, knowledge, and understanding, then The Student of The Path asks The Source for Virtuous Knowledge, True Understanding, and Wise Compassion.

The Mystic Virtue comes from cultivating warm heartedness within yourself, and then with others. This may take the form of speaking, reading, or sharing The Great and Noble Truths. This may take the form of living a Virtuous life--- nurturing, encouraging, teaching, and mentoring those around you without dominating, gloating, or possessing. This may take the form of Cultivating Compassion within, bringing yourself into an emotional condition of Compassion, and then spreading The Light of Compassion into Vastness. The Mystic Virtue comes from that place where

Virtuous Knowledge, True Understanding, and Wise Compassion are represented as three circles overlapping one another forming a middle singularity...)

Being off The Path is not about failure
It's about the choice to get back on
And the willingness to take the next step

The Dominion of Virtue

(As a planet, we're emerging from a kind of psychological darkness. An ignorance of the past that our history books try to explain, but in whose descriptions are woefully absent of some of the more recent "eye opening" archeological findings--- and their vast implications. As archeologists uncover one ancient relic after another, the history of humanity is pushed further back than many of us are comfortable with. In our current condition, we think this threatens our paradigm, disproves our theologies, subverts our governments, or otherwise harms "The ways of our people". So we shut down, we psychologically disconnect, or otherwise ignore the new information, and carry on with our traditions. Somehow, we think that keeping our heads out of the ground, or our noses out of "those" books gives us familiarity, therefore stability, which equates to safety, and morality. Right?

Maybe this is one reason why all these relics are buried in the first place. Perhaps we're not digging up the things that the sands of time have buried, as much as we're digging up what our ancestors intentionally buried, because they too couldn't bear the weight of the relic's implications. If this is so, and if we elect to do as they did, then the old sayings will be true forever--- "He who forgets the past is doomed to repeat the same mistakes of the past". "Those of us, who are enlightened before the others, are fated to pursue that light in spite of others." Thus, relegating mankind to a constant cycle of digging and burying, and nations rising and falling. However, in the same manner that light removes the dominion of darkness, so too The Light of Virtue removes the darkness of these proverbs. The Mystic Virtue is about recognizing the past, and using the dominion of our gift of Virtuous Knowledge, True Understanding, and Wise

Compassion to change the verdict of the past by using their power to forge a bright new future.)

(The Mystic Power we seek, which possesses far more dominion than fire and electricity, makes its first appearance in The Light of Virtue. Pure Virtuous Consciousness, without any trappings of materialism, labels of social order, or the need for equipment to complete a task. The personal choice to connect with, think on, and multiply The Light of Virtue is our first step to creating miracles everywhere we turn our attention. Do you remember The Arthurian Legend? Lancelot "The Invincible" was defeated by his own desires for Lady Guinevere. While Percival "The Virtuous", was the only one worthy to find the Grail. Percival had a Mystical Quality that Lancelot didn't.

Virtue begins as a set of moral guideposts with which to attain direction for one's daily decisions. Virtue grows into a means of internal guidance. Eventually, Virtue becomes a Power that creates a field of influence, a field of dominion (Δ), which directs and defends one's connections, thoughts, and actions toward a Life Path lived in accord with Divine Providence.

As the cultivation of Virtue within one's prayers and meditations allows Virtue to mature inside an individual, one will note that The Light of Virtue reveals the knowledge to discern The Light from the void. The Power of Virtue gives one the understanding of internal guidance. The Inspiration of Virtue gives one the wisdom to remain tranquil within the storms of life. The Enlightenment of Virtue gives one the transitory ability to observe that which is invisible, to sense that which is illusive, and experience that which is over the horizon of the human perception. This is because The Elixir of Virtue has no limit to how often it can be nurtured, multiplied, or shared with others. Thus, The Secret of Virtue becomes cultivating it within, so you might multiply it with others to create The Vastness of Virtue, a multiplicity of Virtue that travels through time and space to become untouchable by those who would extinguish it. Although this maturity doesn't happen overnight, the spark of discernment at each level of understanding occurs in the twinkling of an eye.)

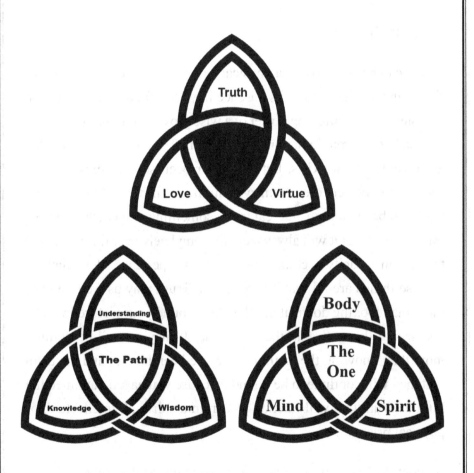

Truth

What is Truth?

(Truth can be as simple as a physical item resting in the palm of your right hand, or the truth of its absence in your left hand. Truth can be the intellectually aligning power of a wise proverb, just as truth can be the intellectual manipulation of deception. Truth can be as complex as something that exists, but has never been seen or experienced, such as an undiscovered country or luminous heaven. Alternatively, truth can be an unseen ethereal truth; something that exists, but is so transcendent that it will always remain completely over the horizon of the human capacity to comprehend or even experience. Nevertheless, if these things are all that Truth is, then Truth may as well be little more than looking down at the shackles around your tortured wrists, and seeing the truth that they're bound. It may as well be nothing more than knowing the truth that they've been bound, and the truth that they will continue to be bound, because you haven't attained the kind of Truth that will liberate you from a spiritual, intellectual, or physical prison.

As common as truth is sought, as universally as it's embraced, and as often as it's purported from every teacher, master, and prophet around the globe, Truth has shown itself to be an elusive concept, which few can peacefully agree on. In our day, the fever of envy is filling the whole world with the sickness of greed. In our time, the obesity of gluttony is dragging us down into the quicksand of sloth.

The rage of wrath is running us over the cliffs of pride. While the fires of lust are leaving us with the emptiness of envy. In addition, social and religious fanaticisms are making blood enemies of blood relatives, and the honor of integrity is being bartered for anything that promises personal progression... In this day and age, it seems as though Truth is buried between the yellowing pages of yesterday. It seems as though Truth is camouflaged behind the confusing static of our hectic lives. Moreover, it seems as though Truth will only be stumbled upon within the dark circuitous passageways of an abysmal future doomed to emanate failure. Under these conditions, any earthly goal becomes as empty as the blowing sands of a wasteland.

In these increasingly desperate times, The Elixir of Truth is exactly the kind of medicine we could really use, but no one seems willing to drink the remedy themselves. They keep demanding that others consume it before they do. In this, lays a hint of understanding to the rationale of their darkened reasoning. "When everyone cheats, only moral people lose." "It's dangerous to be ethical in an immoral world." Yet, in the same manner that cliffs do not discriminate against the sighted or blind, so too there is a human predilection where everyone looks toward the light of a single candle in a darkened room. They long to spark The Fire of Virtue, to evaporate their ocean of tears. They seek The Flashlight of Truth, to illuminate the darkness of despair. They hunger for The Nourishment of Honor, to fill their empty hearts. And everyone; sighted or blind, thirsts for The Water of Compassion, to extinguish the fire of venom roaring through their veins...)

(While it's not the master's job to give into lies, no one can tell them not to be wise about deception. For, The Paintbrush of Truth requires the darkness of deception to be so black, so as to make The Light of

Truth shine so brightly. In the same manner that the honorable hero requires a villainous scoundrel, so he may reveal the bedrock of his integrity amidst an ocean of lies, so too the deception of yesterday needs to be so depraved, so The Golden Path of Truth can be made so Honorable tomorrow.

It's the student and master's job to find greater meaning in suffering, greater light in darkness, to locate that last ounce of Honor in the wasteland of absolute depravity. It's their job to sift through the lies, to refine deception until the truth reveals itself, and prove beyond the shadow of a doubt that truth persists in the midst of lies, compassion persists in the midst of rage, life persists in the midst of death, and light persists in the midst of darkness.

Together, it is the student and master's job to find a better way. Not just transcend into the panacea of a new world, but to lay out a golden path, which guides the master, student, and newcomer into that bright new tomorrow, where the opportunity for something better exists for one and all. As One, their job is to use the paintbrush of creativity to prove beyond the shadow of a doubt that the magical "something", which allows all of us to overcome the most desperate conditions, was always with us from the beginning of The Path to the end of The Chamber of Initiation. On The Path of Truth, that special Light--- that special quality, is Honor.)

A New Horizon of Truth

(Quite often children think of the world as being only as big as their humble home, their joyful play place, or the long journey to their favorite grandparent's house. Then, they go on their first trip to the snow capped mountains, to camp in an emerald forest, or to see the blue sapphire sea span toward the infinite and untouchable horizon. Another vague step toward vastness is taken when their benefactors point to the distant horizon and explain how there is still a vast world that lies beyond even this expanse of new knowledge.

Eventually, the day arrives when the children desire to trek beyond the borders of their past adventures, to make it to the top of that mountain that they can see, but have never been to. To explore the inner depths of that vast forest that they have heard about, but have never trekked. To discover the inner depths of the oceans, which they know exist, but have never ventured. Yet, when they arrive, and even after they've explored to their heart's content, they once again find that there is greater vastness yet to be had.

When Bodhidharma came from India to China, Emperor Wu asked, "What is the first principal of spiritual teaching?"

Bodhidharma replied, "Vastness, not holiness."

"Who is the one standing in front of me?" Emperor Wu asked.

Bodhidharma responded, "*I know not.*"

Bodhidharma's, "I know not." reply wasn't the void of ignorance, nor was it the counterfeit of corrupted knowledge. It was like that child who expanded their horizons only to witness greater vastness.

Bodhidharma had traversed many spiritual horizons, and yet, he only saw ever-greater vastness to be had. He was trying to say that he understood who he was, but only to the degree of the horizons he had thus crossed. Therefore, with an infinitesimal amount of horizons in the realm of vastness, no one could possibly be sure exactly who they were. Thus, this single idea placed vastness above of holiness.)

(At each stage of life, the most important step along The Path of Truth is when one finds a New Horizon of Truth. This is because, while each New Horizon of Truth unveils a great new vastness, which gives us new perspectives about ourselves and the world around us, each New Horizon of Truth also points the way toward more horizons yet to be crossed. This prospect of venturing into immense vastness calls on something at the core of mankind that gives our natural inquisitiveness direction, it fills the emptiness of menial daily tasks with greater meaning, and it instills a new hope for something better yet to come.

This concept of a New Horizon is as vast and ubiquitous as the concepts of light and dark, or the two-way door of dominion. It doesn't require an axis of cohesion, from the model of the wheel, to find common understanding between spokes of separated disciplines. A New Horizon can be found in all disciplines, because it's a profound intrinsic quality in every aspect of life. In the same manner that one doesn't so much as begin the journey out of the darkness, as much as one begins The Path toward The Light, so too a New Horizon of Truth doesn't so much as lead us out of the paths of bondage, but toward the paths of greater Truths and more meaningful freedoms. It leads us to a singularity of vastness, where Physical Truth, Intellectual Truth, and Spiritual Truth amalgamate as One Universally Transcendent Truth; A Truth with transitive notions, and a two-way door of dominion. This unity of Truth is known as The Great Truth.)

The Three Realms of Truth

(Like the substantive nature of the light, and the absolute absence of the void, Truth is the difference between that which is, and that which is not. However, Truth exists both on the right hand with light, and on the left hand with the void. Both are True, because both exist, even in the intellectual Truth of the absence of the void. Absence is still genuinely and truthfully present by being absent.

On the right hand of substance, one might ask, "What is over the next hill?", and the reply would be, "The earth". One may ask, "What is beyond the earth?" and the reply would be, "The moon, the planets, the stars, and the universe". "And beyond that?" Because this is where our horizon of knowledge ends in the realm of the substantive world, the answer would be, "I know not".

On the left hand of absence one might ask, "What is the ground made of?" and the answer could be, "Dirt, rock, or water." "What is the water made of?" and the answer would be, "Oxygen, hydrogen, protons, neutrons, and electrons." "What is beyond the empty space between their particles?" and the answer would be, "The profoundly real, yet curiously elastic emptiness of space-time, which encompasses both eternal vastness and infinitesimal smallness." "And what is beyond this elastic emptiness of vastness and smallness?" Because this is where our horizon of knowledge ends, in both realms of the substantive and non-substantive world, as well as the eternally vast and infinitesimally small world, the answer would once again be, "I know not".

When we exhaust our accumulated knowledge, or attain the point that is beyond our capacity, and declare, "I know not", we speak the truth of that which resides in The Three Realms of Truth. Like a vacationing child looking toward an unexplored horizon that expands in all directions, we're declaring that we recognize the existence of something beyond eternal vastness, within infinitesimal smallness, and yet this obscure quantity still exists between here and there. Remember, this "void of knowledge" is not the absence of knowledge, it's not counterfeit knowledge, and it's not the darkness of ignorance, nor is it the irrational reasoning of suffering. We're trying to express that we sense the presence of something greater, but also that it's somewhat out of our grasp of greater understanding, which would allow us to label, define, or categorize it.)

(Independent of any label of theology, the word "Faith" is often defined as "The evidence of unseen things". In any language, Faith is a human expression that tries to point to that location where the "I know" and the "I know not" overlap to form a third value. The declaration of "Having Faith" is the acknowledgement of current knowledge, that points to the existence of interrelated knowledge and truth, which yet mysteriously resides over the next horizon of understanding. Faith, is a label that's trying to express a condition of intellect, where half of the equation of knowledge is here, and half of the equation of understanding is there, and we don't quibble about labeling the overlap with much more than a word that indicates a kind of (presence + absence). "Something", that lies between the light in our right hand and the void in our left hand, something that lies in each of The Three Realms of Truth.

For good or ill, faith is the beginning of any path, the belief that there is something out there to know, understand, or be wise about. It's the hope of an achievement at the end of an endeavor, or the belief in some new horizon that will bring about a better future. Knowledge comes along the journey of a path, you learn as you go. However, knowledge has a soothing effect on faith; knowledge tends to put faith to rest. As we continue along life's paths, faith might fall into such a deep sleep that it seems to have disappeared all together, but faith doesn't die, it only slumbers for a season.

For, just when you think you've achieved your goals and arrived at your intended destination, there comes a time when you realize that The Path continues beyond--- beyond. There are detours, dead ends, and u-turns along any of life's paths, and it's at these strange points in life that faith must reawaken. We must again have faith that turning left or right will move us in a better direction. A new bit of knowledge, whose understanding is incomplete, must emerge. A new horizon will become apparent, and the journey to that horizon will fill in the blanks of knowledge as we go. Therefore, faith and knowledge walk hand in hand in The Way of The Path.

"The evidence of unseen things" can be expressed in another manner, by observing the two-way door of dominion, where light and dark interact with intelligence and entropy. Before the appearance of intelligence, we have something that we call the void, dead, element, or just matter in the form of a wave, particle, or photon. This might be a pool of water, dirt blowing in the wind, or photons from the sun. After the appearance of intelligence, photons and waves, elements and forces begin assembling in twisting torsion fields, building geometrically interrelated shapes that are mathematically congruent in relationship to one another. This might be thought of as an embryo, the sprout from a seed, or some other basic life form in its first stage of expressing itself. The photons (C^2), energy (E), and matter (M) begin responding to a greater inner sentience, which goes from "something blowing in the wind", to a self-regulating, self-determining, and self-conscious (thing + a different label). In short, an awareness makes an appearance, which seeks to work with its environment, rather than being governed by it, or merely changing its expression as it moves through it.

It is at this stage that we label something as alive, a "life form", and we watch it mature through its life cycle. Then, intelligence leaves this life form, the torsion fields break down allowing the photons (C^2) to evacuate the elements (M) and forces (E), and the material begins behaving as it once did while under the dominion of entropy. Repeatedly, an expulsion of photons (C^2) has been rigorously measured upon the death of any living thing, and as we know, after the movement of intelligence goes to the realm of "I know not", all of the matter ($E=MC^2$) it's nested within also returns to its original dance within the confines of its environment. The photons (C^2) dissipate, the matter (M) decomposes, and the forces (E), which are said to hold the life form together, simply dissipate. In the absence of the "Intelligence of life", the absence of entropy takes over all aspects of the ($E=MC^2$). Einstein's ($E=MC^2$) tries to answer for the three general expressions of matter, forces, and photonic behavior, yet his equation fails to incorporate the faith of Intelligence, which we cannot see, but know must be present. In other words, the knowledge of Einstein's equation lacks faith and knowledge in Intelligence, even though we can detect it via the absence of entropy. Thus, revealing another intellectual game of leapfrog between knowledge and faith.

The movement of a New Horizon, from faith and knowledge to greater understanding lays within the light in the right hand, the absence of light in the left hand, and a void between an unknown horizon. We witnessed an unseen force come from over the horizon of the "I know not". We observed this invisible force cooperate with photons and waves, elements, and forces ($E=MC^2$) to cause the addition of a third peculiar Euclidean type reaction within our realm. Then, we witnessed this intelligence move over another horizon of the "I know not", when photons and waves, elements and forces remain, and yet without the dominion of intelligence, they act and react under the dominion of entropy rather than the dominion of intelligence. An ethereal, and yet very real force, passed through all Three Realms of Truth, created a new Euclidean Common Notion--- "In the same manner that the addition of one thing to another inevitably leads to the addition of a third thing to both, so too the absence of one thing from another inevitably leads to the absence of a third thing to all"--- (the evacuation of (C^2), changed the status of (M) and (E))-- and left us with a Path where faith and knowledge are the foundational repeating steps of the Trivium and Quadrivium. This leads us to a singularity where Physical Truth, Intellectual Truth, and Spiritual Truth amalgamate as One Universally Transcendent Truth; The Great Truth.)

The Architect of Truth

(Let us begin our understanding of "The Architect" by comparing it to the electricity that runs a computer and the software that tells the device what to do. Observing the electricity of a computer is like observing The Force of The Architect. The Force of The Architect governs what type of program is being run, by the type, condition, and intensity of The Field of The Architect. Observing the software that runs the functions of a computer is like observing The Program of The Architect. The Program of The Architect governs the coming and going of everything in the "machine" with an {(If this), (then this)} "computer" programming loop. Like a virtual world that is governed by the conditions of its power source, as well as the stages of its programming code, The Force of The Architect and The Program of The Architect bind every particle of matter, every ethereal force, and even dictate the intellect of the characters, by virtue of The Architect's changing conditions.

{(If 1), (then 1)}
{(If 1), (then 2)}
{(If 2), (then 3)}
{(If 3), (then 5)}
{(If 5), (then 8)}
{(If 8), (then 13)}
{(If 13), (then 21)}
{(If 21), (then 34)}
{(If 34), (then 55)}
{(If 55), (then 89)}
{(If 89), (then 144)}
Infinity».

The next sequence can always be attained by adding the two previous numbers. Such as, (34 + 55 = 89) can attain (55 + 89 = the next integer in the sequence).)

(The beginning pattern of The Architect "{(If 1), (then 1)}", can be expressed by the repeating spin pattern of a double helix, as well as the repeating shapes of a crystal's lattice structure. For every 1 thing, there is 1 more thing that is "made" alike. This 1 to 1 relationship can progress one energetic step further, and be expressed as "1 Mandelbrot" to "1 Mandelbrot", with the repeating function of The Mandelbrot Equation ($F(Z) = z^2 \times C$). This is where we have the program energetically calculating and recalculating "{(If 1), (then 1)}", with the Mandelbrot equation inserted in the place of the number 1--- "{(If F (Z) = $1^2 \times$ C)), (then F (Z) = $1^2 \times$ C))}". This mathematical expression will build the same expression of intelligence repeatedly, except in an advanced expression of itself, by one energetic step. It will replicate itself in physical, energetic, and ethereal forms into infinitesimal smallness or eternal vastness.)

Physically

(At the initial 1 to 1 stage--- The torsion field that is architecturally assembling bytes of intelligence, takes the form of a double helix (Page 10, Double helix formulas). Like the repeating steps of a spiral ladder, a double helix is a self-similar structure that replicates itself in an identical manner at each step of the ladder, no matter what it's building with. This typically expresses itself in carbon-based life forms as stromatolites or coral. These basic living constructs are identical to one another. They are "self-similar", because the condition of the energy field constructing them stays with the same stage of the programming code.

Layers of sediment don't form Crystals, as we think of the earth's crust. They're life forms, whose Architect Energies grow and mature their physical structures, by replicating their lattice structure within the energetic steps of The Program of The Architect. At this initial energetic stage, the lattice structure replicates itself in a self-similar manner. Crystals grow in a self-similar format like the repeating steps of the ladder of the double helix. However, rather than getting "that which they are composed of" twisted in the spirals of a torsion field, they build self-similar Platonic Solid shapes--- one Platonic Solid layered upon another identical Platonic Solid. For instance, if the energy of The Architect expresses itself as an octahedron, then it will continue to form another octahedron on the exterior of the first octahedron--- at this stage of energetic expression.

(

{(Double helix = Biological life forms) = (Lattice structure = Crystalline life forms)}
{(Torsion field = Biological life forms) = (Platonic Solids = Crystalline life forms)}
{(Wave = Biological life forms) = (Particle = Crystalline life forms)}

$$C^{2L} = C^{2G}$$

)

(At The Mandelbrot Stage--- The Force of The Architect modifies its expression causing Intelligence to move matter; ($E=MC^2$), toward the hexa or octa forms of insect and arachnid patterns. This can be seen energetically and physically as One, by overlaying the energetic mathematics of the Mandelbrot Beetle with the physicality of the Egyptian Scarab Beetle (Khepera). These are energetically advancing life forms who stay very close to the initial self-similar architectural pattern, but whose physical designs appear less self-similar, because they've taken the first step of energetic progression within The Program of The Architect. While they replicate themselves in a self-similar expression, that self-similar expression looks a little different, because they're taking an energetic step forward in the expression of the program--- not because of a physical change. It is the energetic step that causes its physical aspects to appear "different" from other more exacting self-similar life forms, such as stromatolites.

Both carbon and silicon based life forms don't so much as undergo physical evolution, as much as they undergo an Architect generated energetic evolution, which happens to be seen by us physically. If our eyes could see in the spectrum of The Architect (The Source Field), we would observe the energetic change, and witness the resulting physical alteration caused by the energetically progressing programming format. However, we don't, thus our spectrum of perspective causes us to mistake the physical alteration for some kind of physical change. Such as, (DNA sequencing change) + (whereby genetic spelling "mistakes" in the amino acids of [A.G.C.T] create genetic alterations over time) = Darwinism.

This line of thought begs the questions--- "If Einstein's ($E=MC^2$)". And, Newton's First Law of Motion, "If that which is in motion tends to stay in motion unless enacted upon by an outside force." Then, what was the force that enacted a DNA's "spelling mistake"? What was the energy @ (E) that caused the equivalent change of Mass @ (MC^2)? Why did "that which was in motion", change its direction, and what was the change in energy, or its equivalency in mass, that caused the effect? Simply put, it was enacted upon by the energetic progression of The Force of The Architect, which altered its energetic expression of progression, and thus modified the The Program of The Architect, which in turn modified the physical expression of that which it is nested within.

Looking for a physical answer from the result of a physical change is idiosyncratic to the lens of a singular perspective. It's no different from blaming water for falling out of the sky, water for spinning in an eddy, or water for evaporating into the air. Behind every physical thing there is an energy that makes it the way it is. Behind every physical change, we observe an equivalent modification in the energy to make it change. Moreover, it is the two-way door of dominion in The Force of The Architect moving through The Program of The Architect's rising and falling energetic expression, which governs the modifications to all mass (M) to energy (E) to photonic (C^2) relationships.

In the same manner that the spectrum of colors is a change in the expression of energy we call frequency (f), so too the difference between life forms changing their physical makeup, is the result of an energetic change in the expression of The Architect. In the same manner that there is a two-way movement toward "manifesting", and then a new movement toward "vanishing" rainbows, so too the two-way door of dominion causes The Field to "manifest", "vanish", or otherwise "modify" The Energetic Expression of The Architect. The Architect manifests from a collapsing Field into two self-similar expressions (∞) then into an energetically and frequency altering wave, into torsion fields, and then into a "physical" expression that we call particle. This physical expression is further modified energetically by the continuing progression of The Program of The Architect. These conditions go through the Platonic Order, and then nest Platonic Orders within each other. This can express itself differently over the maturity of the expression, depending on many factors, but it may modify itself based solely on the condition of The Field in a given location, nested condition, or quantum condition (X, Y, Z).

"The physical expression of an energetic change" ---is not only a representation of devolution or evolution, but also a measurement of the condition we call "aging". To see this in real time, all one need do is measure the ohms in a person's anatomy with a high quality voltmeter. Kids and teens naturally express more Ohms than aged persons. The expression of their aged condition is more about the expression and condition of The Force of The Architect as it moves through the two-way door of dominion, than about telomeres or the operations and function of DNA. This process can also be used with the ill or infirmed where energy patterns are erratic.

Darwin had eyes and a rudimentary writing utensil to record his observations with. When we compare this with the instruments "cavemen" were using, the only difference is the interpretation of the same environment. As smart as he might have been, Darwin wasn't afforded the technologies that allow us to see what the human eye cannot. Thus, because of this change in perspective, we can arrive at new conclusions, which he could not. So, while his observations might have a foundation within the observable world, as it directly relates to the function of the human eye and a degree of intellectual ability to interpret one's environment, the Darwinian model becomes irreparably flawed when we observe a "more primary" dominion behind all change is "The Conditional Emergence of The Architect from The Field", "An alteration in the energetic expression of The Source Field", and "The manner in which The Program of The Architect functions under given nesting, nested°, or un-nesting conditions (X, Y, Z)." Darwinist Evolutionary thinking must give way to, "The physical expression of an energetic change, within the two-way door of dominion of The Program and Force of The Architect, which expresses itself from a collapsed Field of pure potential into changing energetic and particle patterns."

This is no less true for carbon and silicon based life forms, than it is for crystalline life forms. In the same manner that carbon and silicon-based life forms take an energetic step forward to change their physical properties within the progression of The Architect, so too crystalline-based life forms move from identical self-replication of one geometric shape, into flipping back and forth between Platonic Solids. However, always repeating that self-similar pattern within the advanced step of the pattern itself. For instance, at this "second stage", if a crystal began with an octahedron it would move to a cube, then back to the octahedron, and repeat that cycle as the life form matured.

This Platonic Nesting pattern energetically matches the nesting construct of The Periodic Table of Elements, as interpreted by Dr. Moon, as well as Kepler's models of the geometrical nesting function of the solar system. If there were a difference in the models, Kepler would be saying there are energetic geometrical nesting constructs that compose the solar system in eternal vastness (Y), as if the solar system were a life form after the nesting manner of a crystalline life form. While Dr. Moon would be saying, there are energetic geometrical nesting constructs that compose our Periodic Table of Elements in infinitesimal smallness (X). Together, these three models suggest that there is an infinitesimally small and eternally vast energetic Field that changes conditions, whereby things within that Field alter their expression based on the changing energetic condition of The Field, and this is done in a transitive two-way door of dominion in all directions of vastness. The Force of The Architect's changing expression within of The Program of The Architect governs what is expressed, how it's expressed, and the manner in which its constants function.)

Energetically---

(In the same manner that The Intelligent Architect will construct particles of matter with self-similar formats, so too The Architect will form the same patterns with what we might consider "more ethereal forces". Intelligence can be seen marrying itself to torsion fields, twin toroidal vortices, and toroids. Intelligence will blend those energetic geometries as one with other forces; such as electricity or kinetic energy, and manipulate all three as One.

In the same manner that energy can be contained within, or move through, the fluidity of ocean waves, so too intelligence will blend itself with a particle of matter (M) or the energy (E) of a wave. The Force of Intelligence will be within, or otherwise around and among, the particles that composes the water--- to modify its behavioral expression. At the tips of large enough waves, a torsion field can be seen to torque the water back into itself, twist it slightly to the side into the beginnings of a horizontal vortex, and then rationally fractalize each particle of water into smaller self-similar versions of the primary wave.

At this time, the operation of an ocean wave is thought to be the accumulation of energetic waves catching up with one another within water, the energy bouncing more frequently off an ever-shallow shoreline, and all of it collapsing into a single wave that expresses itself near the shoreline. However, the crucial observation that allows us to conclude that intelligence is impregnated within the wave, along with kinetic energy, as well as molded within the particle of water in a trifecta of connectivity is--- the energy is forming the torsion patterns after the blueprint of The Program of The Architect. While kinetic energy forms chaotic patters, such as a rock rolling arbitrarily down a hill, The Architect consistently forms shapes, patterns, or designs, which follow the increasing mathematics of the program.

Waves don't form circles, or capital C's, look closer, and you'll see they form the exponentially changing curve caused by the program. The increasing Force of The Architect moves The Program of The Architect from a 1 to 1 self-similar ratio toward a 1 to 1.618 ratio. The "event" reaches an apex of expression, $\{(\text{If } 89), (\text{then } 144)\}$, the wave reverses its flow, function, and its remnants reveal the scattering program as it again moves toward $\{(\text{If } F(Z) = 1^2 \times C)), (\text{then } F(Z) = 1^2 \times C))\}$ » » $\{(\text{If } 1), (\text{then } 1)\}$ and back to a 1 to 1 self-similarity of the beginning of the program. Simply put, The Architect expresses itself in an ever-changing condition that flows in both directions of The Two-Way Door of Dominion. Ocean waves behave like the program, because the program, in the form of energetic intelligence (Source Field Energy), is imbedded inside the expression. (Fractal Particle Motion; the collapse or un-collapse of the wave or nesting function; aka, the manner in which a product of the Field functions while The Architect is in a Fractal condition. For further reference, study Katsushika Hokusai as well as Dr. Masaru Emoto, both have done extensive work demonstrating how this functions in water. I also go into detail in The Path, Chapter 14: The Code of The Veil, Part II, The Intelligent Universe.)

{(If 1), (then 1)}
{(If 1), (then 2)}
{(If 2), (then 3)}
{(If 3), (then 5)}
{(If 5), (then 8)}
{(If 8), (then 13)}
{(If 13), (then 21)}
{(If 21), (then 34)}
{(If 34), (then 55)}
{(If 55), (then 89)}
{(If 89), (then 144)}
{(If 55), (then 89)}
{(If 34), (then 55)}
{(If 21), (then 34)}
{(If 13), (then 21)}
{(If 8), (then 13)}
{(If 5), (then 8)}
{(If 3), (then 5)}
{(If 2), (then 3)}
{(If 1), (then 2)}
{(If 1), (then 1)}
)

Energetically---

(In the same manner that its two-way door of dominion functions in the construct of water, so too The Force of The Architect can be seen and measured in the arms and behavior of lightning bolts. All the while, possessing congruent ascending and descending ratios, as the event swings through the two-way door of The Program of The Architect. This energy carries with it the basic programming of whatever it desires to construct in the physical or energetic realms, because the programming is within The Force of Intelligence itself. It is not the electricity (E), photon (C^2), or particles of matter (M) that determine how the Field collapses into the expression of a lightning bolt. It's the degree of intelligence, and condition of the expression of The Program of The Architect, working within the elements or forces, which are compelling the electricity (E), photons (C^2), or particles (M) to obey, collapse into, or otherwise express through the numerological, and geometrical patterns of the program that shape the lightening. Its presence or absence can be observed moving through The Two-Way Door of Dominion by watching the patterns of the program form inside the elements, move toward an apex of expression, reverse the function, and "collapse"--- or more accurately, to "un-express" or "un-collapse the expression".

In other words, the event will begin as a field of potentials with many "things" within its arena of activity. The Program of The Architect starts out as a field, spread out, yet imbued within anything in the expanse of the field. Intelligence initiates the collapse of the field; The Program of The Architect begins a movement of expression that can be interpreted with rising numerical patterns. The field continues to collapse, expressing itself as a wave function. This wave function operates as a communications device that transmits and receives, connects and directs The Architect, forces, and energies as One toward a singularity of their particle expression. Because electrons are impregnated with The Force of The Architect (Source Field Energy), as the electrons flash into photonic particle expression, their expression forms after the collapsing pattern of the program. Like the crash of an ocean wave, it will be seen to dissipate in such a manner that its field yet exists, but we aren't able to determine its presence. Emphatically, once again, we realize this is not because it no longer exists; our eyes just aren't able to detect it. Thus, rather than say it no longer exists, in The Way of The Path, we just say that it has traveled over the horizon of our perception.)

(Intelligence moves from this initial form into a greater expression when our {(If 1), (then 1)} program begins to increase with greater numerical values of {(If 1), (then 2)}, {(If 2), (then 3)} ad infinitum-». This can be expressed mathematically by The Fibonacci Sequence (1, 1, 2, 3, 5, 8, 13, 21, 34, 55, 89, -»), where each number of the program is equally divided by the next number in a vice versa, or Flip Function. Pause here; take some genuine time to scrutinize the numbers carefully, to see how the value of .618 » comes to express itself with an undulating wave pattern. At first, the wave goes too high, then too low, the wave pattern moves continually into a smaller nested expression that always moves toward a number, which it never actually achieves. The wave behaves like a snake circling itself around a pole; whose coils get tighter and tighter the further down it goes (X). The numeric pattern of the program "waves" itself in a torsion field "around" this central nothingness.

(1÷1=1) (1÷2=.5) (2÷3=.66) (3÷5=.6) (5÷8=.62) (8÷13=.615) (13÷21=.619) (21÷34=.617) (34÷55=.618) (55÷89=.6197) (89÷144=.61805) (144÷233=.61802) (233÷377=.61803) -» ∞ = .61803399

Looking at the numbers following the underlined number in each equation, note the internal wave of numbers, which flow up and down until they match the programming code, and create another wave out of nothing that follows the same wave pattern, except at a smaller decimal point (X).

In reverse: Look for the mathematical movement toward the expression of 1.618 ».

$(1 \div 1 = \underline{1})$ $(2 \div 1 = 2)$ $(3 \div 2 = \underline{1}.5)$ $(5 \div 3 = \underline{1.6}6)$ $(8 \div 5 = .\underline{1.6})$ $(13 \div 8 = \underline{1.6}25)$ $(21 \div 13 = \underline{1.61}5)$ $(34 \div 21 = \underline{1.61}9)$ $(55 \div 34 = \underline{1.61}76)$ $(89 \div 55 = \underline{1.618}1818)$ $(144 \div 89 = \underline{1.61}79)$ $(233 \div 144 = \underline{1.618}055)$ $(377 \div 233 = \underline{1.6180}257)$ infinity-» $(\Phi = Phi) = \underline{1.61803399})$

As we can see, the division of these numbers is a constant movement toward an infinitesimally small expression of .61803399, or eternally vast expression of 1.61803399. Nevertheless, as the division of increasing numbers continues, the function never actually reaches a constant value. With an undulating wave pattern, they just keep moving closer and closer to a value that it never actually achieves, as though it's coiling tighter and tighter around something that's not there.

Although the mathematical expression of the programming code seems complex at first, once you catch onto its repeating patterns of layered replication, you begin to see the patterns in everyday life. As you see this effect here and there, you begin to see it emerge in every living construct. Then, one day you cross another horizon to see that although it's a simple repeating program, what it builds is magnificently complex, and divinely diverse. Suddenly a New Horizon of Truth emerges from the "I know not", and a smile comes to the side of your face as you realize that this "Unity of Truth" was always there, right in front of you.)

Physically---

(In the same manner that The Force of The Architect governs the swirl of galaxies after the manner of The Program of The Architect in eternal vastness without anything seeming to physically connect anything (∞), so too the physical circling construct of seashells duplicates The Force and Program of The Architect in infinitesimal smallness while seeming to physically connect the particles of which its composed (∞). We see bird's physical forms obey the Program of this Force, even with their many breeds, diversity of shapes, and multiplicity of sizes. This happens in the same manner when we look at all of the varieties of fish, mammals, reptiles, or plant species, because even within the diverse nature of their anatomies, their proportional measurements are built by, and therefore reflect, The Force and Program format. The Program of The Architect builds many shapes and designs throughout nature, but behind the diversity of each physical expression, every single one of them obeys the same compelling Force that can be expressed with the mathematics of The Programming Code, or the expression of a universal Architect.)

Non physically; $_\wedge$---

(Birds can be seen soaring in the air, circling after the same {(If this), (then this)} programming loop. As they rise up, their circle gets wider, and as they descend, their circle gets proportionally smaller. This isn't arbitrary; they're harnessing and riding the torsion field patterns impregnated within the invisibility of the air to get more lift, as well as to be impregnated with more levity by the torsion field, so as to fly with less effort. Ducks are doing the same thing when they fly in a V Λ formation. The downward swoop of their wings causes the ascending and descending patterns of this program to impregnate, swirl, and torque the air sideways, in the same manner that the ascending and descending patterns of this program impregnate waves in the ocean into a crescendo and then a collapse. All of these "bird brained" birds are smart enough to know where the torsion fields are spinning at their optimum swirl, and like a surfer riding ocean waves, they place themselves at a precise location, so as to harness the lift of its levity, and ride the waves of its torsion. Whether horizontal or vertical, are we smart enough to find these invisible fields, place ourselves at their optimum swirl, and harness their benefits? ((^{G}) « » (^{L})))

Non-Physically $_B$---

(Intelligence can be found to express itself with the exact same program within the untouchable population growth patterns of anything that's alive and procreating. Logic and reasoning might lead us to think that 2 procreates to 4, and 4 breeds to 8, and 8 multiplies to 16, to 64--- Binary ad infinitum. Logic and reasoning might also cause us to consider that some offspring don't make it to maturity, accidents happen, and some offspring replicate more while others replicate less. Given a long enough time line, these variables would cause us to reason that the patterns would become too erratic or impractical to be interpreted mathematically. However, no matter how erratic the quantities may seem begin with, reproduction in any species always rises and falls, expresses and un-expresses itself, according to The Two-Way Door of The Architect's Programming Code.

Even in extremely high population numbers, such as the number of cells in a forest, the number of stars in a galaxy, or the layers of thoughts in the collective unconscious--- the pattern always collapses into the nested layers of the program, because The Intelligence of The Architect governs it. Within the flowing pattern of the equation, there's an internal ebb and flow of numbers that matches the programming format. This mathematical expression reveals a layering of The Program of The Architect, which extends itself to infinitesimal smallness and eternal vastness. The relationship between the "frequency of wave" and the "particle of number" follow The Architect in the exact same relationship whether expressed as a wave (E) or particle (M), a galaxy (E) or seashell (M). In the same manner that a single drop of water relates to the rise and fall of The Program of The Architect within an ocean wave, so too a single tree cell has the same relationship with a branch, and that branch has it to its tree, and that tree has the same relationship to its forest.

Said in another way, in the same manner that energy waves in water have an "Architect relationship" on distant water, wherein energy traveling through water over here eventually affects the water over there. So too, the same wave pattern that's found in the particle of a tree has "a wave Architect relationship" to its forest. Even if the cell of a single tree, and the rest of the forest, does not seem to be physically connected, the wave effect will traverse the two-way door of dominion, and cause aftershocks on the distant life forms. This has less to do with the physical expression of a nesting wave, and more to do with the change of direction in its energetic expression, and the two-way door of collapse «-» un-collapse, of degrees of Superposition $((^G)« »(^L))$. And that's phenomenal! That is profound... Moreover, the idea that this is a universal expression of all things is the very definition of Vastness, especially as it directly relates to the origins and causality of Universal Truth.)

(As if someone removed the illusion of a scholastic divide that separated science from theology, and mathematical logic from musical art, we can see A New Horizon of Truth that forges the ethereally spiritual as One with the physically scientific in The Middle Way of The Path. Suddenly, we see theological and secular unity in the shape of a fish, where the physical parts of the life form are constructed by The Intelligent Architectural Force of its spiritual aspect. We see the spiritual intelligence of that fish shape its unique breed or design after the scientific and mathematical ratios of what we express as an energetic computer-programming loop. A layered programming loop and a field collapse that is the mathematical expression of an ethereal Force. A Force that forms repeating wave patterns with perfect nesting geometries, linked with emergent harmonies (f), even among different species, and between seemingly disparate disciplines. As though Truth itself was imbued within all things via the vast presence of Architectural Intelligence, we see that Intelligence; The Force of The Architect, is "The Universal Truth"--- it has a transitive nature in all Three Realms of Truth, beyond the horizon of the unknown, and even in those Realms of Truth that yet lay beyond the human capacity to comprehend.

If we modeled this concept with a geometric shape, the Triquetra would have three arms labeled Virtue, Truth, and Compassion, which were governed by a singular Force in the center of the model. If we modeled this concept within a different discipline, the geometry of the Triquetra would have three arms labeled energy (E), mass (M), and photons, (C^2); or $\{(E=MC^2)\}$ where their unity of function is governed by a Force revealed by the overlapping center of the Triquetra. If we modeled this concept with different expressions, the Triquetra would have three arms labeled distance (D), rate, (R), and time (T), where the unity of function of these variables are governed by another Value in the center of the Triquetra. At the center of each model is the two-way door of dominion of The Force of The Architect.

In the discipline of statistics, this force can be experienced as the thing that causes the Bell Curve to function so reliably, rather than just to express itself chaotically. In Philosophy, this is where metaphysical objectivism of the way we see things meets empirical idealism in the way things actually are. In the way of The Path, this New Horizon of The Fruit of Awareness is the revelation of The One Universal Expression. It's a paradigm changing moment, a brief taste of that which cannot be tasted, a fleeting feeling of that which cannot be felt, a distant echo of that which cannot be heard, and a memorable glimpse of that which cannot be seen.

No longer do we just see a discipline as a form of expression, which has common doorways with other disciplines, or a philosophical proverb that is ubiquitous to all disciplines. We now have a truly universal expression that moves seamlessly between disciplines, as well as can be seen manifesting itself in all things at every level of existence. The Architect of Truth is The Great Truth, to experience the point of unity of all things, a condition one attains as one moves into The Middle Way of The Path.)

Thunderbolt of Enlightenment!

(Dorje or Vajra: {"Door-gee"} Eastern theological symbology--- can symbolize objective and subjective truth. A Dorje represents "The Thunderbolt of Enlightenment", an abrupt, dramatic, and vast change in consciousness. The Dorje represents that pivotal episode in the lives of those who transcend into mystics, Saints, and Precious Ones; Rinpoche'.

The experiences of transformative enlightenment are recounted in the various religions. In the Christian tradition, the conversion of Saul of Tarsus has "a blinded man"--- a man living in darkness--- suddenly "struck by light", after which he could "see the light", and therefore understand his purpose in life. In Hindi and Buddhist theologies, Siddhartha was struck by a moment when The Light of Knowledge vanished the darkness of ignorance, he became Enlightened by The Middle Way of The Path, and taught it for the remainder of his years. In The Way of The Path and from the Creations of The Source, The Thunderbolt of Enlightenment is a sudden and unexpected movement from darkness into a brilliant blinding Light. It's not taking "the next step on The Path", nor is it an epiphany of greater understanding; it's a gigantic leap from one paradigm to another. In every human experience, bound by the borders of a language and a label, The Thunderbolt of Enlightenment is the experience of an abrupt realization, a vast shift in perspective. Moreover, to anyone who experiences it, it's such a powerful occurrence that the rest of their lives are transformed by the effects of this pivotal moment.)

(The Atheist says, "Everything that is here is everything that is here, and nothing that isn't here is here". Inclusive in that statement, the Honorable student will use the two-way door of dominion between faith and knowledge to find that--- As we journey from the darkness of ignorance into the light of knowledge and understanding of experience--- As we travel over one new horizon of Knowledge and Truth after another--- As we grow and mature into the dominion of vast perspectives and eternal paradigms--- We always find one thing: Vastness... Moreover, it is in this Vastness that we find those things that we didn't know existed, or previously believed could be existent. However, this is never because it suddenly manifested into reality just because we became aware of it. These things, which exist in vastness, were always there despite the condition of our belief systems.

The first step along The Path of Truth is the moment when one finds A New Horizon of Truth. The second step along The Path of Truth is when one's Faith must reawaken, to move one toward a New Horizon. The third step along The Path of Truth is finding when and where the physical, intellectual, and spiritual amalgamate as One Universally Transcendent Truth in The Middle Way of The Path. As the virtuous student travels through The Journey of The Path, these three steps bound one over another. A new horizon reveals a new level of faith, a new faith reveals a new unity, and a new unity reveals a new horizon. With every New Horizon of Truth, the student is liberated from the bondage of the borders of a realm, and dichotomies of perspectives that they were once bound by. With an ever-expanding horizon, there comes ever-greater Light, increasing knowledge, further understanding, and eventually the solemnity of wisdom in embracing Vast Truths. As this progresses, the compassionate student receives new insight, which reveals a new unity between those things they once considered separate. They find their "common doorways", and come to understand their ubiquitous expressions.

However, when we sense a New Vastness of Truth, which extends over both horizons of our present perspective, or particular paradigm--- This very special moment in life becomes "The Moment of Truth", and possibly the "Thunderbolt of Enlightenment". This "Heureka!" moment is what faith's ambition, the seeking of science, and the organizing of secular and theological social orders strives so valiantly to bring to the next generation. This is The Fingerprint of Intelligence--- The Architect--- The Design of The Construct. In this single respect, our belief systems are not so much as changed, as refined. Our decisions are not so much as better, as more comprehensive. In addition, our Life Path is not so much as less treacherous, but more resolute.

When you least expect it, "The Thunderbolt of Enlightenment!" flashes brightly in the darkness of the student's night, scattering the darkness of anger, the ferment of fear, and angst of aggression with fractured and radiant arms that extend their brilliance in every direction. The student's intellect is irrevocably refined as they gulp down The Elixir of Truth, which vanishes the darkness of doubt with The Enlightenment of Vastness. With a word and a prayer, the student breaks loose the bondage of suffering. In the blink of an eye, he reincarnates out of the ashes of doubt, and glows with the power to ascend to A New Order of Existence. With every beat of his hammering heart pounding its rhythms in his heaving chest, he can feel the warm fire aglow within as The Phoenix Within stirs to awaken.)

This is The Way of The Path...

Love...

**There are many Paths to the top of Mount Fuji
Nevertheless, there is only one summit**

The Path of Love

(While it's not the lover's job to give into lust, no one can tell them not to be wise about desire. For, The Paintbrush of Love requires the dark side of desire to be so black, so as to make the light side of Love shine so brightly. In the same manner that the honorable hero requires a villainous scoundrel, so he may reveal the bedrock of his Chivalry amidst an ocean of depravity, so too the abomination of yesterday needs to be so decadent, so The Golden Path of Altruism can be made so Compassionate tomorrow.

It's the lover's destiny to find greater meaning in suffering, greater companionship in darkness, to locate that last ounce of affection in the wasteland of universal hate. It's their job to sift through their feelings, to refine the meaning of love until Altruism reveals itself. And by doing so, to prove beyond the shadow of a doubt that truth persists in the midst of lies, compassion persists in the midst of rage, love persists in the midst of aggression, and light persists in the midst of darkness.

Together, it is the lover's purpose to find a better way. Not just transcend into the panacea of a new world, but to lay out a golden path, which guides the lover, absconder, and the unrequited into that bright new tomorrow, where the opportunity for something better exists for one and all. As One, their job is to use the paintbrush of Compassion to prove beyond the shadow of a doubt that the magical "something", which allows all of us to overcome the most heinous conditions, was always with us from the beginning of The Path, through The Three Great Quests, and into the solemnity of The Chamber of Initiation. On The Path of Love, that special transitive quality is Compassion.)

(In the same manner that a cloud must billow and eventually burst, because it keeps absorbing water, so too The Next Step of The Path must burst forth into the student's life, because they keep absorbing Truth, multiplying Virtue, and nurturing Love. When the right amount has been connected with, thought upon, and acted in accord with, the showering blessings of the next step will emerge from the "I know not" of a Vast and distant horizon, yet the student will witness it as though it had always been present. This special moment will fill them with a euphoric serenity, The Thunderbolt of Enlightenment will shift their perspective into a vast new paradigm, and their reward will be to savor new flavors in The Banquet of Ten Thousand Horizons.

With their faculties alive with The Fire of Intelligence, the student of The Path feels as though they're experiencing life through new eyes that reveal an unseen realm, which had always been mysteriously veiled behind the world of their daily life. They have new eyes that can see right through the camouflage of a hectic society, to see that serenity comes from within themselves at any present moment. The milk and honey of life carry new meanings; they become sweeter to the taste, and more satisfying to the soul. The student finds intrinsic value concealed between the yellowing pages of a dusty ole' manuscript. They witness greater meaning in the carefree play of little children. They discover new wonderment in the secrets of the tallest trees. They suddenly see wisdom in the diversity of life of a coral reef. They pause and snicker at the fact that it was always there, but somehow they'd never seen it before. Then, like a child who's caught the spark of a firefly out of the darkness of the night, they're eager to show others the fascinating illumination of what they've found.

While some will pay no heed, and pass by without so much as a glance, others will suddenly sit up and take notice. An eyebrow of curiosity lifts as they see the wonderment of discovery sparkling in your eyes; they feel the tranquility of something illusive in your presence, and like a bee seeking the sweet nectar of greater meaning they desire to partake of this glowing blossom of life. The spark of a connection is made with a warm handshake, the flickering light of a thought is multiplied when the story is told, and a moment of enlightenment is shared while the illumination of their world becomes a little brighter.

At a little distance, the Master sits calmly with patience and the fidelity of honor observing his student become the venerable teacher. With the warm embers of joy refining The Light of Compassion in his spirit, he recalls the first time he tasted this elusive Fruit of Light, and soon he too shares his story with his student and the newcomer (∞). They all smile, laugh, and tell the magnificent stories about the paths that led them to this moment. They turn as One, and take the next step on The Path of Vastness.)

This is The Way of The Path...

(In The Banquet of Ten Thousand Horizons, the following flavors would be called "The Spice of Comparative Etymology". This is where we amplify the zest of an individual word, by spicing it up with equivalent words from other languages and cultures. When we comprehend the multiplicity of a single word from the paradigm of many cultures, perspectives of vastness become quantifiable observations, which amplify the meaning and significance of each word. This singular act renders an altogether new perspective of each word. It incontrovertibly demonstrates that they are all spokes in the same wheel of greater understanding. It reveals that they are all gears of the same machine, they are all parts of a larger device that possess a greater purpose, and more marvelous significance (Page 12).)

Intellectual Love

Amae, 甘え Japanese; to depend or presume upon another's benevolence. Amae is a form of helplessness of the individual's reliance on collectivism that possesses the desire to be loved, served, or assisted. Amae is a request of another for an indulgence of one's needs or desires without the remuneration of worldly compensation. Amae is a call for some form of compassion, but not necessarily genuine Compassion.

Unlike western cultures, where this kind of dependency is embraced for children and seniors, yet frowned upon for those who are seen as capable, the Japanese culture embraces this form of love in all stages of life. Not only because every person has different needs, but because every person has different challenges that effect them to a greater or lesser degree at each stage of life. Therefore, even if it's frowned upon, camouflaged as something else, or done behind the veil of privacy it's still practiced.

The western equivalent to Amae's acceptable continuance in the capable years of life can be likened to a seasoned veteran who will take in a newcomer, and guide them under the wing of their greater experience for no additional compensation. Although the newcomer might be fully educated, physically capable, and mentally competent, this kind of "extra social care" is seen as a necessity to prevent the mishaps of inexperience despite their capable status.

The difference between the two, in western cultures this form of love will be withdrawn after due consideration of the purported need, and any further Amae will be seen as ethically questionable if not morally wrong. Yet, for better or worse, it's traditionally continuous in the Japanese culture under the idea of collective tolerance. After all, the actions of the individual could spoil the needs of the many in the blink of an eye. Thus, the weaker individual is watched over whether or not they need or deserve Amae, not only for their own intrinsic value, but also for the utilitarian greater good of the collective.

In the same manner that too much honey becomes bitter, too much Amae becomes crippling to both the giver and receiver. Too much Amae creates a form of reliant servitude. It turns one party into unnecessary dependents, and the other party into unnecessary obligators. Like honey on warm bread, serving to one degree of Amae leaves a sweet taste on your pallet, a warm feeling in your heart, and an uplifting sentiment in your spirit. However, excessively serving others with a "cradle to the grave" mentality leaves the irritation of an itch that you can't scratch, and makes you wish you were never kind in the first place. Like counterfeit virtue that seems to begin well, yet ends in tragedy, this second type isn't Genuine Amae, it's Amae's corrupted opposite; a form of amae' that enslaves rather than liberates.)

(Ren (or Rén) 仁 = pinyin, Confucian, Chinese: is the notion denoting *the good feeling* that a Virtuous person experiences when *behaving* rightly: especially toward others. Like degrees of increasing light, the growth and maturity of Ren can be measured in terms of degrees of collectivism. This may range from something as small as exercising Ren with one other individual, to a family unit, a nation, or the greater human family as a whole.

Like the root of a vine, Ren grows from the love that a child has for its mother, to family love, and eventually into adopting outsiders as one of the clan. Ren grows into a parental love where one feels obligated to care for neighborhood children as if they were their own. Ren may mature a person into the diplomat who directs and guides his community, or it may lead a person to help communities of opposing interests or beliefs to get along.

Remembering that it's easy to love those who are pleasant, and near impossible to get an entire community to Ren love those who are downright mean, socially intolerable, or culturally fanatical, we realize that it's somewhere at this stage that most people's vine of Ren love stops maturing or is sheared off entirely. Should the student be able to overcome the incessant bombardment of conflict that the world seems content to renew itself with daily... If the teacher can cultivate and mature Ren Love enough to envelop an adversary... Then, the master will possess the insight to avoid their assaults, and guide them toward The Path that is One with the laws and ways of Heaven and Earth.

One will find that the Ren lover refrains from taking sides when those they Ren love are at odds with one another. They see no value in taking sides if it's in the name of harming someone which they,

77

or others, perceive to be on "On the other side of the fence" of life's complications. They do this, not because they're unpatriotic or don't love "Their own kind". To the contrary, they might be considered quite patriotic and full of Love, because they know the innocent surrounding populations are the ones that pay the heaviest price for the violence of aggression. "Their own kind" is seen as being one big family that's bickering among themselves, and they want everyone's best interests to be served by preventing conflict all together. In the same manner that cliffs do not discriminate between the sighted or blind, so too the fires of war do not discriminate between the innocent or guilty.

Unlike someone who only has Ren love for particular collectives, they don't want anyone to suffer... Yes, they seek the welfare of the black sheep of the family, the pigs who relish rolling in the mud, the faking opossums, the wolfs who try to blow the house down, and the dogs of The House of Capulet. For the Ren lover who has matured into the full expression of Ren, it becomes just as difficult to harm another, as it is for their right hand to punish their left hand for being its exact opposite.)

(Ren is the ideal inward expression of Confucian thoughts. Yan Hui, the most outstanding student of Confucius, asked his master to describe the rules of Rén. Confucius replied:

See nothing improper
Hear nothing improper
Say nothing improper
Do nothing improper

The culturally adopted symbology of the three monkeys covering their eyes, ears, and mouth has them moving in a direction of sequestering their talents and abilities for fear of misusing them. Rather than using them in a positive or empowering manner, which creates value and multiplies their Virtue into Vastness. Like any false path that may seem good in the beginning, sequestering our talents in the name of "the fear of their misuse", is not The Way of The Path.

The Way of The Path is not so much about what should be put down, as much as what should be picked up. The Path doesn't so much concern itself with that which shouldn't be done, but more with that which should be done. One rids their thoughts of something, not by trying to forget the matter, but by focusing on something else, which replaces the initial thought. One rids themselves of evil visions, not by turning off bad television programming, but by paying attention to something that is beautiful--- which might just so happen to be on TV. One rids themselves of evil speech, not by being silent, but by speaking benevolent words. One rids themselves of evil sounds, not by plugging their ears, but by listening to inspirational teachers. One rids themselves of the fear of negative connections, thoughts, and actions by connecting to The Source, thinking of solutions, and cultivating, polishing, and refining positive emotions. One removes the darkness of anger, fear, and aggression by cultivating The Light of Ren within, and then echoing it into outer vastness.

By focusing on that which is Virtuous, by embracing that which is Truthful, and by expressing that which is Loving one creates an echo that is a movement into vastness. Whereas, the three monkeys who are trying to "do good", via the inaction of bad things, are creating nothing to spread into vastness. They're leaving the world in just as much light or darkness as when they entered it, and cannot be blamed for any wrongdoing. However, they also can never be rewarded for any "right doing" either. They haven't enslaved anyone, but neither have they liberated anyone. They haven't blown out any lights to create greater darkness, but they also haven't removed the darkness by creating more light. By embracing Virtue, by speaking Truth, and by demonstrating Compassion The Child of Light is creating empowering waves in the oceans of our collective Karma that echo into a vast untouchable future (^{L}).

Confucius believed Rén to be a natural quality inside every person; he also believed humanity to be good at its core when he said…

Rén is not far off
He who seeks it has already found it

Like the decision to take on Virtue's Compassion or Truth's Honor, in the same manner that a candle takes on the light of the flame, so too one takes on, radiates out, and multiplies toward eternal vastness The Intellectual Love of Ren.)

(The Way of The Path is a movement into a condition. It's a recognition of that condition in others. The value of The Path is the multiplication of that condition with others into vastness.)

The Path of Rén and Amae

(Although the phrase, "The enemy of my enemy is my friend" is a true maxim, and in truth, it happens very often, yet it's a proverb of the path of conflict. It carries a true power that causes the volatile karma of the paths of anger, fear, and aggression to feed into one another. When people are compelled to cooperate due to a threatening force, the virtue, truth, and love that's shared between them will be found to disappear in conjunction with the absence of the *mutual* opposition. Thus, if one is following the dark path of conquest, perhaps they should use this aphorism, and shout out, "Truth!" when it works for them. However, this is more like the intellectually aligning power of a deceptive proverb, which leaves the emptiness of destruction in your left hand. In the right hand of substance, if the student desires to follow The Way of The Path, they should look at this kind of truth as a warning that the two-way door of dominion is swinging in the wrong direction.)

(Examples of this illusion of comradery can be found replete throughout human history. Once the mutual opponent of the Allies in World War II was vanquished, the Russians, Americans, and British tore off the mask of cooperation, and replaced their accords with their genuine posture of contempt toward one another. This was something that neither the Brits, Americans, or the Russians could afford to do, a truth no one was able to speak, during desperate times of unlimited worldwide warfare. Japan, Italy, Scandinavia, and Germany were no different. They had never cooperated before they possessed such formidable opponents, and once the slaughter was over, they've never cooperated in such a manner again.

This form of patriotism often looks like virtue, and the veil of this façade is very common. The virtue of unity via the label of patriotism is touted on all sides of the map with an accusatory finger pointing to the opposing hoard that lies just over the horizon of uncertainty. So often staged by those few who desire the conflict in the first place, because of the absence of light within their own hearts, this situation incites and multiplies everyone's fears of the unknown. It angers people to think that the actions of a few are representative of the intention of a country's entire population. In return, the people take on the scrooge-ism of "righteous indignation", and then "righteous aggression", as they rally together and rail back at those whom they're told want to harm them. Then, in the name of self-defense, and personal preservation the other side commits the same fallacy inciting more anger, fear, and aggression among all. This is a truth, and in our day, it's a common and infectious truth, but it is not The Way of The Path.

The important delineation to take away is that the alliances began outside of the individual rather than springing from the inner cultivation of Virtue, Truth, and Love that could be shared and cultivated willingly. This would have formed a kind of union (∞) that doesn't require any semblance of opposition to bring people and nations together. More importantly, it creates a kind of union that can serve to prevent the conflict in the first place. Like a Karmicly driven wheel that feeds into itself, only we can select which direction to spin it. Moreover, which direction that wheel takes us, begins with our choice of the connections, thoughts, and emotions we cultivate within our own hearts and minds.)

(We can see this two-way door of dominion swing back and forth on a smaller scale, by observing the vast difference in outcomes in the wake of the recent tsunami in Japan and hurricane in New Orleans--- When the electricity shut down... When their possessions were destroyed... When the means to maintain order was engulfed in a torrent of mud and debris, and then mercilessly swept out to sea... When radioactivity threatened millions... When the inundation of the ocean wiped multiple cities off the face of the map... And, when the foreboding ferment of fear at the loss of their family transformed into the gravity of desperation, and the anchor of agony that threatened to pull them all to the bottom of the sea, was indeed dragging tens of thousands to a watery grave... ---The People of Japan held it together by holding onto one another.

Like a drowning victim desperately clinging to the last piece of a life preserver, they clung to patience despite emanate destruction. Like old couples who share what little food they possess, they cooperated with their neighbors despite the lack of resources. Moreover, like an honorable father who let's go of the last edifice of order, and dives headlong into the angry waters of hopelessness to rescue a drowning child, uncommon valor was a common Virtue when ordinary citizens demonstrated great courage and selfless sacrifice in the turbulent tidal waves of uncertainty to prevent a greater nuclear catastrophe.

The People of Japan possessed The Genuine Power of Virtue. They were accompanied by The Intelligent-Kami of Truth. They demonstrated The Transforming Energy of Compassion that rises above tragedy, soaring valiantly on the wings of Honor, which kept the survivors afloat both during and after the floods of destruction. The People of Japan possessed "The Pearl of Great Price" which we seek. A Power that's more valuable than the label of their social orders, more powerful than the latest technology, and is just as precious as the salvation of a Divine Wind (神風) in times of individual and national desperation.

The Japanese possessed an inner dominion, which allowed them to see over the distant horizon of the uncertain "I know not", and unveil the Light of that Power that Truly supports and upholds any society. The Middle Way of The Path... The Way of The Gods... In the same manner that Virtuous Knowledge, True Understanding, and Wise Compassion form a greater bond when used as One, so too the union of Virtue, Truth, and Love feed into one another to make each other stronger. Like giant waves of Karma, they echo through our societies, causing our secular and theological orders to function as they are meant to function. God forbid that one-day a larger more horrifying cataclysmic destruction may come to drag the half of Japan into the dark abyss that sits just off the wake of their turbulent shores. Nevertheless, The People of Japan will rise above it, if they will but continue to cling to the life preserver of Virtue, the unifying power of Truth, and the elevating energy of Compassion ([L]).)

(The people of New Orleans didn't build their lives around the same uplifting Force, "The Pearl of Great Price" that upheld the Japanese, was woefully absent from their culture. They relied on manmade walls, manmade forms of order, manmade styles of government, and manmade forms of technology. They relied on the moral code of surrendering a coat because someone has two, and the feigned righteousness of taking other's resources if they were not surrendered in the name of their own needs. Therefore, when the trials of time and the test of fire slammed into their shores in the form of an overwhelming hurricane, they did the same thing as the Japanese. They took that which they harbored in their hearts, minds, and souls and expressed it to their neighbors.

They joined in a clan mentality where individuals of common needs worked together to say, "The enemy are those selfish people who have what we need, if they won't give it to us, we will punish them, and take our resources from them." They then went about looting their brothers, raping their sisters, and pillaging the homes of their fellow citizens, because they embraced vice rather than virtue, and self-love rather than Ren Love or Amae Love. As resources diminished, the infection of conflict festered, irrational reasoning multiplied, and crime intensified, because they harbored the vice of fear of inadequacy rather than the Virtue of Honor and mutual sacrifice. Even when outside help arrived, the prevailing attitude in the wake of the aftermath continued to be an "us against them" attitude.)

(Without a greater Force to sustain us in a time of life and death opposition, we'll always see a form of desperation that's willing to keep any company, adopt any label, or put on any mask to get others to pay attention to it, and give it what it wants. Like a malicious chameleon hiding itself by purporting to be that which it's not, the negative aspects of Amae and Ren are a clever form of vice, which will say and do anything to cunningly beguile its way into surviving one more minute. It is a method of madness that longs to draw you into its tentacles of terror, just so it doesn't have to go down by itself.

As accusatory as these opposites of Japan and New Orleans may seem, and as much as it might upset those who come up on the short end of the stick, we can use the dominion of a greater light of understanding to erase the darkness of the irrational reasoning of accusatory thinking. All we have to do is flip on the light, and take on the perspective that John F. Kennedy proclaimed so valiantly before his sacrifice---

An error doesn't become a mistake
Until you fail to correct it

Failure is not the label of an eternal stain. Failure is like a child learning to walk by making small corrections, all while constantly falling down. Failure is the opportunity to illuminate acts done in the darkness of ignorance, by using The Light of Knowledge and the understanding of experience, to make more refined, comprehensive, and resolute decisions. Failure is an opportunity to transcend a New Horizon of Truth, by learning to tell the difference between the genuine and the erroneous, even when they appear to be mirrored reflections of one another. Failure is learning to see the difference between a path that fails to serve you, and The Path that succeeds in serving one and all. Failure is the opportunity to begin a new day, to don The Light of Compassion, multiply The Power of Virtue, and commune with The Intelligence of Truth. Success is about showing others the two-way door of dominion between the Light and the void, and teaching them how it swings back and forth, so they too may find The Way of The Path, become Children of The Light, and possess their own Power of Dominion to echo into the Vastness of the great and distant future.)

Faith foreshadows a bright new morning
Within the darkness of the abyss.

Obligations are heavy as a mountain
Sacrifice
As light as a feather.

Courage faces the impossible answer
With the improbable solution.

Truth is that light of knowledge
Which divides the darkness of ignorance.

Virtue is that bridge of hope
Which crosses the chasm of hopelessness.

Love is that unstoppable force
Which heaves the immovable object.

All are the light of wisdom
Which escorts us safely through the tempest.

Physical Love

(Eros, Greek; is referenced to the kinds of love as seen in one's physical sexuality. It can refer to an affectionate form of the embrace of copulation, the sincere adoration of another's physical form, or the same act as seen with the intention of sexual lust. The connotation of a self-satisfying form of sexual desire insinuates that one doesn't care for another's physical love needs, another's intellectual love needs, or another's spiritual love needs. They seek only to satiate their own desires or instinctive appetites. However, this might also be seen as a sexual desire that two lovers share, and the only way to tell the difference would be the surrounding actions, the connotation in which it's practiced, or the long-term outcome.

Amō; Latin Southern European; is the basic verb meaning "I love", with the infinitive Amare; "to love". The Romans used this in an affectionate sense as well as in a *roman*tic or sexual sense. Like the Greek Eros, Amō insinuates an overlap of either the use of the label, or the intention behind the meaning of the word. However, the word doesn't actually state it, or specifically delineate between meanings. As with many things in life, Amo is one of those words that has several meanings, and must be understood within the context of its use.

Ishq

(Ishq عشق, (◊) Arabic Dari, Persian Eshgh, Turkish Aşik, Urdu عشق, Azerbaijani; the literal definition of Ishq is the attachment of the heart to something. This description of love is derived from Ashiqah: a vine. A plant that grows, matures, and entangles itself with, and or around another. When love takes root in the heart of a lover, everything other than God is effaced or abdicated. Someone who loves after the growing manner of Ishq, possess a symmetrical amalgamation between the benevolent passion of sexual desire, the intellectual Amae of Ren, and the spiritual love of Altruism. Because of this, Ishq is held up as a Virtuous and healthy form of physical love between two companions. In the same manner that following The Path of Virtue leads to The Path of Truth, so too The Path of Ishq leads to The Path of Ren...

If the European Eros has a duel connotation, which insinuates a difference between lust and benevolent physical passion without stating it, then The Middle East Ishq insinuates three connotations that also must be understood within the context of its use---

1) Much like the story of Romeo and Juliette, wherein the overindulgence of their fiery passion was woefully absent of the tempered moderation of familial and social approval, which lead to their mutual demise--- Ishq can turn from a growing vine that spreads life, to a consumptive vine with a voracious appetite. Its passions become so powerful that it looses sight of all other concerns. It goes from embracing its lover to choking everyone that it is entangled with. It goes from birthing new life into the world, to dragging everyone who's ensnared into the abyss. Truly, Romeo and Juliette is not a love story, but a warning of mankind's habitual nature, which reveals that too much love is just as dangerous as the absence of love.

2) In the amalgamation and symmetrical balance of The Path of The Middle Way, Ishq love is meant to be something that's nurtured in just such a manner, so it grows, expands, and matures into a love of greater significance and vastness of purpose. Like a root to a growing tree, there are always proper proportions between the size of the

root, and the degree of maturity of the tree. In a healthy tree, or in a healthy love life between two "growing trees that intermingle their roots", there exists a harmonic balance that grows in unison between the lovers. When matured, Ishq possesses a Power, much like Virtue, that creates a field of influence, a field of dominion (Δ) that directs and defends one's connections, thoughts, and actions toward a Life Path lived in accord with Divine Providence. Love becomes a vehicle that will carry the lovers from one end of this world into the highest realms of the other.

3) The fiery passions of Ishq indirectly point out its bland and equally unstable opposite. A form of non-rooted love is when one who is *professing* to be an Ishq lover is compelled to rubout or willfully ignore the allure of other potential partners. One is compelled to practice the restraining virtue of faithfulness, because they aren't rooted with their lover. Suddenly, another form of danger is seen to be imminent; cheating, and the absconded lover who seeks remuneration, and the satisfaction of the blood of revenge.)

The Path of Eros and Ishq

(In the Turkish interpretation, the Ishq lover can only be "In Love" with one person from the opposite sex (Aşık). Ishq is not a form of love that is accepted as healthy or Virtuous to feel for one's parents.

Kāma Sanskrit: Devanagari काम Buddhism, Hinduism; can be interpreted as sexual desire, sexual pleasure, or sensual gratification. When used in a broader sense, it can also mean desire, wish, or passion without the sexual connotations. This kind of love is considered in some Buddhist and Hindu faiths to be an obstacle to The Path of Enlightenment. In this faith, The Path of Body Love is considered an inhibitor to The Path of Spiritual Love.

Wait! wait! wait! I feel as though I was listening to a beautifully designed symphony whose composition of diverse notes interwove perfectly to create a consistent fabric of soothing melodies that sang a greater understanding within the reasoning of my mind, brought elations to the warm feelings of my heart, and elevated my soul to rapturous revelries of heavenly delight (Δ). But now, I feel like I'm left with the irritation of an itch that I just can't scratch, because someone just told me that the greatest form of Love was when I was Ishq-rooted to my lover body, mind, and soul--- Yet, there's a major religion out there that tells me I can't reach enlightenment with my Lover by my side, because being united in the physical sense will inhibit my spiritual growth.

Yet, according to some other religions, "Celestial Marriage" is a spiritual, intellectual, and physically loving union between a man and woman that extends into the eternities beyond life and death. Unlike "till death do we part" marriage, eternal marriage is considered to be the ultimate expression of marital union, a path to the highest degree of heaven, and the foundational function of eternal increase. In that religion, The Path of Creation is The Path toward Vastness.

So which is it? A life of abstinence and devotion to meditation in far off monasteries for the opportunity to reach enlightenment and the rainbow body? Or a union with a lover, which might cause one to reach The Celestial Kingdom of Heaven, and attain vastness via the eternal increase of offspring? Before we attempt to answer that question, and subsequently alienate the opposing parties, let's not so much as seek to change our belief systems, as much as refine them. Let's not so much as seek to make better decisions, as much as more comprehensive observations. Let's not so much as seek to remove all danger, but be more resolute in the knowledge that we are seeking and following The Right Path. Let's attain some perspective, and perhaps unveil a new paradigm, which vaults our faith and knowledge over a New Horizon of Virtuous Knowledge, True Understanding, and Wise Compassion.)

Perspectives

A Western Theological Perspective

(To the human psyche, the concept of "Forbidden Fruit" is about that thing which the awareness doesn't desire until the moment it's denied. Moreover, it's about the psyche suddenly desiring the new thing more than that thing which it truly wanted in the first place. Like bait on a hook, the conscious awareness and its motivating desires, completely forgets what it was originally pursuing, and is lured down a false path to the empty rewards of that which it is shown, but always denied, until the trap slams shut, and it's too late.

The Light of Knowledge divides the darkness of ignorance, and like a moth to the flame, we're drawn in by the allure of some new bit of the unknown. If it's false virtue. If it's a truth of the path of conflict. Or even more dangerous, if it's the mirrored illusion of Virtuous Love, we're suddenly in great danger. "The allure of the dark side" always appeals to our needs and desires, while failing to actually serve us. It catches our eyes, before it connects with our heart. It feeds our cravings, before it nourishes our body. The dark side always takes a path that resembles the genuine Path, but it always ends up on an oppositional or destructive path.

"A thing" that is labeled as secret, sacred, or even forbidden is habitually held out like a lure to our psyche compelling us to seek its attainment. In this way, rites of passage are able to be placed in the way, which are said to "test" our devotion, or make us "worthy" to achieve the knowledge, status symbol, or that "Thing" which we "desire", or that "Fruit" which has been forbidden. In reality, each obstacle is used like an investment that one doesn't want to waste by turning away from that which cost them so dearly. In this manner, one is continually drawn deeper into the ploy, with ever-greater investments, and an ever-greater desire not to lose those investments. Eventually, the time comes when they're so invested, that even if they realize the ploy, they still boast of their achievements or new status as part of "the elect group", and inadvertently drag others into the same trap. This becomes a self-fulfilling prophecy that is governed, not by a Deity, or the esprit de corps of real valor, but by the madness of our own psychological mythos. Nowhere, absolutely nowhere, is this psychological snare more universally employed and blatantly abused than with love, emotional desire, and physical sexuality. This, because Love is one of our primary movers, so of course this is the cord that manipulative malefactors will pluck at.

Remember not to forget... The most dangerous path in any endeavor is one that manipulates you in such a manner, so as to make you think you're following the correct Path. When in reality, you're dedicating your life to an erroneous path that is the mirrored illusion of the original. What could be more dangerous than the illusion that "All's well"? The moment the trap slams shut, the hook is in your jaw, and your fate is sealed.)

(In Hellenistic Theology, anything that was not spiritual was considered corruptible. Thus, because flesh was considered "not spiritual", the logical conclusion to this premise was a desire toward the abolition of the needs of the "corruptible flesh" in favor of the subconscious ambitions of the spirit. Hellenistic philosophical conclusions labeled anything of the flesh as negative, evil, or something to be covered, hidden, or overcome via the cultivation of greater spiritual will. Thus, because we find the roots of Judaism, Christianity, and Islam connected through The Hellenistic Culture, and those three theologies cover most of the earth, one sees a common theme of "forbidden fruit" woven in amongst their common storylines, which always insinuate forbidden sexuality.

Even the forbidden fruit of "The Knowledge of Good and Evil" is carried about with sexual connotations. The pictorials, art, and storylines of Adam and Eve always insinuate that the taboo knowledge achieved by Adam was the forbidden fruit of sexuality, via the adoption of shame that "should" accompany the greater awareness of unlawful carnal knowledge. In the story, God notices that Adam is aware of that which he was otherwise oblivious of before the effects of "the apple". God notices that Adam now understood that "nakedness" was somehow wrong, and to become "moral", both of them had to "cover up" the "sin" of being naked in front of God.

The thing that shows us the snare is if we interpret this theosophy in a manner reminiscent of the Confucian Monkey fallacy. Where one attains "morality" by sequestering their talents and abilities, rather than by multiplying The Light of their talents and abilities in a Path that progresses towards vastness. To follow the other path is to miss all the glory that The Tree of The Fruit of Knowledge has to teach us! It's to move in such a manner that doesn't do wrong, but it also doesn't create anything good.

The biggest hint to unlocking the insinuations of the story of The Garden of Eden, as it relates to the "Tree", is "The Fruit of Awareness", which the fruit of The Tree of Knowledge gives. The Fruit of Awareness is "The Light" of The Tree of Knowledge. The Light of Knowledge divides the darkness of ignorance and its dominion of greater awareness altars one's paradigm with its vast perspectives. Not only does it arrest the irrational reasoning of suffering, but also it transforms the darkness into a new illuminated perspective. This act transfigures whoever "consumes it" into a new Paradigm.

In the same manner that The Light transforms one's definition of a darkened room, so too The Light of Awareness can transform the meaning of a story. Rather than a tale about original sin... Rather than an eternal stain on mankind, which must be overcome via rites of passage that you must invest into... Rather than a story about disobedience to a deity who was so obviously standing in the same Light of Knowledge Himself... The tale of the "Tree" becomes a story about mankind's progression--- not so much as out of the darkness of ignorance--- but toward The Light of Knowledge and The Fruit of Awareness.

The Tree of Knowledge represents that Light which allows significant growth, a step out of the darkness of ignorance, by stepping into The Light of Knowledge, and receiving The Gift of Greater Awareness. The Light and Knowledge of something is in itself The Rite of Passage that moves one into a new paradigm. In the same manner that The Connection of Love, The Intellect of Truth, and The Act of Virtue is a movement into a particular condition, so too The Fruit of Awareness is a movement into a peculiar condition. In all forms and interpretations, The Way of The Path is not so much a movement out of the darkness, but a movement toward ever greater Light (X » Y » Z).)

(These are two of the most ancient symbols known to mankind overlaid with one another. In every language on earth, the larger circle is called The Flower of Life, while the other is called The Tree of Knowledge. In the same manner that there's a missing apple from the story of Adam and Eve, wherein there is yet something described, so too there is a missing aspect from this image, yet even in its absence it's still there. That is, if you can detect the absence of something which should be present.)

Our hearts reflect like a mirror
That which we store within them

(From the time he left the lavish comfort of his father's palace, Siddhartha could sense the "I know not" of that Intelligent Force, which possessed greater meaning and eternal vastness. He sensed incongruities between this greater "I know not", and the lesser illusions that overlaid his reality, even though he couldn't fully discern, or completely comprehend it. Just like Bodhidharma, Siddhartha sensed more than the eyes could see, the ears could hear, or the tongue could taste. He sensed something that laid half way over the next horizon of greater awareness, but he couldn't quite reach "The Fruit".

For many years Siddhartha sought enlightenment behind this Intelligent Kami of Truth that lay just over the horizon of his "I know not". He followed several Gurus, joined numerous religious groups, and attained a number of disciples. He sought the path he should follow by exercising several mortification styled austerities. Furthermore, he did all of this in the ambition of finding the answers to his Life Path questions, about the causation of suffering, and the reason for death. Indeed, Siddhartha faithfully stood on many New Horizons of Truth, and valiantly crossed over to the other side to make his understanding One with The Light of their Knowledge.

As the story goes--- And it came to pass, while meditating on the bank of a river in India, Siddhartha heard a teacher speaking to their pupil. "If you tighten the string too tight, the string will snap. If it's too lose, the instrument will not play".

Siddhartha recited the phrase as a proclamation, but he understood this statement as more than just how tight or lose a string should be on an instrument to make it play as intended. He understood how this pattern of "Too much or too little" made an appearance in every discipline. Above and beyond that vast realization, Siddhartha grasped how this concept's repetitiveness in many walks of life revealed an invisible Power that was causing it to happen.

As a student standing on the precipice of vastness, Siddhartha was staring teary eyed into the magnificence of a radiant universe, which was challenging his youth and inexperience to comprehend the immensities of an eternal splendor that had just been uncovered for him. He was struck by The Thunderbolt of Enlightenment when The Light of Knowledge and The Fruit of Greater Awareness vanquished the darkness of ignorance and bondage of suffering. The moment that The Intelligent Kami of Truth appears from over the horizon, envelopes your awareness, and expands your realm by expanding the veil of the "I know not" from the intellect of your mind. For Siddhartha, it was an emergent awareness, where a concept of balance and imbalance applied just as equally to the physical, the intellectual, or the spiritual. In the same manner that Bodhidharma spoke The Great Truth in recognition of a greater vastness that lay beyond his "I know not", so too Siddhartha was correct in labeling this Power "The Middle Way" when he replied to himself, "The Way of The Path is The Middle Way."

As the story continues--- And it came to pass, Siddhartha broke his fast with a bowl of rice milk, which he was given by a passing village girl. Upon witnessing him break his fast and disavow his austerities, his disciples felt betrayed. They thought Siddhartha had given up The Quest for Enlightenment, and in doing so, had failed as their Guru.

The disciples were still in the darkness of ignorance, and were therefore under the dominion of a different manner of reasoning; a different paradigm. The Light of Knowledge had not expanded their awareness over a New Horizon of Truth. They had not yet experienced the eye-opening phenomenon of The Thunderbolt of Enlightenment. The veil had not been lifted from their minds, and they had no Fruit of Greater Awareness. They yet slumbered in a kind of dark ignorance that governed their reasoning. So of course, they reasoned differently, came to different conclusions, and treated him as a social pariah. However, like any good teacher, Siddhartha said the same thing in a simpler manner, "To learn is to change". Nevertheless, in the same manner that the word "water" cannot replace the many experiences that water has to offer, so too Siddhartha's mere words couldn't replace the many Horizons that The Thunderbolt of Enlightenment has to illuminate. His disciples yet remained in darkness, and still couldn't comprehend the abrupt change, so they left him concluding that he was the one who was on the wrong path.

Kneeling by the water, this abandonment by his friends and disciples brought a degree of uncertainty about the genuineness of what he'd just experienced. Looking for The Fingerprint of Intelligence via a test of authenticity, Siddhartha put the empty bowel into a flowing stream and said, "If I can reach Enlightenment by following The Middle Way, may this bowel float upstream", and it did! Thus, Siddhartha began to walk and teach The Path of The Middle Way, where The Intelligence of Truth causes all things come together as One.)

(Like a candle that passed its flame to another, Siddhartha connected with The Source of Intelligence in a manner that united physical Truth, which invigorated the matter of his body... The communion sparked an intellectual Truth, enlightening the intellect of his mind... In addition, the bonding awakened a spiritual Truth, which empowered The Intelligence of his Spirit. More significantly, the Force behind this event united these three faculties as One, and awakened a greater more Divine inborn sentience.

Remembering that neither the question nor the answer is more important than the journey of discovery. At the beginning of his quest, Siddhartha felt compelled to seek the greater good by abandoning his wife and child in order to serve the utilitarian theory of finding the meaning to suffering, which if achieved, could better serve all. He followed several Gurus, but he also left several Gurus. He joined numerous religious groups, but he also left numerous religious groups. He attained a number of disciples, but he also lost a number of disciples. He sought Enlightenment by exercising several mortification styled austerities, but he also abandoned those austerities as well... In the end, rather than continuing to follow utilitarian ideologies, he adopted the moral idealism of The Path of The Middle Way, because it was this Path that revealed the invisible Force, which he initially sought, and we are currently seeking.

Before he made his journey, "the greater good" of utilitarianism took him down one path, while moral idealism eventually showed him another path. However, The Way of The Path is a journey of perspectives, and the difference in perspectives that lay between "Siddhartha the student" and "Siddhartha the master" was not as important as the journey that lay between the two paths he followed. The greater meaning of the journey is to cultivate and polish The Way of The Path with sincerity and watchful care at every step along the way. The journey gives The Light of Knowledge, The Quest unveils The Fruit of Awareness, and Virtue, Truth, and Love multiplies all Light into Vastness. The events that happen along the way, on our own path, allow us to refine ourselves not refine the world in which we reside. Moreover, it is in this process of refinement that gives us a power, which allows us to understand that which cannot be understood, to taste that which cannot be tasted, to touch that which cannot be felt, to hear that which cannot be heard, and catch a fleeting glimpse of that which cannot be seen.)

(A child must travel over many horizons before they find greater treasure in the blue sapphire sea, the hidden secrets of an emerald forest, or the greater meaning to their place in the circle of life on snow capped mountains. Like fumbling about in a dark room, even the Masters who are thought of as the wisest of all teachers, are compelled to use what they have while they reside in the darkness of ignorance and inexperience of youth. It's the human condition that we are compelled to journey down various paths in order to find, understand, and be willing to follow The Middle Way of The Path.

Part of being cultured in life is seeing and learning about what others have seen and learned. Moreover, it's about seeing what both of you have seen and what both of you have repeated. These are the stories of life that repeat themselves of their own accord in every time and every culture. They may take the form of "The Romeo and Juliet Syndrome" of new, lost, or unrequited love. They may look like childhood adventures, or senseless childhood tragedies, which happen in identical manners. They might look like war, conquests, and defeats just as easily as they might look like the Virtue, Truth, and Compassion of the Saints of any given religion.

There are issues between man and mankind, and issues between man and God. Then there are the ringing of familiar bells, the singing of familiar songs, the observation of repeating seasons, and the recognition of many beginnings and many endings. These patterns are just as True for finding Virtue, as they are for finding Love. It is just as true for learning the art of war, as it is for learning the art of peace. And once again, like finding the middle pattern of "too much or too little", this new pattern of "Seeking and maturing awareness", via the growing faith and knowledge of a journey, The Fruit of Awareness of a Quest, and leaping over a New Horizon of The Thunderbolt of Enlightenment emerges of its own accord to reveal its Vast, yet untouchable, presence. This is The Light of Knowledge and The Fruit of Awareness, which have a delicate, but fleeting, taste to them that moves over the horizon of awareness very quickly. Like a rare white flower that only blooms under extraordinary conditions, you must savor this flavor in this moment, and remember how to share it tomorrow.

This is The Way of The Path.)

A Secular Perspective

When we perceive the ways of nature
We remove the conflict within

(Those actions, which constitute Virtue for one physical construct, don't necessarily constitute Virtue for another physical construct. The Cheetah attains Virtue, Truth, and Love with a degree of balance between its kinesthetic intellect of speed, the physical truth of its limited strength, while at the same time it embraces the intellectual Love for its offspring, which it must hunt to provide for. If it doesn't attain a balance between these, it will suffer the consequential dominion of another path. The cheetah must find and follow a Middle Way, which is partially defined by the expression of its physical construct, and what exists in the world around it. If it goes beyond its physical design, becomes arrogant, and takes on the pride of lions, then its end is near.

This attainment of Virtue via "the demands of the expression of one's construct" is True for every life form. The cuttlefish must use the diversity of its skin for attraction, camouflage, and hypnotism. Smaller male cuttlefish must camouflage their skin patterns after that of the females. They use this ploy to gimmick their way past the larger more physically adept males, so they may hand off their seed to the females within the confusion of many intertwined tentacles. A female cuttlefish uses her tentacles to receive and hold several male's seed. She must reach Virtue, via the prudence of selecting which one she will fertilize herself with. If she does not choose well, her offspring will not possess good genes, they will be subject to the dominion of those who do have good genes, and they will not reach the following generation.

As it is with one form of life, so too is it with another form of life. As it is with lesser intelligences, so too it is with greater Intelligences. Just as The Synchronicity of Construct is with one species, so too is emergent congruency with other species. To attain The Path of Virtue within the expression of her construct, the queen bee must produce thousands of offspring in a very short period. Not because copious amounts of sex, or selecting a sexual partner from many "slave" drones is a moral issue, but because this is what her anatomy, intellectual programming, and the societal design of the hive dictates she accomplish. Should a queen bee select the moral code fallacy of abstinence for even a short duration of time, she will not find her genes in the next generation, and the entire hive will pay the consequences of her inaction (Page 79, Three monkeys).

Because their construct is dominated by the expression of feathers, the male peacock must use his feathers in a demonstration of virility and veracity to win the favor of the female of the species. A male deer must run faster than the female deer, and it must be strong enough to fight off other males. Both male and female salmon must swim hundreds of miles upstream, just for the opportunity to spawn once before they die. Plants must release copious amounts of pollen into the air, or cooperate with insets to reach the next generation.

Nature never fails. However, when it fails to produce offspring, nature doesn't fail in killing off the inadequate breed, to allow those breeds who follow The Path to keep going. Thus, even in failure, nature doesn't fail to succeed. Each species of plant or animal obeys the dictates of the design of their construct to achieve the union of The Path of Ishq, attain their form of altruistic Virtue, and demonstrate a greater Truth in the continuing emergence of The Grand Design.

The human construct could never follow these paths and hope to survive, let alone use them to achieve The Genuine Path of Physical Love. However, that's where The Spice of Comparative Etymology can be used "outside of its box" in a secular manner. Rather than comparing words from other languages and cultures, we compare and contrast our sexuality with other life forms. When we comprehend something from the paradigm of many disciplines, perspectives of vastness become quantifiable observations that amplify the meaning and significance of each point of knowledge. This singular act renders an altogether new perspective of each observation. The methodology of reasoning through the two way door of observation incontrovertibly demonstrates they are all spokes in the same wheel of greater understanding, all gears of the same machine with a common function, and all parts of a larger device that possess a greater purpose, and more marvelous meaning. Alternating perspectives gives us insight into The Grand Design, The Middle Way, and proper use of our own sexuality. If one will attain Virtue by embracing patience, and read the previous section again while thinking of human sexuality, then one will be rewarded with great insight, and a vast new perspective, as to what constitutes The Path of Ishq-Love, as well as the illusions of its mirrored opposite.)

A Divergent Perspective

(To gain ever more perspective, and shift the gears of our lives into the paradigm of the two-way door of eternal vastness, let's look closer at the concept of following two paths that appear similar, yet have dissimilar outcomes; "Living to fight, or Fighting to live"... "Living to fight": is an individual who wraps their life around fighting, rather than someone who learns to fight, because they might be compelled every now and then to fight for survival. They follow the philosophy "Let your plans be as dark as night, and strike like lightening from the darkness of the unknown." This kind of incessant attention to conflict produces aggressive outcomes, and boisterous egos that purport themselves as ruler over another, merely because of their fighting skill. They fall in lust with their conquests or accolades, and taunt their opponents into duels, so they may declare supremacy, dictate order, exercise control, or wield worldly power over others who only pay homage by threat of force. In the end, these inflated egos are inevitably knocked off their pedestals, and their "loyal" followers pay homage to the next ego until their time ends as well. This path is violent and short-lived, many suffer, and while the events may be remembered, they will be held up as evil people doing evil things. A path to avoid for The Children of The Light.

"Fighting to live": this is an individual who learns how to fight, and is prepared to use their skills should the need arise. This form of skill produces a movement toward the discipline of one's body, mind, and soul, and becomes a form of self-defense that works toward the common good of all. It spreads the sacred knowledge of advanced personal protection to those deemed worthy of protecting the knowledge, because they follow The Path of Honor. This Path camouflages it from those who do not follow The Path of Truth,

Virtue, or Compassion; those deemed unworthy of Trust. In this condition, everyone is safer because of the fighter's mere presence. Everyone is better off, because everyone realizes their part, high and low, within the accomplishments of the whole: including the pugilist who serves all. Yes, he even serves his opponent with good will; Ren, to destroy "opposition" by making his rival into his comrade. A warrior is not charged with inciting conflict, the warrior is charged with bringing a halt to contention and strife.

The pugilist understands that "Martial Arts" means to "gather together": the skill of leveraging all resources. This is not just the tools and resources for the execution of conflict, but also the tools and resources for the prevention of, or elixir to, conflict. This includes marshaling the art of peace via The Dominion of Light, The Fruit of Knowledge, and The Fire of Intelligence to bring about a favorable outcome for everyone. In this manner, one may ensure that a future spark of conflict isn't fanned into an inferno of destruction, which consumes everything they created. Like Ren and Amae, the opponent is taken care of in the name of the greater good of the individual, and the general wellbeing of the collective.

Victory is achieved
When there are no losers

Because "living to fight" appears indistinguishable from "fighting to live", to the uninitiated observer, many people often mistake one for the other and commit the ultimate fallacy. They avoid all forms of the act to the detriment of the absence of the positive aspect. They digress from using their talents and abilities, to covering up their talents and abilities.

In terms of fighting, this fallacy strips individuals of their protection, and can leave entire societies exposed to the viciousness of aggressive entities. In terms of the two-way door of dominion, this is like not using fire or electricity, because someone could be injured by them, and knowingly and willingly suffer the darkness of the absence of their positive dominion. In terms of physical Love, should an entire population avoid copulation all together, because it too carries with it a negative expression, they will soon find themselves following the way of other abstinent societies. These are entire societies that existed, and yet very few even know they existed. Perhaps, not because they failed to do good deeds, but more because they have no descendents to carry on the path they chose.

In all the benevolent holiness of these "Gnostic" like societies, they failed in one regard, they did not attain The Path of Vastness. They did not follow the precept of lighting the candles of others with life itself. This precept of multiplicity is just as True with igniting the spark of life in a woman's womb, as it is with multiplying into vastness the condition of Virtue, Truth, and Love.)

(To be successful on the path of conflict one is compelled to practice the arts of distraction and deception--- To arrive unexpectedly, attack suddenly, kill fiercely, and win decisively. To be successful on The Path of Truth one is compelled to distill the illusions of deception (∫)- -- To seek out greater Truth, find greater meaning, and reveal the big picture of Vastness--- and pass on it onto others. This oppositional design compels the individual to choose between following one path or the other, or suffer the consequences of attempting to follow two oppositional forces at once. In the same manner that one cannot choose to douse the lights and expect to live in the Light, so too one cannot live in the Light and think they can get away with deceiving those who possess The Fruit of Awareness. On this path, one will be rejected by one side, and then cast out by the other.

Yet, it's not only about choosing to follow one path or another. In the same manner that darkness is only the absence of Light, so too vice is only an absence of Virtue. In the same manner that a lie is the absence of Truth, so too lust is only an absence of Love. In the same manner that one may avoid the path of conflict by adhering to The Way of The Path, so too may one avoid being compelled to follow the negative path of physical love by following The Genuine Path of Ishq Love.

In the same manner that One cannot violate The Path of Virtue and hope to attain The Path of Love, so too one cannot ignore The Path of Truth and hope to attain The Path of Virtue. One weaves The Path of Truth within The Path of Virtue, The Path of Love will emerge from the "I know not", appear as though it were always present, and lead to The Path of Vastness. If one is seeking love, companionship, and a counterpart to enjoy life with, the next step of The Path is attained by connecting with, thinking about, and acting upon The Paths of Virtue, Truth, and Love. Its proof of dominion will be a revelatory New Horizon of expanded awareness, a new taste in The Fruit of Knowledge, and a movement into greater Vastness with The Fruit of Awareness. Then, your companion will arrive from the "I know not", appear as though they were always present, and both of you will move into vastness by creating a new life.)

Love

If love were a Fire
Then a lover's face
Would not be drowned in tears

If love were an Ocean
Then a lover's heart
Would not burn with desire

If love were a Paradise
Then a lover's veins
Would not coarse with venom

If love were a Poison
Then a lover's lips
Would not drink its elixir

Love's Circle

If love is infinite
Why has my lover gone?

If love is a season
Why does my lover not return?

If love is so fulfilling
Why do I feel so empty?

The sting of love has become a dagger
In the heart of my dreams
The bug of love has become a plague
In the sickness of my mind
The elixir of love has become a poison
In the passion of my soul

If I could but love for a single second
I would make that moment last 10 lifetimes
I would live in a world
Where a single moment in time
Was an eternity of blissful ignorance
Of the emptiness of the following morning

In that world
The science of love would be a raging fire
That burned away the ocean of my tears
In that world
The magic of love would be an eternal ocean
That quenched the fire in my veins
In that world
The alchemy of love would be the elixir
That cured the sorrow of my soul,
The paradise that healed my broken heart,
And the rising sun
That illuminated the darkness
Of my soul's eternal night.

In that world
Though I were dead
I would gather my heel and my leg
I would gather my arms and my backbone
I would gather my dreams
Crackling in the dark cave of my skull
I would knit myself together in secret
And come forth from death
A Bright and Shining Thing,

Born anew, my face aglow with radiant heat

In that world
Before me would stand my love
Within me would be my warmth
Returned to me would be my reason
In my heart would flow my nourishment
In my chest would rage my passion
In that world
If love were the day I would never sleep
If love were the night I would never awake
The world would spin west to east
The seasons would come and go
The grass would be green
The sky would be blue
And water would flow downhill
I would once again be whole
And life would be worth living once again

Love Duality

Seek the wine press as though
The flowing wine would fill thy heart with love.

Know the vineyard as though
Your heart were the root itself.

Seek the daybreak of love as
The grapevine longs for nourishing light.

Seek love's evenings as
The lunar spectacle rises in her full beauty.

The grape trembles before the winepress
The heart's root cries out when pruned
Daybreak voids the lunar beauty
And the sun dries the pressed grape.

By the crushing of the grape
Is the flowing wine of love made

By the pruning of the root
We are reminded of whom we love

Lunar beauty will return
With her many phases

And though dried out
The grape is just as sweet as a raisin.

True love cannot be overshadowed
Pruned
Nor dried out
For if it is over shadowed
The light will shine through

If it is pruned
It will cry out for its lost

And if dried out
The nectar of love becomes sweeter to the taste
And more satisfying to the soul

True love lasts in life and death,
True love endures while it is loved and hated
True love determines destiny

If love be a word, let it be spoken
If love be wine, let it be drank
If love be Luna's beauty, let it shine

If love be all things of my vineyard,
Let it quench my famished lips,
Fill me until I can drink no more
And let its glory transcend all eternity.

Love Is

Love's Passion

I am the thief in the night
Picking the lock of her modesty
With the key of my words

I am the hunter sparking the flint and steel
To ignite the bonfire of her passion

I am the bee making honey
From the sweet nectar of her beauty

I am the Romeo to her Juliet
I am the Paradise of her elixir
I am the flame a-top her fire

But, she...

..... is the moon to my midnight
She is the water to my thirst
She is the treasure of my desire

The love we make
Is the warmth in the cold night
It's the logic to our insanity
And the fulfilling light
In the darkness of loneliness

Because life without love
Is like a flame without heat
And life without you
Is like a bird without wings
The light of my passion
And the heat of your desire
Ignite the wings of our phoenix
To soar to heaven's top spire!

Spiritual Love

Love is the messenger of God
He who obeys God and His Messenger
Has already attained the highest achievement

Islam

You shall love the Lord your
God with all your heart
And with all your soul
And with all your mind (Δ)
This is the first and greatest commandment
And the second is like the first
You shall love your neighbor as yourself

Christianity

(While Islamic Sufis believe that Love is a projection of the essence of God to the universe, Hebrews call The Source of all Energy and life giving force "Eil". In The Way of The Path and from The Creations of The Source, they are describing a Force, Power, and The Pearl of Great Price of The Path of Love. In the same manner that many cultures have their own stories about The Thunderbolt of Enlightenment, so too we can think of these descriptions as different cultures experiencing the same thing, but using the etymology of their own language to describe and pass it on. Thus, by any other label, Love is a Force from The Source, which is One with the amalgamation of {The Three Powers of Virtue Δ (180 f), The Three Powers of The Intelligence of Truth Δ (180 f), and The Three Transforming Energies of Love Δ (180 f)}.)

(<u>Agape</u>, Greek Theosophy; from Greek Theosophia, from Theos = divine + Sophia, wisdom; literally "<u>Divine Wisdom</u>": *The decision to love, being an act of Godly wisdom.* It's a charitable, selfless, *altruistic*, and unconditional kind of love, which is yet practiced with Virtuous Knowledge, True Understanding, and Wise Compassion (Page, 34). Although it's seen as the positive side of parental love, The Romans used it in both this affectionate sense, as well as in a romantic or positive sexual sense. Thus, insinuating a *duality* behind the meaning of its label, similar to Amae and Amō, or Erotus, and Ishq.

<u>Ai</u>, Japanese Buddhism (愛): Is a passionate or caring love. Ai possesses the ability to grow toward the selfish form of Amae, the physical side of Ishq, or mature toward The Benevolent Altruism of Celestial Enlightenment, which is a core idea behind Compassion. Like the growing vine of Ren or Ishq, one's degree of adopting this

form of Love reflects one's capacity to love and embrace small or increasingly larger collectives. Like the ubiquitous nature of light and dark, it also reminds us there's a Pro or Anti duality, which makes its appearance in all labels of love.

Karuṇā, Buddhism, Hindi Theology/Tradition: is that Compassion and mercy which reduces the suffering of others. Pāli is complementary to wisdom, a necessary ingredient for the attainment of enlightenment, and the correct employment of all forms of Love.)

(Divine Compassionate Wisdom, can be likened to burning your hand on a hot stove, or using that same stove to cook your food with. Like Prometheus handing man fire, one must take caution with their application and practice of the different forms of Compassion. You desire to multiply The Light of Compassion within others. You don't want others multiplying the darkness of their hate and discontentment within you. In the same manner that too much Amae can make slaves out of obligates, so too having your candle of compassion blown out just one too many times can transform you into an old scrooge at a young age.

Remember not to forget, The Child of Light cultivates Virtuous Knowledge, True Understanding, and Wise Compassion as One within their prayers and meditations, then they echo it into the open arms of the universe (∞). Just like "Eil". However, when it comes to lighting other's candles, one should hold out their candle, and allow its light to shine in the darkness of hopelessness. Those who no longer desire to live in darkness will come, and those who yet desire to live in darkness will remain consumed with their own concerns.

The Child of darkness does not follow this path; they say and do things to try to force their will on others. They don't enlighten, they extinguish. They don't multiply, they divide. They compel others to obey their ways; they threaten, spread fear, and withhold all forms of life's necessities to coerce others to follow their ideologies.

None of the great, loved, and revered masters follow the path of The Child of Darkness. Within the realm of each New Horizon, The Child of Light practices the wisdom of caution, using Virtuous Knowledge to understand how best to approach each situation, even if that means maintaining a certain distance from those involved. At the same time, they practice Wise Compassion for individuals who suffer from the form of reasoning that the dark ones tend to use as their moral compass.

The Children of The Light must remember that the dark ones are not really their anger, nor are they their hate, nor are they their fear, nor are they their dark ways of reasoning... They are the Force behind the flesh, the intellect behind the face, and the spirit that slumbers in the darkness of ignorance. They are a divine being that just so happens to be suffering from "the absence of the positive aspect"--- The Guidance of Virtue, The Direction of Truth, and The Service of Compassion. They suffer from too few New Horizons, they lack The Light of Knowledge, and they haven't tasted The Fruit of Awareness.

The Child of Light possesses a measure of all of these things, and while it's not the Child of Light's job to give into hopelessness, they must learn to understand and be wise about despair. They must find greater meaning in suffering, greater light in darkness, and locate that last ounce of hope in the wasteland of absolute hopelessness. It's the Child of Light's job to be patient, to come up with the right solution, and prove beyond the shadow of a doubt that life persists in the midst of death, truth persists in the midst of lies, and light persists in the midst of darkness. It is their responsibility to find a better way. Not just to transcend into the panacea of a new world, but to lay out a golden path that the master and student can follow into a bright new tomorrow. The Child of Light's job is to use their paintbrush of creativity and prove that light, hope, and that magical "something" that allows us to overcome all odds was always with us from beginning to end. This venture can only be achieved in that singularity where Virtue, Truth, and Love are One with Knowledge, Understanding, and Wisdom.)

(Ishq-e Haqīqi, حقیقــــی عشـــق, General Arabic: Literally means "The Real Love", but on a spiritual level, it means "The Love of God".

Al-Wadud, Arabic Islam; Is "The Loving One". In the continuing nature of The Declaration of The Basmala, "In the name of God, the most Gracious, and Merciful", "The Loving One" is one of Allah's (تعالی و ســـبحانه) 99 names.

Adveṣa & Mettā, Buddhism (Eastern): Refers to *detachment* and *unselfish interest* of one's own needs in favor of other's welfare. Kāma, prem; refers to elevated love.

Altruism; French/ Latin/ Southern European/ Christianity: Speaks of a behavior of Love. If Intelligence and The Architect cut to the heart of dominion of life over death, then Altruism cuts to the dominion of The Force of Love over the absence of love, The Power of Virtue over the empty cup of vice, and The Architect of Truth over the destruction of anger, fear, and aggression. Like the sun that goes about its Life Path shining, radiating, and multiplying, so too The Child of Light goes about their Life Path shining, radiating, and multiplying The Energy of Altruism: cultivating it within and echoing it without. In the same manner that the sun doesn't try to oppose the darkness of outer space with some kind of activist crusade or jihadist struggle, but merely follows the path for which it was designed, so too The Children of Light follow The Path by shining "The Projection of The Essence of The Source", multiplying The Life Giving Force of Eil, and radiating a beacon of The Power of Love. To think of this in another way, envision the devastation of a battlefield of war, which represents the culmination of anger, fear and aggression. Now, see the sprout of a seed that seems to emerge from the nothingness of the dust of the earth, and observe as its vine grows over the rusting hulks of weaponry. This is The Architect going about its Path without regard to those who are following "another path".

In the same manner that it is The Path of Virtue to multiply without the loss of giving something away, so too is it The Path of Altruism to multiply without loss. Just as it is The Path of Truth to multiply Truth without loss, when you speak a profound Truth into someone's ears, so too is it The Path of Ren, Ishq, and Altruism to multiply without loss when you share their light with others. In the same way that one candle multiplies its flame when shared with another candle, so too The Energy of Altruism is multiplied when one absorbs, cultivates, and then echoes the projection of the essence of God to the universe. One takes in, and radiates out "The Love of God".)

One Force

(The Way of The Path is not a rite of passage, where one is adopted if they accomplish a certain task. The Path is not a social order, as in a political party in whom someone is adopted, and seeks to climb the ranks to become a representative. The Path is not a rank, brand, or badge to be worn for bravado, boasted about, or shown off. Neither is The Path a location to where one must make a pilgrimage. In the same manner that one does not so much as move out of the darkness, as much as move toward the Light, so too The Way of The Path is not so much the abolition of anger, fear, and aggression, as much as it's a movement into a condition of Virtue, Truth, and Love. A state or modality of Oneness, where the condition itself is the point, purpose, goal, and reward all rolled into one glorious package.)

(Independent of the brand of social order into which they are born, a baby is in absolute need of the Compassion of its mother. Babies are subservient to and completely reliant upon the condition of altruism within their families, communities, and the good will of neighboring communities. Independent of their culture, children seek the condition of Virtue in the realm of fair play and Queensbury Rules when they play in the illusion of fantasy and make believe. If something is pretended for them, it is equally pretended for all others within borders of the game on a subconscious level of mutual understanding. Ironically enough, kids even have the innate unspoken moral code to allow other children to opt out by calling "Base", "Out of bounds", or even "Do over" if something is amiss. Like calling the front seat, "I called it", these universal rules are an unbreakable, but natural, code of ethics to kids.

"You will know that you are my disciples if you have Love, one for another." Even if we removed the label of Christianity, and replaced it with a new label such as Islam or Buddhism, the meaning would remain just as pertinent for one theology as it would for the human condition. Christianity embraces the idea that "Faith, Love, and Charity" brings them into a condition, in the same manner that Japanese Shinto's embrace the idea that "Truth, Courage, and Compassion" puts them into the same condition. Taoists embrace The Three Jewels of "Compassion, Moderation, and Humility" to bring them into a condition, in the same manner that Hindu's couple Ahimsa with "Compassion, Charity, and Self-Control" to bring them into the same condition. In the same manner that Jesus understood how Virtue, Truth, and Compassion are Paths that are inexorably intertwined, and it is in following those Paths that cause one to "be" a disciple, so too is there is a universal recognition that humans seek a movement into a common condition, which is reflected in the orders of our theologies, and regulations of secular laws.)

(Being a disciple of The Path is not a rite of passage into an order, it's a movement into a condition of Oneness with a Force. A condition where The Power of Virtue, Truth, and Love illuminates and amalgamates one's body, mind, and soul. It's The Light of Knowledge that possesses dominion over the darkness of ignorance. It's the wise sharing of The Fruit of Awareness, which has dominion over irrational reasoning. It's the oneness of all Forces, which gives us a symmetrical tool of dominion in emergent congruence. In the same manner that every Horizon of Truth is like another Light that illuminates the darkness of ignorance, so too every expression of Love, Virtue, or Truth is the lighting of another Light which makes our world just a little brighter.)

(It doesn't matter where you're at, what your age is, or whether you're a boy or a girl, a man or a woman. It doesn't matter if you're a Fascist, Communist, Socialist, Capitalist, Theocrat, Aristocrat, or Anarchist. It doesn't matter if you're a street sweeper, an industrial worker, a philosopher, or philanthropist. It doesn't matter if you're a Jew, a Buddhist, a Muslim, a Zoroastrian, or a Christian. All orders of mankind, all forms of government, and all expressions of livelihood have their strengths and weaknesses, their purpose and misuse, their tyrants and their shepherds, and their rise and their fall. Only when we're at One with The Source of all Energy and Life Creating Force will we find no flaw in the expression of any system.

Although it is often a proponent of one model that decries the negativity of another model, the value of a given model is not found within the models themselves, nor does their interpretation of benevolence or malevolence lie in the good opinions of its proponents or the bad opinions of its detractors. No model of mankind possesses an intrinsic value of good or evil, benevolence or malevolence. Like a wrench or a screwdriver, they only possess potential value, which matches the intent of their purpose, and whether or not those users employ them in accord with their design and intent.

If we call ourselves disciples of an order, such as Christianity, yet leave behind the condition of "Faith, Love, and Charity" which causes one to "be" a Christian, then we fail to attain Christianity, even if we've graduated through every rite of passage this religion has to offer. If we call ourselves capitalists, yet misuse the revenue we acquire, then that venture will eventually collapse, because it lacks the powers of dominion that will hold it up during times of distress. If we label ourselves an aristocrat, yet fail to properly provide for our surfs, then we've only attained a pomposity, which the surfs will eventually tear down, and replace with a new model.

Although some orders tend to work better in the short term while other orders function better over the long term, it doesn't matter nearly as much as to which model we practice, as much as in what manner we use those models. Do we use them with Virtuous Knowledge or vicious vice? Do we use them with True Understanding or deceptive distraction? Do we use them with Wise Compassionate Love, or with a form of love that that only drinks to the satiation of its own appetite?

In all lands and in all times, people fall into the fallacy of labeling a model as good or bad because of how they see others use it. On the other hand, some commit the ultimate fallacy by decrying a model as "all bad", and suffer the darkness that is the absence of the model's positive aspects. But remember, in the same manner that spoons do not make one fat, and pencils do not misspell words, so too it's not the models that are intrinsically good or bad, but their values are determined by the individuals who are using them. What causes a model to be good or bad, empowering or disempowering, is the condition of the moral fiber of the individuals running the model itself.

This is why the absence of law and order didn't matter one bit in Japan, and was so disastrous in New Orleans. Independent of what a few individuals may have had in their hearts and minds, the vast majority of the Japanese people had The Power of Genuine Love, a greater understanding of Truth, and an Honorable sense of Virtue in their heart, mind, and soul. So, the Japanese could've had any form of government that ceased to function, and they still would've been just fine. It is the Power that they shared, which possesses the real

Dominion, even when the government was functioning. It's The Force of Intelligence, within the two-way door of dominion, which makes all forms of secular or theological orders function as they are meant to.

When we disingenuously embrace the labels of Virtue, Truth, and Love in a physical, intellectual, or spiritual manner, without embracing or following The Genuine Path of their meaning, we do not attain them or the Power of their dominion. By all accounts, the labels of any order may appear genuine when they're not under the stress of duress, or the careful eye of scrutiny. However, when the trials of time and the stresses of changing situations put these labels through the refining furnaces of "The Test of Fire", the erroneous paths of virtue, truth, and love will be seen to collapse either during, or shortly after the duress of the test. Their virtues will be found to have no Guiding Power. Their truths will be found to possess no Increase of Intelligence. In addition, their form of love will be found to possess no Transformative Elixir to cause the individual or collectives to move toward something better.

Most importantly, neither their love, virtue, nor truth will be seen to multiply and spread toward vastness. This is The Mystical Love... Is it contagious? Does it catch others on fire, like the "The Fire of Intellect", and move toward the vastness of multiplication? Alternatively, does it expand and grow, only to divide its users, and implode on itself?

If it's the negative form, it will warp into a lower condition of life that will tear off the mask of the disingenuous labels, and reveal the form of vice that was truly sequestered in the individual or collective. Anger, fear, and aggression will prevail, suffering will multiply, and like the inception of a terrible tempest that threatens to wipe them all from the face of the earth, and drown them with the anchor of agony in the angry waters of hopelessness, they will attain the next step on their path, because this is the karma of the path they follow.

We know what the next step is... Hatred, suffering, bondage, and an Anti movement into the divisionism of the darkness of ignorance, as men and women who are The Guardians of The Fruit of Knowledge parish by the hundreds along with the burning of their repositories of knowledge. Then comes war, murder, and midnight raids of revenge. Eventually the situation ripens into famine, and pestilence as mass atrocities are committed by all sides in the name of righteous indignation, where the innocent on all sides are labeled as combatants, and blamed for the death of loved ones who themselves engaged in these activities. Then, when all material is exhausted, when all the men are dead, when the women are raped, and the land is pillaged there comes a desire for peace. However, not because the survivors desire Peace for the sake of Peace, but because everyone has a sickness in their stomachs, and can no longer tolerate where the karma of the path of conflict has taken them. This leads to even more sadness and ever-greater suffering later, because they never attained that which is Genuine in the first place. They'll rebuild, they will rearm, and the cycle of suffering will recommence. And why? Because they're following the same path, spinning the wheel in the same direction, and receiving the same karma. "The desire for peace, because you are sick of war," is not The Path.)

(What is The Miracle of Love that illuminates the darkness of the abyss? What is the phenomenon of love that heals open wounds? And, how do we get someone as voracious as a lion to lay down with someone as fragile as a lamb? Few things in this world provoke our passions as much as The Force of Love. Like a full tank of gasoline, love contains great potential to thrust us forward or burn us alive. In the same manner that our lives would be consumed with the misuse of fire, so too we could burn ourselves into oblivion with the misuse of love's fiery passions. In the same manner that our lives would be in darkness in the absence of electricity, so too we would suffer from the darkness of anger, fear, and aggression in the absence of love and compassion. So, not only must we learn how The Light of Love divides the darkness of apathy, but also we must learn how to use love wisely, to create abundance rather than destruction.)

(Like any other model of mankind, The Model of The Triquetra of Love has a positive side, and an equally negative side. In the same manner that The Path of Ren, Ishq, and Altruism overlap in The Path of The Middle Way of Love, so too do their opposites overlap in the same manner. Where the karmicly positive model spins in what we call a counterclockwise direction, the negative aspect spins in a clockwise direction. Ironically enough, this is True with all models, all social orders, and all paths. Virtue, Truth, and Love must come from within, they begin with an inner strength of character to cultivate them from within, and then it must be shared into the multiplicity of vastness without a desire or expectation for remuneration, which could spoil the Elixir. When this is done, when one has become One with The Force of this Power, all models and social orders will function as they are supposed to for the benefit of all their parishioners.)

(Remember not to forget; to eliminate some negative aspect of one's life it's not so important to put something down, as to pick something else up. It is not so important to remove the label, as embrace the meaning behind the label. It's far more important to pick up the recognition that there are virtues, truths, and loves that move different parts of us in different manners, than to get rid of a kind of love, truth, or virtue, because it might be perceived to contain some negative aspect. It is more important to learn how to use the Pro empowering portions of Love to benefit us, than it is to label these irremovable aspects of ourselves as malevolent, and therefore commit the ultimate fallacy--- To avoid any form of _____ to the detriment of the absence of their positive aspect.

There are Intellectual Loves that govern the movements of The Mind. There are Physical Loves that inflame the passions of The Body. There are Altruistic Loves that multiply The Intelligence of The Self. There are always Genuine and mirrored paths that karmically spin each of these aspects in a positive counterclockwise direction or negative clockwise direction. The most dangerous paths are always those which *purport* themselves to be something other than that which they truly are. It will be the fruits of their labor, illuminated by The Fruit of Awareness, which removes any disingenuous labels, and comes to identify their real karma. The most empowering Paths of Love are those that follow the symmetrically emergent Paths of the other models of The Path. They will contain a Force that causes a layered consistent emergence, which one will come to identify as congruent in all Three Realms of Truth, eternal vastness, and infinitesimal smallness, as clearly as if they were all one in the same in The Middle Way.

Just as with great power comes great responsibility, so too does The Empowering Triquetra of Love, and the disempowering triquetra of love possess the responsibility of directing and guiding great volatility. The Empowering Triquetra of Love possesses a Celestial Purpose, a Divine Power, and great rewards if used as the model suggests. Whereas, the disempowering triquetra of love possesses great danger, a perpetuity of bondage, and soliloquy of suffering. Like nitroglycerine, both paths contain the opportunity of great volatility. While one can be used to move one forward on one's Life Path, the other could very well end it at the drop of a hat.)

(Virtue, Truth, and Love begin as a set of moral guideposts with which to attain direction for the student's daily decisions. These signposts grow into a means of guidance. Eventually, they mature into a Power that creates a field of dominion. The Oneness of their Field directs and defends the student's connections, thoughts, and actions toward a Life Path multiplied in accord with Divine Providence. As the cultivation of Virtue, Truth, and Love within the disciple's prayers and meditations allows them to grow and mature, they'll note a certain Inner Illumination that allows them to see that which cannot be seen, to feel that which cannot be felt, and transcend those horizons that cannot otherwise be transcended. This is the essence of The Nectar of The Elixir found in The Chamber of Initiation. It carries a Force that can change the hearts and souls of mankind. While this maturity doesn't happen overnight, the spark of discernment occurs in the twinkling of an eye. A projection of the essence of The Source to the universe, a Force, a core emotion that is a movement into a condition where the condition itself is the point, the reward, and The Way of The Path all rolled into one glorious package of brilliance. It divides the darkness of hate with its golden glistening trail of magic; it renews corrupted souls, heals festering wounds, and reincarnates us out of the ashes of life's tragedies into a new world of endless possibilities.)

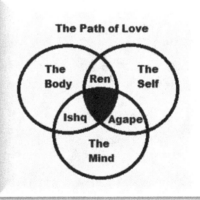

If a man dwells on the past
He robs the present.
If a man forgets the past
He robs the future.
The seeds of our future
Are nurtured by the roots of our past
And the growth in our present.

The Three
Great Quests

The more you get in touch
With your higher consciousness
The more you become
The Living Master

In the forests
There is no December.
On the mountains
There are no appointments.
In the oceans
There are no schedules.

The mountains do not think to possess
The snow that lays upon them.
The trees do not think to guide
The sun that shines across them.
The oceans do not concern themselves
With the many life forms living within them.

Think not to stop a rising tide.
Rather, enjoy riding its waves.
Lament not the changing seasons.
Rather, revel in each season's celebration.
Regret not a sitting sun.
Rather, marvel at the splendor
of the starlit night.

The Quest of Identity

Attaining The Quest of Identity is like manipulating a mystical barrier that governs the expanse of your horizon. Every day that you are on The Path, your inner divinity refines its own inner Force. This causes your inner divinity to shine brighter, illuminating your world, and expanding your awareness over new horizons. It is the maturity of this inner divinity, which moves the mystical barrier over the next horizon. This event does not join two halves into a single whole, but reveals that all horizons have always been one. It is only the veil over our eyes, and therefore our inability to spark The Divine within, which causes the illusion of separateness, and thus the need to interpret life through the lens of so many horizons.

The Quest of Identity is The Elixir.

When we meet life with preconceived notions, we fail before we begin. Virtue becomes clouded, Truth becomes uncertain, and Love becomes a list of expectations rather than a mutually shared emotion. The opportunity before us is not to say, "It can't be done", but to ask, "How can the impossible be accomplished?" for this is the mantra of all those who broke down every impossible barrier. There is great power, freedom, and opportunity in letting go of expectation. It allows the doors of possibility to open. If you will allow The Middle Way of The Path, The Power of Observation, and The Paradigm of Perspective to be your teacher, then no New Horizon will be withheld from you.

Illusions

(Has it ever dawned on you, why does a child explore their body when that body designed itself, and grew every cell within it? Why must children explore their bellybutton, as it were for the first time, when it was the child that created every body part it explores? Furthermore, why is it that although a child's intellect seems as hollow as a basketball, yet their mind and bodies possess more natural genius than the most educated scholar? After all, scholastics are only a medium of expanding a portion of our intellect about, "That which is already intelligent enough to happen of its own accord". Yet, at the same time, another, more inborn, portion of our intellect already knows millions of things of its own accord.

The hardware of our mind and body come preprogrammed with innate bio chemical, and (Source Field + Electrons = "energetically") driven software, that knows exactly how and when to create. It comes with its own program that knows how to grow, what cycles to go through, and even when to shut itself down. This innate program knows its proper blood sugar, it knows how to digest food, and excrete waste without its conscious awareness being privy to these functions. The program even knows how to connect and disconnect dendrites, to build neural pathways, and attain different cognitive operations. It knows how to beat a heart in an ever-changing fractal rhythm, and maintain a proper blood pressure long before its intellect knows what the transcribed label of fractal is, or that it even has a heart. It knows how to modify its genetic entry and exit keys to prevent external viruses from destroying the structure of its anatomy. It is well aware of the kind of energy drive systems that cause it to function, as well as how to drain those batteries, such that they become stronger when it recharges them. Most importantly, all of this functions independently of the child's cognitive intellect. An innate dissonance exists between the program of the body, mind, and the conscious awareness of every living being.

Although the intellect of a child seems to be devoid of The Light of Knowledge and The Fruit of Awareness, a parent can see the ethereal character of that child's inner Spirit periodically shine through the mask of their childhood faces. Therefore, this "un programmed" portion of our intellects is not completely devoid of something greater. A child's character is like the air that fills the basketball, we can tell that it is there, but it must be quantified differently than the basketball, even though it's considered part of the ball itself. One would have to spend a lot of quality time with the child, just to observe it flash into view, and disappear just as quickly.

By design, the genius behind all of this programming serves the ignorance of the intellect and hidden inner character of a baby. Allowing something so magnificent to be operated by the ignorance of an infantile being is like putting a five year old behind the wheel of an expensive racecar. Initially, it seems to be a very dangerous and irresponsible move. That is, unless we understood that there was some greater purpose.)

Intellect

Two Umbrella Intellects

(There are two umbrella intellects, and seven subset intellects currently labeled in our textbooks. (1) Fluid Intellect: requires no previous knowledge, or experience, and relies solely on deductive reasoning skills (connect). (2) Crystallized Intellect: the ability to use that which has been learned, and relies on one's ability to access learned information from long-term memory (think). One might think of this as the difference between the speed of a computer verses the storage space of a computer. While some individuals can be thought to possess greater speed and less storage space, others can be thought to possess greater storage space (gigs) and less speed (hertz). While some will rely more on deductive reasoning to manage problems, because they have greater speed and less storage space. Others will rely on recalling the information they learned from their scholastic endeavors, because they have more storage space and less speed.)

Seven Intellects

((1) Logical: This area of the intellect has to do with reasoning. Though traditionally excelling in areas demanding mathematical type abilities, this intellect is more adept at logically reasoning through puzzles or abstract patterns, because mathematics, puzzles, and abstract problems require this kind of intellect to solve.

(2) Spatial: This intellect is the ability to visualize with the mind's eye. To see that which is not yet fabricated, and produce it based off the interrelatedness of one's Fluid and Crystallized reasoning abilities.

(3) Linguistic: Individuals with this intellect are good at reading, writing, and telling stories. They learn best by taking notes, listening to lectures, and discussing subject matter.

(4) Kinesthetic: Superior control over one's musculature, or an ability to handle objects skillfully. This includes a sense of timing, goal of physical action, and an ability to train non-natural responses so they appear to be natural reflexes.

(5) Musical: This intellect possesses sensitivity to sounds, rhythms, and tones. Individuals with this intellect can sing, play instruments, and compose music. A linguistic intellect is typically developed in conjunction with a musical intellect.

(6) Inter personal: Or social intellect, is the ability to work well in groups. Though typically thought of as leaders, these individuals also make good followers, and enjoy discussion and debate.

(7) Intra personal: An introspective and self-reflective intellect. These individuals decipher their own feelings, motivational roots, and understand themselves very well. These are the philosophers, theologians, and writers.)

(Like degrees of logic, different levels of ability to play instrumental Music, and or different kinesthetic aptitudes, everyone possesses a degree of all of these intellects. However, there is always one intellect that an individual can employ with an uncanny degree of excellence. The student should endeavor identify whether their Fluid or Crystallized Intellect is dominate or recessive. One should endeavor to identify their primary, secondary, and tertiary intellects of the seven-subset intellects. Link your dominate intellect with your first subset primary intellect, and link your recessive intellect with your secondary intellect. Then, list the third subset intellect as a situational variable. Like perspectives, learning your own intellects can be achieved through observation of how one learns best, by how one expresses themselves the most, and in the reflective qualities of one's chosen friends or occupational fields.)

The Emergence of Intellect

(Although ancient life forms appear to be very alien from our perspective, if we look at them from the vast point of view of Intellect and The Program of The Architect, we can unveil that they are no different from any other life form. From the construct of a Tyrannosaur, to the most ancient of Nautili, dinosaur's bones and physical proportions follow The Intelligence pattern of The Program of The Architect. In the same manner that a human baby's intellect is separated from the programming of its body, yet its construct is in possession of all it needs to run its life cycle, so too a dinosaur's intellect is separated from the programming of its body, yet its anatomy is in possession of all of the programming it requires to run its life cycle. In other words, independent of its brand of intellect, or the cognitive dissonance between its conscious awareness and the programs of its construct, ancient life forms were imbued with The Intelligent Force of The Architect, which grew them according to The Program of The Architect. Moreover, this cognitive dissonance and growth pattern are universal formats for all known life forms in all periods of earth's existence.

A dinosaur that is far older than what we typically think of as a "dinosaur", the cuttlefish's intellect appears as it directly relates to a genius contained in its skin and the malleable manipulation of its anatomy, which is found within its design metamorphosis when it executes certain behaviors with particular intentions. When the cuttlefish prepares to attack, it will transform from a squid looking creature, into something so exotic that it seems extraterrestrial in nature. Its tentacles form a singular crescent with the outer tips pointing inward and toward its prey, its skin turns into a bluish white pulsating hypnotizing light, and it hovers around its intended target like an alien spacecraft using a lights show to attract memorized attention. Then, in the flash of a millisecond, it strikes with lightening speed, and kinesthetic coordinative excellence.

The cuttlefish's primary intellect has developed into a spatial or visually oriented means to an end. Its spatial intellect has been spread to another portion of its anatomical structure; its dermis, rather than only being stored in a central brain like structure. While most dinosaurs moved their Kinesthetic Intellects into their anatomy, to outgrow their opponents, the cuttlefish moved its spatial intellect into its anatomy, to out "visualize" its opponents. It created an intellect that manipulates the strengths of its opponent's eyes, which are rooted in the coordination of all its other intellects, to entice them into its "Dermis Spatial Intellect". In short, it turned its prey's intellects against them. Unlike other intellects, which are either designed to move themselves around their environment, or their environment around them, the cuttlefish's "Spatial Dermis Intellect" is designed to move an opponent's intellects around them.

What if this cunning cuttlefish should come up against another animal whose eyes functioned within the invisible or infrared spectrum, like the Bee? This most cunning and ancient of Nautili, which has survived at least five extension level events, could no longer use the superior intellect possessed in its skin to hide or fight so creatively. The new species would be immune to the cuttlefish's spatial dermis wiles, which only function within the range of the visible spectrum. The infrared vision of its opponent could tell the temperature variances between the cuttlefish and anything it should hide against, and the cuttlefish would be easily picked off.

Isn't this pattern, of moving a type of intellect to the program of the anatomy, how dolphins use echolocation to identify fish camouflaged just below the surface of the seabed? Like our cunning cuttlefish, isn't this another example of moving a portion of one's intellect into another portion of one's anatomy? Weren't there ancient aquatic dinosaurs that looked just like the dolphin, and filled the same survival niche? Although the Ichthyosaur is classified as reptile and the Dolphin is classified as a mammal, aren't both species teeth congruently spaced, so as to attain the same sonic echolocation function using the skull and teeth to send and receive sonic information, and translate that data to the neuro fibers of the construct? Is this transference of Dentem Musical Intellect, from the musical centers of the mind to the bones of the anatomy, not the same as a Nautilus transferring the Spatial Intellect of its brain to its skin to create a Dermis Spatial Intellect? Can we now use this common emergence of intellect to create a kind of species list, which interrelates those emergent intellects that meet the same specifications? Yes...)

(In the same manner that we witness identical intellects symmetrically emerge between species, so too can we understand that we need to look for vestigial and analogous intellects between other species. We need to look for them in the same manner that paleontologists look for vestigial and analogous emergence in ancient anatomies. We will find them where we observe any life form within its life cycle (body), intellect cycle (mind), or energetic cycle (soul). We will be looking for intellect to express itself somewhere between the mind and the anatomy, somewhere between the mind and the energetic centers, or somewhere between the anatomy and the energetic centers.

In the same manner that the Dolphin and Ichthyosaur share a congruent emergence of dentem musical intellect between species, so too the Cheetah and Velociraptor share vestigial kinesthetic intellects of lightening speed and analogous claws for gripping between species. In the same manner that the cuttlefish would be left behind, because another life form expanded its intellect into its anatomy in a new or unique manner, so too the tyrannosaur could've been left behind on the evolutionary ladder, because it didn't multiply the veracity of its anatomical intellect with a lightning fast kinesthetic intellect. The tyrannosaur may have gone from being cock of the walk, to something with a nasal intellect like a hound dog that only tracked down the scraps of packs of faster more agile beasts, to something that was a rarity before it disappeared all together (Page 64, Two-way door of The Architect). Simply because of the emergence and interplay between intellects and the expression and collapse pattern of The Architect. This is the real "Process of Extension", where animals come and go, not necessarily based on an event that cripples their habitat, but by the very nature and function of {(That which is within the habitat itself) = (The Design of The Construct)}.

The same vestigial and analogous intellects are replicated in an eagle and pterodactyl. The eagle's kinesthetic intellect of flight will be directly connected to its spatial intellect of telescopic sight. Both of those intellects will be directly linked to its analogous instinctive intellect to naturally know where to go to hunt. Additionally, all of these will be used in the analogous coordination of both species' flight, speed, and talons laying hold on prey. Thus, in the same manner that a cuttlefish, Cheetah, and Ichthyosaur must coordinate their primary intellects with other less developed aspects of their intellects, so too must eagles, pterodactyls, and humans. Just as all of these life forms will function to their optimal capacity during a Condition of Symbiotic Intellect, so too will mankind's intellect operate to its optimal capacity when we coordinate our combination of intellects into a condition of symbiosis.

In the same manner that paleontology records vestigial and analogous physical similarities that emerge or repeat within the animal kingdom, so too we can plainly see that Intellect itself is an emergent vestigial and analogous phenomenon. This comparison of intellects "In Action" is just a glimpse at how design and intellect morph into something more significant--- Not based solely upon the physical design of its construct, but by the constructs of other intelligences, and or similar environments around the life form (The Design of The Construct). It teaches us a valuable lesson as to what kinds of intellects might emerge through the diversity of a given environment, as well as how competing intellects within the bandwidth of that given environment might compete for resources.

Perhaps in the distant future, an air breathing aquatic insect will adopt a musical spatial dentem intellect. It will extend its cognitive musical intellect to its evenly spaced "teeth" to create, send, and receive a pleasant harmonic lure. It will move its cognitive spatial intellect to its thorax's "dermis" to create an attractive and hypnotizing lights show. While this might be used for hunting in packs of thousands, it might just as well be employed for mating rituals, or other more esoteric Life Path purposes. For instance, what would happen if thousands of pods of dolphins were to stop all over the planet, and begin communicating with one another by squeaking through their Dentem Musical Intellect, and some other "Analogous tool", which allowed them to communicate over truly vast distances?)

Intellect's Spiritual Emergence

(Emergent properties of a system are a function of synergy, where the sum of the parts creates a thing greater than the number of parts. This is a thing that otherwise wouldn't occur if the total sum of the parts were aggregated individually. For example, a human being has many parts, but to see the synergistic function of the individual body parts, they must come as one, in a living, and operational condition. This could be seen as the difference between the micro and macro, where the micro comes to be seen as being human, and the macro comes to be seen as being humane. While we can all see the synergistic effects of the collective body parts coming together to create a functional human being, the real synergy of a human being is in large numbers of human beings behaving in a humane manner. At every level of this expression, there is a greater collective synergy occurring that is creating "things", which would not otherwise occur, if the individual parts of the whole were not cooperating and working together. The micro must cooperate with, and have a meaningful relationship with the macro, or else the macro cannot create something greater than the sum of the micro.

We don't always understand how the micro fits into the macro, or how the macro applies to the micro. However, the micro and the macro, the portion and the whole, can be seen as One when we look at The Force of The Architect. The Program of The Architect can be seen in the micro spiral of a seashell, just as easily as it can be seen in the macro spiral of a galaxy. The Architect can be measured within the micro construct of one's blood vessels, or the macro "whole" of the human construct, or humanity. The Program of The Architect is that Force which builds the macro in the same manner that it builds the micro.

At each layer of its expression, this program is the function behind the cooperation between Quantum Physics (X), Galactic Physics (Y), and Field Physics™(Z). The Architect is the world behind the world, the reality behind each reality, The Force that moves between The Three Realms of Truth, and the causality behind the diverse expression of intellect. When we see our realm through the lens of this perspective, it changes our Paradigm. We suddenly demand that all things fit into a larger model while yet remaining congruent with the smaller model (Page 6, Dominion of Relativity).

In the case of intellect, we're dispelling the micro perspective that intellect is a product of a life form or a species, in favor of a macro perspective where the ubiquitous nature of intellect's emergence forms a synergistic effect in and between all expressed life forms. In the same manner that the nested layers of The Architect permeate everything at all levels of understanding, so too intellect becomes an emergent program that repeats itself within all life forms. A micro expression of Intellect, which repeats itself with macro patterns. A micro expression of identical forms of Intellect, which emerge in and between species in a macro manner. A macro expression that does not contradict or leave the micro out of the equation, but at the same time it dispels erroneous myopic points of view about intellect.)

Through mathematical disciplines, the soul has an organ,
Which is purified and enlightened.
An organ that is better worth saving
Than ten thousand physical eyes
Since Truth becomes visible through this alone.

Plato

(The Mystery Schools, and men such as Plato, Pythagoras, and Ptolemy, were well aware that the Pineal Gland is far more miraculous a masterpiece than just another gland, which happens to secrete hormones. The soul has an organ, called the Pineal Gland. Mathematical disciplines purify and enlighten (^{L}) the Pineal Gland. Truth becomes visible through the purified and enlightened Pineal Gland.

The Pineal gland is a link between the micro and the macro, a connector (∞) between the individual, and the collective. While the mind extends its programming into the anatomy in vestigial and analogous manners, it also extends its intellect into the construct of its spiritual and energetic expression, via the Pineal Gland, in vestigial and analogous manners. In the same manner that a martial artist moves Chi around in his body, so too moving chi up the spinal column and through the antenna (∞) of the Pineal Gland can activate the connective expression. This design allows life forms to connect with an Intellect that is One with The Path of Vastness.)

(According to our initial textbook definitions, Nikola Tesla's primary intellect was Spatial. He "saw" his inventions with a portion of the brain in charge of vision. Tesla's secondary intellect was Logical; he reasoned what he saw into fabricated functionality based off learned

Crystallized Engineering Knowledge, and Fluid trial and error reasoning. Tesla's third intellect was Intra personal, not only because he suffered greatly in his social interactions, but also because he was very cognizant of what was happening within his own heart and mind. Tesla's introspective intellect allowed him to be self-knowing enough to realize what was happening during these special moments of insight. That self-awareness taught him to set up conditions that were to his advantage when he wanted to "invent" (connect). He knew he possessed a spatial intellect, so he knew to "look" (think) to see what he wanted to "create" (act), when those special moments were the focus of his intention.

In a vision, that was *the instrument of action behind a moment's intention,* Nikola Tesla's spatial intellect coordinated with his Pineal Eye to "see" his inventions with his mind's eye in their completed forms. In an instant, he could comprehend the invention's intricacies long before other aspects of his intellect could fabricate, or fully comprehend each part's quantifiable make up or collective purpose. In the moment in which Tesla saw his alternating current device, he claims to have seen it as a singular complete image. He claims it was as though it had already been built, was in operation, and flipping in a circle back and forth. He quickly scribbled it down, and then went about reverse engineering the vision with the coordination of his other intellects.

One form of inventing that most people consider "inventing", is if one were tinkering with different designs, and through trial and error, came up with an Alternating Current Device. Like a child exploring its belly button to eventually comprehend an umbilical cord, this lone wolf approach would be built line upon line and precept on precept. After this manner, the inventor would not see *the object of their intention* in its completed form from the very beginning. The inventor would be compelled to reason through portions of their creation until they eventually put all the pieces of the puzzle together. However, if one suddenly had a vision of an Alternating Current Device, with all its intricacies already put together, and functioning--- this would be an entirely different form of inventing. Not to mention calling into question how anyone could see something that was not yet invented, in its completed form, and somehow still have to go about reverse engineering it even though they saw it in its completed form. Yet, this is how Tesla did it, and he is far from being alone in this methodology.

In the same manner that the cuttlefish extended its spatial intellect to its dermis, so too Tesla's spatial intellect was extended to his pineal gland. In the same manner that the dolphin extended its intellect into its bones, so too Bach's musical intellect was extended into his "Pineal Ear" (♪). Bach couldn't have visions of engineering prowess in the same manner as Tesla, because his spatial intellect wasn't extended into his Pineal Gland in the same manner as Tesla's intellect. Nor was his Crystallized scholastic knowledge the same as Tesla's. While focusing *the instrument of action behind a moment's intention* on musical composition, Bach claims to have heard the music as though it were coming from afar (connect), he would grab a quill and parchment (think), and quickly translate what he could hear into a written language of notes, lines, bars, and rhythms (act).

Symbiotic Intellect is the coordination of various forms of intellect with one's anatomy, after the manner of the form of their extended expression in each life form. Genius is the coordination of Symbiotic Intellect, with the combination of intellects extended into their spiritual or energetic aspects, which creates something greater than the sum of the parts. In humans, the pineal gland is that anatomical antenna ---of intellect--- that extends our cognitive intellect to our spirit or energetic aspect. Like energizing a computer with electricity, sending conditioned Chi through the frontal lobe or crown chakra activates our Pineal Antenna with The Force of The Architect.

For instance, if one's three primary conscious intellects were spatial, logical, and intra personal, those intellects would be seen as the arms of one's Intellectual Triquetra, while The Pineal Eye would be the Divine activator in The Middle Way of The Triquetra. The functional synchronicity of those intellects would be The Chamber of Initiation sparking The Genius of The One. This condition of Genius would be the spark, while the Symbiotic Intellect would be the collective talents and abilities that allowed one to build The Fire of Opportunity. In this model lies The Objective of The One within The Quest of Identity, to learn how to unlock this Genius inside of yourself, and use synchronicity and synergy to fulfill your Life Path's purpose.)

Managing Genius

(Claiming pontifical proof via one's own methodology will never withstand the oppositional differences of others who possess the liberty to express different perspectives or unique ideas. While scholastic knowledge is going to appeal to the Crystallized Intellect, reasoning matters through on their own accord is going to appeal to the Fluid Intellect. While the Crystallized Intellect of a scholar is going to ostracize the Fluid Intellect of the basement genius for their lack of formal training, The Fluid Intellect of the basement genius is going to ostracize the Crystallized Intellect for their lack of original thinking. Once again, each will boast their claim to the proof of correctness, the throne of righteousness, or the supreme authority of verification. Yet, they will equally bear the weight of ostracism by those who are absent the perspective of their brand of intellect (Page 5).

The Genius of The One, is the sparking of greater intellect wherein there is a coordination of all of one's intellects. While Fluid Intellect is more of a method of reasoning things through and sparking new horizons of "Heureka!" via moments of contemplative inner solitude, Crystallized Intellects advance their knowledge from outside themselves in a scholarly manner of aggregation of knowledge to cross New Horizons. It is in using both, as One, that we find greater meaning of the parts and the whole.

When we comprehend something from the paradigm of many intellects, perspectives of vastness become quantifiable observations that amplify the meaning and significance of each kind of intellect. This singular act renders an altogether new perspective of each intellect. The methodology of reasoning through the doorways of

Intellects incontrovertibly demonstrates they are all spokes in the same wheel of greater understanding, all gears of the same machine with a common function, and all parts of a larger device that possess a greater purpose and more marvelous significance (Page 12, 75, 106).)

(One of our greatest strengths lies in our ability to coordinate our personal combination of intellects as One through the antenna of our pineal gland. The following individuals came to master their own combination of intellect over a lifetime of trial and error--- Trying to get into that special condition that causes the program of intellect and Intelligence to move into a functional condition of greater expression. They then used this greater more unified intellect to tap into a kind of library or super conscious state where nothing that their *intent* focused on was denied to them. They attained The Fruit of Knowledge, which was the instrument behind a moment's intention, by repeating a process that they themselves created or became familiar with.

By inadvertently failing in scholastics and being compelled to go on long contemplative walks, aimless bicycle rides, or creating what he called "thought experiments" (connect, think), Albert Einstein learned that he "created" best outside of the traditional classroom of recitation and lectures. More important than learning that his Fluid Intellect was his dominate trait, Einstein learned how to set up temporary conditions to coordinate his intellects, and unlock his personal Genius. Einstein's "Thought experiments" might be thought of as meditating on an eccentric postulation, such as imagining what it would look like if he were a photon shooting through space. By taking the time to reason these thoughts through to a new horizon of understanding, in an undisturbed state of solemnity, and for an indeterminate amount of time, he was able to get into a *meditative condition of consciousness* whereby the answers just came to him. His Fluid Intellect reasoned things through in a very personal manner that engaged his Crystallized Intellect, coordinated his top 3 subset intellects, and created a greater macro expression of his Intellect.

Albert Einstein learned how to set up environmental conditions that employed his intellect in a particular manner, which helped him coordinate his personal forms of intellect into a synergistic Oneness. He learned how to set his conscious mind into a condition that activated his Pineal, coordinated mind, body, self-intellects, and flipped on his genius. Then, he was able to {(connect with) + (think upon) + (act in accord with)} marvelous, extravagant, and very real, but postulatetively exotic things, which allowed him to singlehandedly redefine how humanity thought about reality. It was a paradigm shift, and everyone exclaimed, "What a magnificent brain he must have!" Yet, when we remember that Einstein was a failure at life until after he became a patent clerk, we can see that his intelligence quotient had less to do with the quality of his physical brain, and more to do with the manner in which he learned to employ it.

We're bound by the energetic condition of our brain, more than by its design. For instance, some think they are Little Einstein's by virtue of the construct of their brain, while others think they're idiots because of the construct of their brain. After all, following his demise, Einstein's brain was spirited away for what the thief thought was a valid reason. He thought it was Einstein's brain that made him a genius, not the manner in which he used it, or the condition that governed its function. That is, the manner in which he "conditioned" it with his thought experiments.

Like so many species, who only know the world through the lens of their own perspective, we're so preoccupied with what our eyes can see, and what our hands can touch, that it bleeds into our mythos in manners we don't comprehend until years after the fact. In the same manner that scientists connect dozens of electrodes to their specimen's heads, while idiosyncratically leaving the rest of their construct bare, so too this methodology of thought of stealing Einstein's brain reveals a kind of thinking that only takes into account a portion of the overall puzzle. Our construct is run by Source Field Energy, which is imbedded in everything that's operating each system. Like a bolt of lightning, the electrical pulses in our nervous system have The Force of The Architect nested within the electrons, and they are directed via The Program of The Architect through the system, which branches out after the two-way door of The Program of The Architect. If The Source Field Energy were not nested in the electrons to direct the electricity through our system in an ascending and descending pattern of The Architect, the electricity would focus, and fry our nervous system one cell at a time. We can see this operation nested in the growth pattern of our kidneys, nested the fractal construct of our blood stream, and even in the ratios between each system of the body. So, before DNA, before electrons, and before all material things "of that which we are composed", we are made by The Source Field and governed by The Architect ---Hooking our heads to electron governed electrodes, and stealing brain specimens are a representation of a certain lens of perspective--- past methodologies. They're conclusions based on less than all of the facts, or the use of equipment capable of seeing the brain while it was in a macroscopic functional relationship with the other portions of its anatomical, energetic, and collectivistic construct.)

(One doesn't need to climb a mountain, or prey at the feet of the masters to get their creativity flowing again--- although these things have been known to help. However, never underestimate the intrinsic value of just taking a long shower. Enjoying long aimless baths, or reveling in soothing bathhouses, is a wonderful mechanism *to divert the mind, relax the body, soothe the soul,* and get the creative energies coordinating with one another again.

This "busy work", or repetitive mindless tasks, such as a patent clerk might do, should not relate to the task at hand. Spatial intellects may want to look at random scenery to get their spatial intellect doing "anything else". A kinesthetic intellect may want to go dribble a basketball, go for a walk, or otherwise do something physical without actually playing their personal sport. In the same manner that bicycle riding and aimless walks had nothing to do with Einstein's thought experiments, none of these behaviors should relate to the task you are trying to accomplish. Yet, at the same time, they should be something personal to you, something you "just do" when things aren't going as you think they should in the learning or creative process.

With all of these methods, there is commonality that can be built into a model, Connect, Think, and Act. Where we synergistically connect with something greater, meditate in accord with our postulations, and take immediate action when the moment of, "Heureka!" strikes. However, you should identify what works best for you, and your personal combination of intellects. Learn how best to make your adopted methods accessible when and where you may need to call upon them. Recall times in which genius has happened in the past and experiment on recreating those conditions.

By understanding how the combination of their intelligences functioned as One, these individuals were able to experience moments of what some of them labeled Divine insight. They looked for optimal times and triggering mechanisms behind their Symbiotic Intellect to employ and trigger their Genius Symbiotic Intellect. They then *focused their intention* during these moments to attain the "I know not" that empowered their Life Path's purpose.

Whether they understood what was happening in its totality, or like Siddhartha, if they only understood a degree of the "I know not" during a moment of insight as they crossed over each new horizon. What matters for us is that they *grew; they matured over time,* and came to *understand* how their personal combination of intellects went about bridging the barrier to connect with something possessed of a greater magnificence. They *learned* to make their Genius Intellect function to its greatest capacity through a *concerted and coordinative* effort. Then they repeated that process until they had it down to a science, and then down to an art. In the same manner that the godly skill of a martial artist can flow and pounce with the grace and agility of a Buddhist Monk, strike with the force and precision of lightening, and roar with the ferocity of the inner Tiger, so too unlocking your genius becomes an Art possessed of Crystallized skill and Fluid talent, where the mere thought of the spark of the divine will cause the perfect stroke of a brush on the tapestry of the artist's project (Introduction, A Taste of The Fruit of Light).)

The Quest of Truth

Mechanical Advantage

(In all its majesty and natural skill of flight, a falcon will never reach mach five without a mechanical advantage. So too, we may never attain the altitude of our full potential, unless we harness a mechanical advantage, which amplifies our natural abilities. Thus, we must learn to harness the energetic advantages of The Source Field, The Architect, and Intellect in a union with natural and mechanical advantages.

The Way of The Path is our natural method into an amplified condition. Following each Path imbues each aspect of the student with a transformative elixir that is One with The Projection of The Essence of The Source, The Source Field, and The Architect. The Quest of Identity is our second natural method. Like a steel hammer pounding on intellectual flint, sparks of natural genius offer the opportunity to forge Thunderbolts of Enlightenment, and feed bonfires of innovation with the black powder of our dreams.

The Quest of Truth is a journey that allows us to meld our naturally amplified genius with mechanical and energetic advantages--- To condition "of that which we are comprised" into a higher state of being. Imagine the difference between cavemen seeing fire, and Prometheus showing mankind how to make fire. Now, imagine Prometheus showing mankind how to harness the natural fire of The

Source Field with a mechanical advantage that thrusts our intellect into hyper drive--- with his tools--- with his technology. The degree of change in our paradigm would be the same radical difference between the Stone Age and modern cities. The Golden Race will emerge from the "I know not", appear as though we were always present, and life as we know it would never be the same again.)

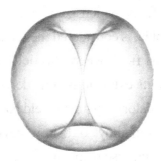

The Torus Field

(In the same manner that The Architect is everywhere between infinitesimal smallness and eternal vastness, so too the torus field is a universal expression, a fundamental part of nature, and can be found everywhere we "look" (Z). The torus field is an energetic egg, and like The Program, it's a self-organizing system of The Architect. The torus field is a geometrical energy field that gives as it receives, and receives what it gives. We can think of the torus field as moving around itself, into itself, through itself, and out of itself in an ever-repeating cycle. In the same manner that Light, Intelligence, The Architect, and Intellect are expressed dominions, so too we will come to think of the torus field as an expressed field of dominion within the two-way door of dominion.

Torus fields initially express themselves as an invisible, but perceivable, force field of energy before they express themselves in a union with particles, waves, energies, or forces. While some torus fields will only manifest themselves energetically, others will manifest themselves both physically and energetically. While some toroids will be flatter, others will be rounder. While some will appear thick and corpulent, others will appear as a thin spherical ring.

The top of the torus field, which spins counterclockwise into the center of the torus' bubble, is considered the female end, or its left eye. The bottom of the torus field, where the field spins out of the torus bubble to wrap around its exterior, is considered the male end, or its right eye. Throughout history, the torus field has been represented by the swastika, as seen from above or below, and depicted as spinning counterclockwise or clockwise respectively. While recently hijacked in the Western mythos, this multicultural worldwide symbol of peace and prosperity can be drawn with curved lines indicating the feminine or straight lines with right angles, which are representative of the masculine. The Chalice, or sacred feminine, can be seen three dimensionally as the V, or cone shape at the top of the torus. The male, or penis, can be seen as the chevron Λ, or three-dimensional cone at the bottom of the field. In the same manner that a man's seed must "come out of the masculine" and "go into the feminine" in an ever repeating cycle of life, so too the energy of the field goes into the feminine, and comes out of the masculine in an ever repeating cycle of life of torus fields.

Torus fields can come in two main categories; natural and unnatural. These two categories can come in three subcategories--- physical, energetic, and the physical amalgamated with the energetic. Some naturally existing torus fields are red blood cells, hurricanes, and galaxies. Torus fields, and their central vortexes, pass through, overlap, encase, or otherwise imbue themselves within solid or semisolid particles, forces, fields, waves, and energies. This amalgamation can be seen in everything from a magnetosphere, to water spinning down a drain, to a dust devil dancing across the desert.

Dolphins create torus air bubbles as if they were analogous aquatic hula-hoops. From the lens of our own perspective, we might initially reason that they're just playing with these "vestigial" air bubbles as they frolic in the water. However, when we understand how the symbiotic coordination of their Dentem Musical Intellect, combined with the frequencies of their squeaks, interact with the function of a torus field--- something quite marvelous comes from over the horizon of the "I know not", appears as though it was always here, and takes us over a New Horizon of Vastness.

In terms of eternal vastness, torus fields express themselves as black holes. This is an energetic and physically amalgamated torus field that's so vast, nothing in this realm can make its energetic construct appear solid. Like whirlpools that suddenly, and sometimes inexplicably appear in large bodies of water, black holes are naturally occurring torus fields of energy manipulating the fabric of space time$_{1\,2}$.

In terms of infinitesimal smallness, there is the "Morula", also known as "you" near the beginning of life. After the number of your cells multiplies between 13 and 21, the nesting function of The Program of The Architect moves into a new condition that modifies its expression, and thus the relationships between its geometric (D) and harmonic (f) function. The cells change their geometry from a cube of eight spheres, multiply, and the energetic nesting function transforms their harmonic (f) and geometric (D) resonance into that of a sphere $\{360°(D) = 360(f)\}$. The change in expression of the nesting function causes a change in energy, geometry, and even space, time; and ironically enough velocity. Thus, a duplicitous central vortex forms down the middle of its expression. The sphere transforms the torus field, once again modifying its harmonic and geometric functions, and eventually it develops into a "more developed" life form.

Magnets are also torus fields. We're used to thinking of magnets in a flat, one, or two-dimensional manner, through positive and negative charges, or north and south expressions. Yet, we've all seen the photos of flakes of steel that form a circle around a magnet, which reveals how the polarities form a torus field around the magnet itself. We just have to remember that all of this is happening in a three dimensional toroidal sphere, and that even though the metallic flakes appear to our eyes to be stationary, the nesting function in which they're expressed, and the energies flowing through them, are always in motion.)

Torus Labeling Chart

Top	Bottom	Middle
Female Path	Male Path	(Golden) Child or Conception
Curved lines	Straight lines	Circle (The Flower of Life Geometry)
Left	Right	Third Eye (Psi + Phi) ($\psi + \Phi = \infty$)
Emotional	Logical	Coherent Union (∞)

The Triquetra of The Apple

(Peer through The Eye of an Apple and you'll see how it's One with the torus field. If you'll overlay the shape of the torus field with that of an apple, you'll see how the protective skin of the apple is both physically and energetically working in unison with the apple's torus field. Like a magnet, the energy of the torus field is flowing through the particulate matter of the apple, as well as energetically shielding the inner living portions of the apple from outside influences. In the same manner that a Mandelbrot Beetle reveals the energetic dominion behind the design (D) of the Egyptian Scarab Beetle, so too the torus field reveals the energetic dominion behind the shape (D) of an apple (Page 52, Mandelbrot Beetle).

If you chop an apple in a side-to-side fashion you'll see that the horizontal placement of its seeds match the geometry of a pentagon. Hovering in the middle of the torus field, yet encircling the central ring, there's a flat field of energy shaped like a pentagon. The amplified energy at the nodes/corners of this energetically expressed pentagon are changing the function of matter at the points of amplified energy. The seeds are expressed physically where the energy increases at the nodes of the energetic geometry. The seeds aren't creating the pentagonal field. Remember, energy (f) determines particle (D) behavior before particles (D) can guide energy's (f) behavior. The Egg of Energy came before the chicken. In the expression of the apple, the energetic field comes before everything else, even the torus field.

If you chop an apple down the center from top to bottom, you'll see a slight green discoloration in the white portion where the female and male torsion vortices are pressing in, through, and out of the particulate matter. Like the pentagonal energy nodes at the seeds, there's another energy node at the middle of the apple's torus field. Rather than expressing itself as a series of five spherical nodes, which vibrations wiggle around or transfer through, this node expresses itself as a circular ring around the central hollowness between the two adjoining vortexes. It's an energetically rich, but physically voided, location inside of the apple. The ring possesses an ongoing energetic spinning torsion movement, which creates an amplified energetic condition of increased local coherence, increased local acceleration, and increased local energy.)

{(Amplified Energetic) (Inviscidly Conditioned) (Uniform Acceleration)}

$$\Delta$$

(Acceleration, coherence, and energetic amplification operate much like the spinning coils of a Tesla Tower. Tesla Coils spin electricity through ever-smaller conduits that are coiled into ever-smaller spins. In this manner, the electrons are not so much as accelerated, after the manner of squirting water out of a garden hose, but the electrons are "energetically enhanced", "energetically amplified", and "energetically accelerated into uniform coherence". It was the model of the torus field that helped Nikola Tesla understand that, "energetically enhanced inviscid acceleration" doesn't so much as supercharge the nature of the electrons that he was trying to manufacture, but it changes the function of their very nature. The conditioning, caused by this behavior, modifies the fundamental constants in this realm.

For some reason, the Tesla Models we have don't add enough coils. In any Tesla Coil; Tesla Tower, there should be at least 2 coils. If you spun 2 coils that initiated their spin from equidistant sides--- Or, if you spun 5 (Penta) -6 (Hexa) coils initiating each coil from equivalent geometric sides--- If you designed them after the manner of a Tesla Coil, adding the downward sloping patterns of the torus' torsion spins, in accord with The Hemisphere Effect--- Then, the effects could be amplified exponentially, and a new fundamental constant of Field Physics™ (Z) would emerge. An effect Tesla was well acquainted with. Note, our current models of Tesla Coils don't address The Hemisphere Effect of coils aimed at one another into a central ring. Nor do they address the flat pentagonal energy nodes that hover its bubble when these two vortexes are aimed at, or torsioned through, one another.)

{(If 1), (then 1)}
  {(If 1), (then 2)}
    {(If 2), (then 3)}
      {(If 3), (then 5)}
        {(If 5), (then 8)}
          {(If 8), (then 13)}
            {(If 13), (then 21)}
              {(If 21), (then 34)}
                {(If 34), (then 55)}
                  {(If 55), (then 89)}
                    {(If 89), (then 144)}

(With "The Model of The Apple", we're talking about two kinds of energy effects that render different modifications. First, we're talking about Source Field Energy being harnessed by, and or otherwise focusing at, the nodal points of a Platonic Solid; the flat one-dimensional dodecahedral points of a pentagon. These five nodal points of energy behave like an antenna to Source Field Energy, and manifest a degree of energetic amplification of matter. In this case, the energetic amplification tells the intelligence of the apple that it should generate its seeds at the location of energetic enhancement. Another biological advantage based on geometric (D) and harmonic (f) resonance relationships (Page 63-64, Birds).

Second, we're talking about the conditioning of an energetic field by moving it down a vacuum vortex. The combination of "Amplified Energetic, Inviscidly Conditioned, Uniform Acceleration" conditions the energetic field, the fabric of the location, and anything else in its torsion field. The Conditioning of Source Field Energy, not only amplifies the function of particles, waves, and energy, but it changes the properties of their physics, and causes them to behave in different manners as they move toward the central ring.

Under the first condition---, all matter in our realm can be expressed as waves or particles flowing through a two-way door that exists below the "real" speed (R) of light. Mathematically, we can express the real speed of light as (inhibited velocity minus inhibitions), in order to attain light's "more real" expression. When particles or waves get an extra dose of Source Field Energy, such as in the pentagon, they operate better. However, they aren't accelerated, and thus cannot become more "conditioned", so as to transform their properties into a fully uninhibited state of Field Physics™ (Z).

They lack an added degree of coherence that something like a Faraday Cage attempts to address, by blocking interference (agitation) that can cause "incoherence", but not necessarily by adding something like a torsion field, which will actually cause, increase, and condition coherence. Under the first condition, things such as codons or dormant genes may flip on like light switches, and the emergent expressions of intelligence and intellect will manifest themselves in an amplified manner. However, because there's no acceleration to remove "that which inhibits", no inviscid state caused by the lack of agitation, and because there's a lack of uniform acceleration, there's no greater "magic" in the change of fundamental constants.

Under the second condition---, when particles or waves are placed in a location of energetic amplification and inviscidly conditioned accelerated coherence... When Source Field Energy is drawn in, uniformly accelerated, and conditioned via the ever-smaller spinning conduits of a torsion field... In addition, when they also get an extra jolt of Source Field Energy by {The Design of The Construct ≥ The

Backster Effect}, and the pentagon hovering at the equatorial belt...
Particles or waves can accelerate toward true light speed and attain
greater degrees of uninhibited velocity. In this special condition,
we begin to break the bonds of Quantum Physics (X) and Galactic
Physics (Y), and step into the realm of Field Physics™(Z).

Amplified energetic inviscidly conditioned uniform velocity allows
particles and waves to move into a condition that modifies their
expression, so they can make a jump from our realm of space-time$_1$
into another realm of time-space$_2$. Under this specific condition,
they transform their properties to ever-increasing degrees, such that
the fundamental constants governing their expression begin to slip
their bonds, and they can move toward different behaviors. The
fundamental constants governing their expression in our realm$_1$ begin
to change from what we know them to be, to "that which they really
are" under "uninhibited" conditions. Light speed changes velocity,
physics modify, and what we once thought were rock solid constants,
such as water freezing at certain temperatures, begin to transform
into something quite magnificent.

Under the first condition---, The Source Field is able to manifest a
physical change to matter. Remembering that the Field came first,
the special self-similar, equidistant, and entanglement properties of
Platonic Solids become physical harnessing points of Source Field
Energy that nests The Force of The Architect, and amplifies the
function of The Program of The Architect at that given location.
Under these conditions wounds heal faster, the clockwise spinning
torsion fields of poisons are weakened (R) or reversed (R), light isn't
scattered it's absorbed, and "things" just generally function for the
better in these regions.

Under the second condition---, the state of amplified energy, increased coherence, and uniform acceleration changes the operation of fundamental constants. Not because it changes the constants in a given realm, but because it's changing the nature of the thing within a given realm$_x$, and given area within that realm$_x$. The new condition within the ring transforms particles, waves, energy, fields, and forces into "something with a different label", causing them to operate differently than expected in their previous condition. This can be likened to the two-way door of dominion, not so much as being present or absent as with Light and darkness, but more like spinning in one direction or another; like a whirlpool. Its either spinning clockwise toward a given expression (collapse), or counterclockwise to undo that expression (uncollapse). In the same manner that the wheel of Karma spins in a creative or destructive direction, so too the concept of which direction a torsion field is spinning will become more significant to the concept of the two-way door of dominion as we continue.

The Einstein Rosen Bridge Theory says that great amounts of mass tend to bend the very fabric of the space-time continuum. It's in this manner that we believe light isn't so much as being bent around a star, as much as it's flowing in a straight line around a bend in the fabric of the space-time continuum. In The Einstein Rosen Bridge Theory, space-time$_1$ can be bent, and in this region, things can begin behaving strangely, but these "strange functions" are still operating pretty much the same as they would in a "non-distorted" location of space-time. Particles are still particles, waves are still waves, and stars and planets keep spinning as before.

Under the second condition, rather than a contortion of space-time$_1$, we're seeing a gateway function that opens a hole in the fabric of space-time$_1$. This allows particles and waves to "make the jump" through the ring to another dimension$_2$. Rather than bending the space-time$_1$ continuum, after the manner of The Einstein Rosen Bridge Theory, under amplified energetic inviscidly conditioned uniform velocity, the fabric of space-time is breached, opened, or otherwise unlocked. Like Neutrinos that appear to be blinking in and out of existence, The Architect is able to enter and exit this realm$_1$ at the central ring of torsion fields, because of the natural conditioning provided by hyper-specific geometry, hyper-accelerated energy, and hyper-coherent condition of torsion fields. As the mass of a product is collapsed into a greater expression, if it is not conditioned in just such a manner, The Einstein Rosen Bridge Theory says that it pushes on, or otherwise bends the fabric of space-time. Like the opposing direction of the two-way door of dominion, it's when "things" are in a movement toward a particular condition that they begin operating differently than we presently expect.)

The Apple of Earth

(In the same manner that the "Triquetra of Condition" is about three kinds of conditioning used as a singularity, so too the "Triquetra of The Torus Field" is the union of physical, energetic, and Intelligent Force of The Architect amalgamated as One in The Initiation Chamber of The Middle Way of The Path. The Triquetra of The Apple is its union with the torus field, The Source Field, and whatever particle/wave aspect it happens to be manifesting in, or being decelerated, and nested within. "The Triquetra of The Earth" is One with the map of an apple. Like one big electromagnetic force field that surrounds "The Apple of Earth", the magnetosphere is an energetic torus field that protects and encases the expression of intelligence nested within it from certain outside influences. Also like the apple, we can see that all life on planet earth resides nested within the protective egg of the magnetosphere. However, unlike the apple, while we're residing within a torus field that's much bigger than the earth, we can witness all manner of smaller torus fields functioning under the dominion of the earth's larger torus field.)

Eddies

(If we imagine looking down on the counterclockwise spin of the magnetosphere's central vortex, as that vortex moves into the earth in the northern hemisphere... If we follow that counterclockwise spin, as it continues through the central exchange ring at the center of the earth, and then out of the other side into the southern hemisphere... Then, we will observe the flow of energy never alters its direction; it never changes from clockwise to counterclockwise. It's only because we change our posture and position on the surface of the earth's sphere from right side up to upside down, and thereby look at it from a particular perspective, that we perceive a change from a counterclockwise flow of eddies in the northern hemisphere to a clockwise spin of eddies in the southern hemisphere.

From top to bottom, "That which is in motion tends to stay in motion"--- and in this case, even though there's an outside force holding the magnetosphere in place (∞), there's no outside force to modify the vortex's directional expression. The variable that changes the function of the expression is determined by--- whether the torsion fields are moving into tighter spins (female, left eye) toward the central ring, or in widening spins (male, right eye) away from the central ring. The difference between the spins, not in direction of flow, but in direction of the tightening or loosening of each vortex, is that which modifies expression and creates The Hemisphere Effect.

In the northern hemisphere, we say that aquatic eddies spin counterclockwise, and leave a unique rippled fingerprint on the water. We say their kinetic flow travels toward the earth's center, independent of its angle on the surface of earth's sphere. We also say the kinetic flow of the material, which eddies are imbued within, such as water or air, always flow downward in the direction of gravity. However, in the southern hemisphere, the energetic flow of the torus spins out of the earth contrary to gravity. While the water can still be seen to drain in the direction of gravity, because of its degree of collapse, we can perceive the reversal of the torus' spin, as well as the change in the reverse fingerprint of its ripples.

This reversed shape, which the torus forces the water to take on, reveals that the exiting vortex of the torus is maintaining its initial direction, and that it's moving independent of gravity. The torus field is moving freely through the material of the planet, yet, it's controlling matter to a degree, in that it's governing its energetic directional flow. However, gravity seems to be a bit stronger, since the water continues to flow toward the center of the planet. Somehow, the energy seems to be independent of gravity and matter, since it passes through the planet, while still being able to manipulate particles expressed to a degree of collapse, which are subject to gravity and the field.)

(While torus fields maintain obedience to their own field, and flow independent of what we currently think of as gravity, torus fields do not flow independent relative to other torus fields. Like two particles of the same type that won't pass through one another, or similar waves that will interfere with one another, so too torus fields affect the function of one another. In the same manner that all eddies on earth are obeying the flow and direction of the exterior torus field, so too the magnetosphere is subject to the torus field of the system or galaxy in which it resides. All nested torus fields maintain their obedience to the two-way door of dominion of the exterior torus field.

Because we've observed torus fields harnessing and drawing in ambient energy into their vortexes, we can see that the magnetosphere is injecting Source Field Energy; and all manner of other energies that it's related to, into the earth. The magnetosphere is pulling it in from beyond our planet, drawing in Source Field Energy with the vacuum of its vortex, and injecting it directly into the planet. Every eddy, hurricane, or any other label we have for a torsion field, vortex, or toroid is behaving in the same manner.

Plants are then pulling that life force energy of The Source Field out of the earth, as much as they're living off the nutrients found within the particulate matter of the dirt. Literally, their life force is sustained by the energy that is injected and stored inside of the planet, by the planet's torus field, and its interconnectedness with other relative fields. Other life forms are then drawing energy out of them, and or the herbivores that consume the plant's life force. Moreover, any planet or being that is seen or labeled as dead, is only so, because it lacks torsion fields sufficient to inject or enliven them with particular kinds of energies. Torsion fields are an integral function of Intelligence, and where there is one, there is typically the other. However, with the two-way door of dominion, where there is entropy; or the absence of Intelligence, there is typically the absence of a torsion field.)

Hurricanes and Typhoons

(Hurricanes and typhoons begin at or near the earth's equator. One reason the storms get started at this location is the ample availability of heat and water in a liquid form. However, the storms grow so massive, because it's at this location that they're closest to a 90° angle in relationship to the earth's torus field. At or near this angle, the earth's magnetosphere gives the storm's energy two kinds of energetic "help along" pushes.

The first push comes from the dominion of the exterior placement of the earth's torus field that envelops the planet, and thus the storms. Like directing the flow of eddies, the first push determines the direction of the storm's spin, but this flow will actually continue to add to the kinetic energy already present, and increase that energy via a constant push that continually accelerates the storm's energies. For example, think of two sprockets, one sprocket is driven by wind and heat that creates the storm and its fields, while the second sprocket constantly adds an additional push to the first. In this manner, no matter what speed the initial sprocket is moving at, the other sprocket always adds more kinetic energy to constantly drive the first one just a bit faster. Rather than teeth on a metal wheel, its parallel lines of energy moving lines of energy on the side of each torus field in a crank like fashion.

The second push comes from the direction of the energy flowing up the exterior bubble of the earth's torus field. The exterior bubble of the magnetosphere has a concave, crescent shaped, westward sloping angle that flows in energetic lines from *south to north*. Like thousands of energetic railroad tracks headed to the north pole, which encompass the circumference of the earth, these energetic guidelines direct the storm's field as it moves through and across the surface of the earth. While being nested at a 90° angle within the magnetosphere's torus field spins the storm like two sprockets, the south to north flow of the exterior bubble guides the angle and trajectory of the storm across the sphere of the planet (∞).)

(Torsion fields move seamlessly through air and matter simultaneously. Inside the northern hemisphere of a hurricane, the portion of the torus field above the surface of the earth, the torus field and storm will be blowing wind and water. Simultaneously, its southern hemisphere; the portion of the torus field below the surface of the earth, will be moving seamlessly through the crust of the earth; just like the magnetosphere moves seamlessly through the center of the earth. In the same manner that the northern aspect will spin wind and water, the southern portion of the field will be massaging tectonic plates, and spinning magma deep down. Imagine for a moment, the twin torsion fields of an F-5 Magma Tornado or Hurricane injecting and massaging tectonic plates with Source Field Energy. When we consider the decrease in tectonic disturbance in those locations where we see increased torsion field activity--- that really answers allot of questions.)

(Imagine what would happen if a hurricane's pentagonal node encountered one of the pentagonal nodes inside the earth. Some folks think that aligning nodes opens up a gateway called "Temporary Local Risk Factor" or TLR. This can be expressed as a mobile energetic signature from within the earth that aligns with other energies on the surface of the earth. Crossing these nodes seem to bring down aircraft, make boats go missing, or otherwise change one's condition of expression, and thus their "space-time-velocity" coordinates within a given realm$_x$. Hundreds of books on The Bermuda or Dragon's Triangle can address these questions.

For our model, it's widely recognized that the proximity of two nodes can determine how much field energy is present for a given event, as well as in what manner those nodes will interact with one another. When a storm's torus field expresses itself further in the earth, the result will be a smaller storm. However, when a storm's torus field rises further out of the earth, such that its pentagonal plate skims the surface of the earth/water, and the storm's hemisphere is at its widest expression at ground/ocean level, this is when and where we will see Fujita-5 storms. The proximity of the pentagonal nodes to one another can determine the amount of kinetic torus field and Source Field Energy that is added to the event. It is this extra energy that can determine a rise or fall, and or an expansion or contraction relationship to the event's field.

For our purposes, the important aspect to recognize is that when a storm is stronger, so too its vortexes are both stronger as well as more conditioned. The amplified energetic, inviscidly conditioned, uniform velocity of its fields are more "Field reflective", they harness more Source Field Energy, are stronger, and more wide spread. Remember, while nodes, and cooperating nodes, amplify functionality, torsion fields and their central ring "condition" and "transform".)

("The Hemisphere Effect": is a recognition in the changing effects that the nature of a sphere has on the torque of torsion fields within a given hemisphere, or given location within a sphere.)

(In the same manner that magnets will move one another when carefully pushed against each other, but will suddenly flip when the relative angles of their poles/ vortexes/fields change, so too a hurricane's torus field will be sucked into the female end of the inward flowing vortex when the storm moves too far north. This absorption of the field happens, because the storm's fields are moved by the earth's exterior field bubble toward the northern polarity of the earth's magnetosphere. This absorption is able to occur because the earth behaves like a solid magnet, while the torus field enveloping a hurricane only has particulate matter floating within its field, and therefore possesses nothing to anchor to. Thus, the storm's nested field is stripped off, and absorbed into the larger, exterior, and more dominate field. Because the storms no longer contain a torus field, and are no longer at the optimal angle to receive their pushes from the dominion of the exterior field, the storms will be seen to dissipate shortly after it loses its field.)

(If you'll overlay the shape of an apple with that of a hurricane, you'll see that the same functions, which are happening inside of an apple, are also happening inside of a hurricane. Moreover, we can see they're all moving energy, injecting and extracting, in an eternal recycling process that turns positives into negatives, and so-called negatives into positives, which are all said to be determined by which direction the flow is moving, when in reality the flow is always moving in the same direction. "The physical expression of an energetic change" is beginning to sound like a philosophical catch phrase that lays somewhere between the emergence of The Middle Way of Siddhartha's bow string, and the perspectives of scientific observation. It's becoming a common doorway between the philosophical, the theological, and the scientific. A single room with several two-way doors. A common chamber between disciplines, which is erasing the illusion of their separateness, as it joins them as One. Creating a condition of greater understanding that's about to reveal something magnificent, something vastly greater than the sum of its parts.)

(Does all this talk remind you of a few familiar phrases, like "Down the rabbit hole", "The Apple of my eye", or "The Apple of The Garden of Eden"? The clockwise or counterclockwise spinning yin and yang? Could it be that this information has been known for time and all eternity, but was somehow gifted to us, or otherwise encoded in our holy books, and passed on for posterity for those of us who were educated or enlightened enough to decode it? PHD and world scholar Graham Hancock would seem to say so, as he makes an extensive detailed explanation of just such a postulation in his best seller, "Fingerprints of The Gods". Indeed, as we move out of the darkness of ignorance, and into a greater conditioning of conscious awareness, we must come to terms with that which has always been, but with that which has been forgotten, or so misunderstood for so long.

The ring at the center of the torus field is the "Eye of The Apple", as much as it's "The Apple of my Eye", while at the same time, it's the jumping off point between realms. If you halved an apple from top to bottom, and turned it sideways, you'll see a curious eye staring back at you. If you remember the function of the fields while doing this, you'll see even more; even in its absence. If we look at the torus field from the top, it is the Yin female of the swastika spinning in one direction, and if we look at it from the bottom male end, it's the Yang male of the swastika spinning in the other direction: each hemisphere with their own dominion and effects. Understanding The Eye of The Torus, through the lenses of multiple disciplines, languages, and cultures, is the key to comprehending the value of its use...

Reference, The Eye of Horus, The Eye of Ra, and the mathematical equation of $(1/2 + 1/4 + 1/8 + 1/16 + 1/32 + 1/64) =$ where a single portion that is mathematically "elsewhere" seems to be missing from the equation. A portion that has transcended, translated, or has otherwise been "surfed" to the other side of the "I know not". This is seen in ancient texts to accompany the allegorical expression of The Eye in many cultures. In the same manner that all of these things are referencing The Ring of Absolute Conditioning, which is the function of the first circle to The Flower of Life, all of these references are pointing to the vast significance of the torus field.)

Eternal Recurrence

(With magnets, positive and negative polarities must be flipped respective to one another to cause attraction or repulsion. With battery's torus fields, the bottom out flowing vortex$_{male}$ in the southern hemisphere must be placed on the inflowing vortex$_{female}$ at the top of another torus to create a "mutual attraction", which is really an energetic flow between fields (∞). Like magnets or batteries, other torus fields function differently when their relationship to one another's field is altered by posture, position, or nesting. They may relate, repulse, share, flow, or if they're nested, the exterior field will have dominion. Yes, our batteries are designed wrong, they should be nested not lined up.

The torus fields that encase the earth and sun are standing on end with "The Eye of The Horus" facing up and down, respective to one another. As the earth circles from one side of the solar system to the other, the top of our torus field is attracted to the North Star's torus field. As we move from one side of the solar system to its opposite side, the earth is said to wobble between winter and summer. Yet, it's the eye$_f$ of our torus field, which continually points at Polaris, which is causing the illusion of a wobble. Like the shared energy flowing through batteries, it's actually an energetic guideline connecting the two torus fields (∞), not so much as across the distance of space time, but in a kind of energetic connectivity, which is not bound by space or time. But, we'll have to cover the Fuzzy Physics behind that later.

So why aren't we wobbled by the sun's torus field in the same manner? After all, it's much closer, and proximity usually insinuates a greater potential for cause and effect relationships. Whether or not torus fields are nested, if they're placed at 90° angles to one another, torus fields behave like energetic sprocket mechanisms with one another, and if they're side-to-side, they can create a kind of push-pull balance. However, batteries and magnets only transfer energy between one another when their polarities are aligned (north south) to (north south), or (female male) to (female male). It's in this second manner that torus fields possess the potential to energetically interlink in a cause and effect relationship with one another.

Polaris' torus field is positioned in just such a manner that its outward flowing $vortex_m$ is facing our inward flowing $vortex_f$. This creates an energetic flow between fields that guides the angle and direction of our wobble through the 25k+ years of the precession of the equinoxes. This energetic "cord" (∞) creates a Source Field connection, or Source Field flow, which shares Source Field Energies between the two torus fields. Polaris, not only has us lassoed by the magnetosphere in the same manner that a cowboy has a bull lassoed by the horns, but the manner in which the shared energetic effects flow between the two fields is a determiner of The Force of The Architect's energetic potentialities, as well as The Program of The Architect's Codes within each torus field.

Remembering that our $magnetosphere_f$ is injecting the earth with life producing Source Field Energy, and taking a bold step into vastness, we can say that every star in our galaxy has a torus field that's attracted, repulsed, cranked, nested, or energetically wired to, energetically transferring energy between, or otherwise possesses Interrelations to every other star or field encased heavenly body. As our solar system takes its 120 million year trip around the galaxy, we can see that the 300+billion torus fields of stars and planets are energetically Entangled to one another. They're creating a centrifugally flattened disc shaped energetic cohesion, which is holding everything in the galaxy in place, while everything is yet moving at ungodly galactic speeds.

Because we know galaxies possess nested torus fields, we can surmise that each star's torus field will behave differently due to its location within each portion of each nested field within the galaxy, or within a particular Hemisphere of the galaxy. Moreover, in the same manner that apple seeds and apple cores are subject to the two different energetic effects that have a particular dominion over them, so too the behavior of the particles and waves of galactic torus fields are subject to the nesting patterns of each layer of torus field they are nested within. "Relative position within The Hemisphere Effect", is just as significant to the function of Physics as relative position to the pentagonal field, relative position to the central ring of coherence, and relative interlinking of torus fields.

In the same manner that one star energetically relates to another within in its location of its galaxy, so too all galaxies are cohesive to one another after this energetic manner. This goes for so-called rogue planets, wobbling stars, and double stars, which are all being held in place by the fields of other heavenly bodies, by being nested inside of another torus field, or even their relative locations within The Hemisphere Effect. It may not necessarily function in the exact same manner for so-called dead bodies, which don't possess an active or fully functioning field. However, those bodies, such as our asteroid belt, will still be subject to the dominion of the field in which they reside, and therefore will be energetically held in place by default of the dominion of nesting or The Hemisphere Effect in which they reside.

In the same manner that batteries, which are lined up in a row, flow their energy one torus field into another, so too other torus fields between heavenly bodies flow into, share, and are otherwise energetically cohesive to one another. In the same manner that one origin of Source Field Energy, which our Magnetosphere is drawing off, is coming from its present energetic link with Polaris, so too every other energetically connected torus field is behaving in a similar relationship to one another in a given galaxy. That is, unless a torus field should happen to move into another hemisphere of its nested torus field. If the earth should happen to move into the northern hemisphere of The Milky Way Galaxy, Earth's position within another torus field will have changed, in the same manner as an eddy crossing the equator would be compelled to flip its spin. The body would be compelled to flip its energetic fingerprint, and its field will be compelled to make a new connection with a new star with a relative polarity. The Magnetosphere is compelled to switch, flip, move, or otherwise adjust relative to its position within The Hemisphere Effect, and the dominion of its next connection.

Like a Tesla Alternating Current Device that constantly flips back and forth, earth goes through a 25k year Hemisphere Effect Flip, which causes our magnetosphere to be inverted, flipped, or otherwise energetically rewired with other heavenly bodies. Out of 300 billion stars in our galaxy, the Earth cannot be the only torus field encased body that's doing this. In eternal vastness, the Galaxy is acting like two hemispheres of an infinitesimally small human brain, whose energetic dendrites are wiring and rewiring themselves on an eternally vast galactic timescale. This rewiring effect from all bodies, which move between the hemispheres of the galaxy, will have galactically long repercussive effects on all other bodies in the galaxy. It will cause them to rewire their energetic relationships, such that the energetic changes will alter the natural constants to the degree of available transference of energy, or lack thereof.)

(Even black holes can be seen as one end of a massive torus field that energetically gobbles up other torus fields. The vacuum created by the spin of its in flowing vortex, will flip another body's field, such that the out flowing vortex of that body is facing the correct inflowing vortex of the black hole. Then, like two magnets compelled to race toward one another, the stronger field gobbles them up by the trillions, sending them down the vortex to its central ring of coherence. If a gateway can be created by an apple, and a larger gateway can be created by a magnetosphere, one might want to begin asking themselves just how large an opening something as massive as a black hole could create, how much could go through it, and how much could return from "the other side" of a black hole that operates in the other direction. To my eyes, black holes don't look like garbage disposals; they look like a universal (X, Y, Z) two-way door of dominion.

Torus fields, in the form of black holes, do not initially use gravity to pull items into their vortexes. At their inception, there's no significant mass, or relation to a realm, which the field possesses that would allow this to begin; just something that would create the energetic spin of the torus field. Remember, in the same manner that the field is present before the egg of energy, so too the egg of energy is always present before the expression of matter. In the same manner that whirlpools exist, because water is impregnated with the energetic spin of an eddy, so too black holes are first and foremost energetic fields that impregnate the fabric of space and time with a torsion field, before they begin effecting particles or waves. Black holes are energetic fields that manipulate energy fields, and then they push or pull on particles or waves.

A ubiquitous rule of thumb to any discipline in the Trivium or Quadrivium could be the Field Physics™ Rule, "Whether it be infinitesimal smallness, or eternal vastness, nothing is without an energetic attachment via the energetic expression of something else". There's always an energetic link that's interwoven or entangled into the fabric of existence, whether we're talking about invisible microscopic eddies dancing across the surface of an apple, the torus fields called chakras that are nested within a person's anatomy, or the galactic torus field of a galaxy that behaves as a Mother Field to 300billion children stars. All things within those fields are subject to the Nesting Effect, Hemisphere Effect, and the relationships and conditions of other nearby fields, nodes, rings, and inter wiring of energetic flow of torsion fields. This goes for all life forms, and collectives as much as it goes for everything else possessed of an energetic expression.

All torus fields are compelled by their very nature to communicate and link with one another. Torus fields exercise dominion over particles and waves within their fields. Torus fields exercise dominion over torus fields within The Hemisphere Effect of their field. In addition, nesting torus fields, within other torus fields, creates new dominion, and new links.)

(The Signature of The Path of The Three Great Quests is Eternal Recurrence in infinitesimal smallness and eternal vastness. "As above so below" is expressed in all directions of vastness. Observing the function of torus fields allows us to understand how torus fields, fields, and forces maintain dominion without ever touching the thing that it has dominion over. In Field Physics, this is a vastness that transcends Realms. It reveals how the profoundly real, yet curiously elastic emptiness, of what we call "outer space", is actually the inner space of an exterior field, and thus every cubic inch of it is subject to the exterior field's dominion, nodes, rings, and energetic wiring; the Merkaba is expressed in eternal vastness. This "empty fabric" is under the dominion of ever-larger torus fields, such that even if the exterior field never actually touches the thing it's controlling; pushing Intelligence, transferring energy, spinning fields, and transforming forces into, or drawing out of, and exchanging with, it still has dominion. It doesn't matter if they're magnetospheres of planets, stars, or entire galaxies, Nested Dominion and Hemisphere Effects reside in and between the so-called emptiness of outer space, while at the same time it resides in mid air, in the crushing bowels of a planet, or within torrential firestorms of stars. In the same manner that light has dominion over the darkness wherever it's present, so too torus fields dictate the function of reality over anything their fields have dominion over. Like the two-way door of dominion between light and dark or knowledge and ignorance, torus fields modify the laws of fundamental constants within their field of influence and relationships to relative fields.)

(We find a north/south polarity flip in the Atlantic seabed samples in even increments, because our solar system travels across the plane of the ecliptic of the galaxy's torus field in a 25K "Great Year" cycle. The earth's magnetosphere is nested within the galaxy's field, thus it must obey the exterior field and flip to correct itself relative to its position within that field, and the constant direction of the galactic torsion field.

We just passed the galaxy's equator on December 22-25th of 2012. Yet, we've been recording a pole shift since the early 1900's. As our planet continues to shift into our new old hemisphere, we'll see the energetic shift of our magnetosphere continue to move into alignment with dominion of the galaxy's torus field.

It's quite possible, because of Polaris' polarity relative to our current northern polarity, that when our magnetosphere flips, we'll have a precession of the equinoxes that's energetically linked with a new star. Based on Egyptology, this may very likely be Alpha Draconus. However, this will be based on the linking condition of its field, or which star our field is already next in line to link with. The "rewiring alignments" keep changing throughout the galaxy, and with 300billion stars constantly rewiring themselves, like billions of dendrites, the energetic links we once had, may not be what we get next.)

(Thinking along the lines of the location of the seeds of our apple. Like the earth, the galaxy's torus field also has the same pentagonal shaped seed nodes in its torus field. Based on the universal model of torus fields and The Program of The Architect, as these nodes spin through the galactic plane of the ecliptic, they disburse their energy like golden flakes of life giving energetically driven Source Field Intelligence, which spiral out after the manner of The Fibonacci Spiral seeding each layer of the galaxy with life. These nodes could be considered the energetic source of the "Panspermia Theory", which is said to seed the galaxy with life forms.

Like the crossing of or proximity to one another's nodes between hurricanes and earth, our increasing or decreasing proximity to galactic nodes carries the potential to alter our fundamental constants after an energetic manner. We need to look toward Field Nodes for the creation of, or doorway to, life in all its forms. These nodes will express themselves within the pentagonal nodes, the central ring, or even where energetic rays of Source Field Energy intersect. This will be expressed as Ley Lines, Metatron's Cube nested inside a torus field, or even the construct of an apple. This is also a big hint as to the location of healing or restorative waters that flow along, or otherwise intersect with, these areas (See also Ponce De Leon, 36°57'08.06 N 90°59'38.38 W elevation 444 ft.).)

The Alchemists Dream

(It's not good that a man should think to run before he can walk, nor expect to run faster than he has strength. While a student learns a subject at a beginner's level of understanding, they will not be able to see what they have just experienced at its more complete level of comprehension. They'll read over something several times, and may even call it insignificant, before suddenly realizing its vast significance. Very often, the student must spend a great deal of time and devoted commitment to fully understand what the master is trying to teach him before being gifted with the attainment of a new horizon, the epiphany of greater understanding, or The Thunderbolt of Enlightenment. Such is The Path of The Three Great Quests.

We join spokes together in a wheel
But it's the center hole
That makes the wagon move

We shape clay into a pot
But it's the emptiness inside
That holds whatever we want

We hammer wood for a house
But it's the inner space
That makes it a home

We work with being
but non-being is what we use

(There is an ancient saying, "We live in the hollow places of life". As Master Lao Tzu suggests in this excerpt from The Tao Te Ching, it is the hollowness of the pitcher that holds the greatest purpose for that pitcher, and it is useless lest we do something with that void. We build beautiful houses, but it's in the empty spaces between the walls where we find a home, and raise a family. We play beautiful music, but it's the silence between the notes, which holds the greater meaning of the song, which allows us to dance.

In the same manner that a hollow axis supports the value of a two-way spinning wheel, it's in these hollow spaces of life that we find other things revolving around them. In the same manner that a house is meaningless without a family to pass through its hollow spaces, so too a hollow axis is useless unless that which passes through it provides a greater significance. When the student attains a level of understanding, which allows them to reduce many disciplines through a common axis of expression, this newfound skill allows them to translate between all disciplines as if the hollow axis between them was truly absent, but also truly existent. All subjects become spokes in the same wheel of greater understanding, gears of the same machine with a common function, and parts of a larger apparatus that possess a greater purpose and more marvelous significance (Page 12, Same machine).

The Torus Field is the universal two-way wheel of Virtue, Truth, and Love. It's also the counter spinning wheel of anger, fear, and aggression. The Northern Hemisphere Effect can be represented as the positive Karma of The Triquetra of The Middle Way of The Path. The Southern Hemisphere Effect can be represented as the negative Karma of The Triquetra of paths that lead to anger, fear, and aggression. The Central Ring can be represented as the axis mundi, a substantively absent geometrical ring through which all things pass, around which all things revolve, and a void within which we attain a greater significance. The axis mundi of the central ring is that physical, energetic, geometrical, harmonic, mathematical, scientific, and artistic two-way door of dominion through which all things pass. It's our magical "something" that seems to be absent, but was always with the student, master, and even the villain throughout the journey of The Path of The Three Great Quests. It's this hollow place in life where we find great value.)

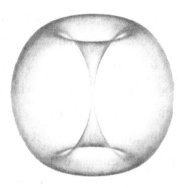

(The Hindi word Chakra means wheel (chakra = wheel), but this is a language misnomer. Rather than a wheel, as one might think of a tire on a vehicle, a Chakra is more like looking at a three-dimensional torus field from the top or bottom. One sees the spinning wheel that is actually the torus' torsion field drawing in energy at a particular location, at a particular frequency, and corresponding to a particular geometry. But remember, the torus' hollow axis also expels particles, waves, energy, and forces out of the other side.

These particles, waves, energies, or forces can be seen to enter and exit the torus field, in the same manner that a driver might enter and exit a tollbooth. They go in one side, and come out the other, they're a few pennies short, but they otherwise exit unchanged. Rather than exiting out of the other side in the same Realm, the "missing change" comes out of another tollbooth in another realm.

Think of two energetically connected torus fields, one existing in $Realm_1$ where we are, and one that's in another dimension: $Realm_2$, over the horizon of our perspective. If energy goes into the torus field in $Realm_1$ it can move from space-time into time-space in $Realm_2$ and exit out of another duplicate torus field on the opposite side in $Realm_2$. Should the particle, wave, energy, or force remain in its own realm ($Realm_1$ » $Realm_1$) or ($Realm_2$ » $Realm_2$), it will be relatively unchanged in the same manner that we remain relatively unchanged when coming out of a tollbooth. The particles, waves, energy, or forces will be more energized and coherent, because of the conditioning effects of The Northern Hemisphere Effect, but otherwise everything will be the same as it was when they went in.

However, when the energy, particle, or force goes into the torus and those lost "pennies" come out of the other side in another realm ($Realm_1$ » $Realm_2$) or ($Realm_2$ » $Realm_1$), wherein they can inverse their properties--- If you injected a particle in $Realm_1$ you could get a wave in $Realm_2$. If you injected a geometric shape, such as a particle shaped after an Icosahedron in $Realm_1$, you could get its inverse geometric shape of a dodecahedron in $Realm_2$. If it makes the jump, its construct can realign, reorder, or otherwise change its relationship with its form in the opposing realm.

Popping in and out or back and forth between realms is a great tool, but we must pause here, and learn to walk before we can run. The diagrams below are some of the "Jump" correlations aligned with those things they transform with between Realms. After all, it's one thing to familiarize yourself with the idea that things are constantly flipping back and forth between the two realms of space-time$_1$ and time-space$_2$, or even to know what they're flipping back and forth as. It is quite another thing to flip them over, change their "geometric music", and then flip them back as something entirely different (Page 5, Geometry and music).

Geometry = (Number in Space)
Music = (Number in Time)

In this manner one could theoretically begin with earth, after the geometry of a cube, and resonating it at 525Hz, push it through a torsion field's central node flipping 1/64^{ths} of it from (space time$_1$) to (time space$_2$). On the other side, it flips over to an octahedral Air at 600Hz. As a wave, we use frequency (f) to change its function to Icosahedron water at 900Hz and flip it back over to space-time$_1$ as a spiritual dodecahedron element at 1200Hz. The transmutation of the elements, The Alchemist's Dream. Yet, what if there was something greater than The Alchemist's Dream? There is, and like the greater significance of the Dolphin's Dentem Musical Intellect squeaking through the hollow ring of torus bubbles, we're rapidly closing in on its absent presence.)

(

Nested Equation

$$(\text{Realm}_1) = (\text{Realm}_2)$$
$$(\text{Space time}_1) = (\text{Time space}_2)$$

$$(\text{Particle gravity}_1)(\text{Wave levity}_1) = (\text{Particle levity}_2)(\text{Wave gravity}_2)$$

$$\{(\text{Frequency})(\text{Particle gravity}_1)(\text{Wave levity}_1) = (\text{Particle levity}_2)(\text{Wave gravity}_2)(\text{Frequency})\}$$

$$\{(\text{Frequency})(\text{Space time})\} = \{(\text{Time space})(\text{Frequency})\}$$

$$\{(\text{Geometry})(\text{Frequency})(\text{Particle gravity}_1)(\text{Wave levity}_1) = (\text{Particle levity}_2)(\text{Wave gravity}_2)(\text{Frequency})(\text{Geometry})\}$$

$$\{(\text{Geometry})(\text{Frequency})(\text{Space time})\} = \{(\text{Time space})(\text{Frequency})(\text{Geometry})\}$$

$$\{(\text{Dodecahedron})(1200\text{Hz})(\text{Source Field})\} = \{(\text{Water or Emotion})(750\text{Hz})(\text{Icosahedron})\}$$

$$\{(\text{Icosahedron})(750\text{Hz})(\text{Water or Emotion})\} = \{(\text{Intellect or Air})(600\text{Hz})(\text{Octahedron})\}$$

$$\{(\text{Octahedron})(600\text{Hz})(\text{Intellect or Air})\} = \{(\text{Earth})(525\text{Hz})(\text{Cube})\}$$

$$\{(\text{Cube})(525\text{Hz})(\text{Earth})\} = \{(\text{Fire})(300\text{Hz})(\text{Tetrahedron})\}$$

$$\{(\text{Tetrahedron})(300\text{Hz})(\text{Fire})\} = \{(\text{Fire})(-300\text{Hz})(\text{Inverted Tetrahedron})\}$$

$$\{(\text{Inverted Tetrahedron})(300\text{Hz-})(\text{Fire})\} = \{(\text{Void})(\text{Frequency})(\text{Sphere})\}$$

)

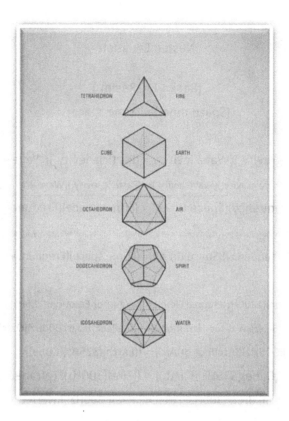

Platonic Solids, their inverse geometry, and accompanying elements.

Geometry	Particle/wave	» «	Inverse geometry	Inverse element
Dodecahedron	Spirit	» «	Icosahedron	Water
Icosahedron	Water	» «	Dodecahedron	Spirit
Octahedron	Air	» «	Cube	Earth
Cube	Earth	» «	Octahedron	Air
Tetrahedron	Fire	» «	Tetrahedron (inverted)	Fire
Sphere	Void			

Ascending pattern

Geometry	Particle/wave	» «	Ascending geometry	Ascending element
Dodecahedron	Spirit	» «	Icosahedron	Water
Icosahedron	Water	» «	Octahedron	Air
Octahedron	Air	» «	Cube	Earth
Cube	Earth	» «	Tetrahedron	Fire
Tetrahedron	Fire	» «	Tetrahedron (inverted)	Fire
Tetrahedron (inverted)	Fire	» «	Sphere	Void

Circle of Sound

(963Hz Pineal activator)

(852Hz Awaken intuition)

(741Hz Consciousness expansion)

(639Hz Connecting or Integrating structures)

(528Hz Miracle and Love)

(417Hz Transmutation or Facilitating change)

(396Hz Liberation from fear)

(285Hz Quantum cognition)

(174Hz Foundation)

And recycle back to 963Hz (These frequencies can be raised much higher than those currently listed)

Comparative table of Chakras and (color = freq)

Chakra	Hindi name	Color	Location	Crystal
Crown Chakra:	Sahasrara	Violet	Crown or top of head	Quartz
Third Eye Chakra:	Ajna	Indigo	Third Eye/forehead	Amethyst
Throat Chakra:	Vishuddha	Blue	Throat	Blue aventurine
Heart Chakra:	Anahata	Green	Sternum/heart	Green aventurine
Solar Plexus Chakra:	Manipura	Yellow	Xiphoid/solar plexus	Yellow aventurine
Sacral Chakra:	Swadhisthana	Orange	Sacral/ Dan-tien	Orange aventurine
Root Chakra:	Muladhara	Red	Base/Coxis	Red Jasper

Interlocking tables

Torus-Chakra	Color	Purpose	Organ/location	Wave-Frequency	Particle-Length
Sahasrara	Violet	Spiritual	Pineal gland	1200Hz	230-250nm
Ajna	Indigo	Psychic/intellect	Pituitary gland	900Hz	333nm
Vishuddha	Blue	Self-expression	Thyroid gland	750Hz	400nm
Anahata	Green	Love	Thymus gland (heart)	600Hz	500nm
Manipura	Yellow	Ego/Emotion	Pancreas gland	525Hz	575nm
Swadhisthana	Orange	Reproduction	Gonad glands	500Hz	600nm
Muladhara	Red	Survival	Adrenal gland	300Hz	1000-750nm

The Torus fields of our chakras are nested within other torus fields, each of a different nature, spectrum, energy, and dominion. There is a singular torus field encasing all our chakras. However, it doesn't end there, we must get used to thinking in terms of vastness. Our torus fields are surrounded by the torus fields of our collectives, the magnetosphere, and the torus fields of the galaxy. When we think of torus fields, we must think in all directions of vastness.

Interlocking tables

Color	Element	Purpose	Chakra location	Geometry
Purple	Source Field	Spiritual	Pineal gland	Dodecahedron
Indigo	Source Field	Psychic	Pituitary gland	dodecahedron
Blue	Water	Expression	Thyroid gland	Icosahedron
Green	Air	Intellect/Love	Thymus gland	Octahedron
Yellow	Earth	Ego/Power	Pancreas gland	Cube
Brown	Earth		Body	Cube
Orange	Fire	Reproduction	Gonad glands	Tetrahedron
Red	Fire	Survival	Adrenal gland	Tetrahedron inverted
	Void			Sphere

Range of Frequency

Chakra	Purpose	Frequency	Length	Geometry
Violet	Spiritual	1200Hz	230-250nm	Dodecahedron
Indigo	Psychic/intellect	900Hz	333nm	Dodecahedron
Blue	Expression	750Hz	400nm	Icosahedron
Green	Love	600Hz	500nm	Octahedron
Yellow	Ego/Emotion	525Hz	575nm	Cube
Orange	Reproduction	500Hz	600nm	Tetrahedron
Red	Survival	300Hz	1000-750nm	Tetrahedron
	Void			Sphere

Conditions or frequencies of the human brain.

Alpha 7.5 to 14htz

Beta 14 to 40htz

Theta 4-7.5htz

Delta .5 to 4htz

Legend:

(Nanometers = nm) = a measure of microscopic distance of a wave.

Red has the longest wavelength, and the slowest frequency. Emotions are heightened by this color as well as its energy.

Purple has the shortest wavelength, and the fastest frequency. Emotions are soothed by this color as well as its energy.

Red is represented at the naval, while Purple is represented at the crown chakra.

A good acronym to remember the colors of the rainbow is through a man's name---"Roy G. Biv" - Red Orange, Yellow, Green, Blue, Indigo, Violet.

The formulas of these pyramids will assist in getting your ratios correct within your designs.

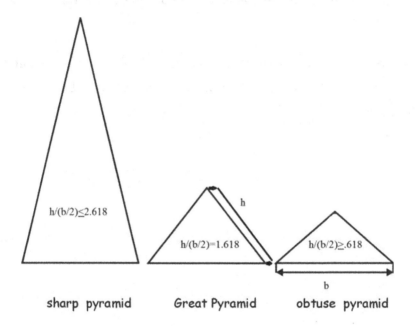

h/(b/2)≤2.618

h/(b/2)=1.618   h

h/(b/2)≥.618

b

sharp pyramid   Great Pyramid   obtuse pyramid

(As a Force, The Veil, which divides all realms, is composed of "passive" or "inactive" energy of The Architect while it's not "constructing". It can be crossed with a movement into a condition of amplified energetic, inviscidly conditioned, uniform acceleration, which torsion fields provide at their central ring.

$$(\text{Realm}_1) = (\text{Realm}_2)$$

The labels of (space time) and (time space) can be used interchangeably with the labels of (Realm_1) and (Realm_2). We can also replace the label of (Realm_1) and (Realm_2) with "that which we find in each realm", and "that which something translates into" in the opposing realm (particle and gravity), or (wave and levity). Particles are subject to gravity, and waves are subject to levity in Realm_1. Particles are subject to levity, and waves are subject to gravity in Realm_2. In the same manner that math can be interpreted via letters or numbers, and the Associative Property of math can be represented by the Entanglement Property of Quantum Physics, so too The Nesting Equation can begin with three different, but identical translations or expressions of language.

$$(\text{Realm}_1) = (\text{Realm}_2)$$
$$(\text{Space time}_1) = (\text{Time space}_2)$$
$$(\text{Particle gravity}_1)(\text{Wave levity}_2) = (\text{Particle levity}_1)(\text{Wave gravity}_2)$$

Within space-time$_1$ and time-space$_2$ particles and gravity behave relative to one another as do waves and levity. While particles are typically seen as subjects of gravity in realm$_1$, they may also be subjects of levity. This expression may flip its value in realm$_2$, an equal and opposite expression of the same value. The opposition of these two can also be expressed as that which creates balance or equilibrium.

Nevertheless, there's something that can change all of this (frequency), which can also be expressed as (coherence°). Think of water in any one of its three states of solid, liquid, or gas. That thing which causes it to function differently is typically thought of as "how hot or cold it is". What that really means is how fast or slow the particles are moving. How orderly the particles are structured. Are they agitated, discombobulated, and in an incoherent state, and thus resonating at a different frequency? Are they energized, inviscid, or uniformly accelerated? What this is really asking is, "How coherent or incoherent something is." "The Condition" of the elements, or measurement of degrees of viscosity. Thus, we nest the formula further.

$$\text{Incoherence°} = \text{Viscosity°}$$
$$\text{Coherence°} = \text{Inviscid°}$$

$$(\text{Realm}_1) = (\text{Realm}_2)$$

$$\{(\text{Inviscid°})(\text{Particle Gravity})(\text{Wave Levity})\} = \{(\text{Particle Levity})(\text{Wave Gravity})(\text{Inviscid°})\}$$
$$\{(\text{Coherence°})(\text{Particle Gravity})(\text{Wave Levity})\} = \{(\text{Particle Levity})(\text{Wave Gravity})(\text{Coherence°})\}$$

In the same manner that levity effects waves, depending on what frequency they're operating at, so too gravity effects particles based on what frequency they're functioning at, or what "condition" they're in. In the same manner that The Path is a "movement into a condition" via the special powers of each Path, so too we're using conditioned Source Field Energy to move "things" into or out of a unique condition using torsion fields. In the same manner that we're transforming waves into particles or particles into waves by flipping them between realms, so too we want to be able to exchange the properties of levity into particles, and transmute gravity from particles into waves in either realm.

Quantum Pinching uses Freon and "room" temperatures to cause the veil (fabric of space time$_{1\,2}$) to be "pinched". The extreme variance in temperatures in a localized region between Realm$_1$ and Realm$_2$ cause a bending of the inactive fabric of The Veil, in such a manner that The Veil itself is the "thing" "trapping" a given object. Scientists are not so much as changing the properties of the thing being trapped, such that it now attains the properties of levitation, they're changing the conditions around the thing being "held in place" "by an outside force" by using extreme temperature variances. In much the same manner that air unequally pinches an airfoil to cause "lift", when an aircraft uses the imbalance of thrust, so too Quantum Pinching is a kind of "trapping" that gives the illusion of levity, while not actually transferring the properties of levity into the particles. In the same manner that a magnet has a natural "magnetic" property, so too we must get a particle to contain levitative properties to truly be called levitated. Looking at the formula, we must get the properties of levity and gravity to flip their relationships with particle and wave, while at the same time leaving the other properties of wave and particle alone.)

(Realizing that the student is undergoing something of a "data dump" at this time, where we have a lot of unfamiliar information, and are trying to compile and comprehend it in large mathematical gulps, we realize that before we can continue, we must pause to reflect. We need to bring past information forward, and meld it with this new information on a conscious intentional level. Recalling the computer program from the chapter on Truth, The Architect of Truth, we remember that The Source Field Energy builds itself with geometric patterns nested within geometric patterns and harmonic waves nested within harmonic waves; and thus, gravity nested within gravity, and levity nested within levity. These patterns can be expressed physically with particles, such as the growth and shape of trees in relationship to their branches. These waves can be expressed energetically as growth patterns of those same trees as a wave function in an expressed, but spread out pattern, within the branches of the forest of the Amazon. Moreover, we remember that no matter if we're looking at infinitesimal smallness or eternal vastness, the expressions of these patterns and waves always collapse, like a quantum wave function, into a given pattern that can be expressed linearly through a common doorway of geometric or harmonic numbers.

Because water is the closest thing we can observe with the naked eye that can universally demonstrate both a particle that is subject to gravity, or a wave that is subject to levity, while yet within the confines of $Realm_1$, we'll look first at the function of this "Quantum Collapse" aka "Quantum Expression" (X) as it relates to our nested equation with the operation of water. Looking back once again, under the caption "The Architect of Truth" within the chapter on Truth (Page, 57) we have the following excerpt---

(In the same manner that The Intelligent Architect will construct particles of matter with self-similar formats, so too The Architect will form the same patterns with what we might consider "more ethereal forces". Intelligence can be seen marrying itself to torsion fields, twin toroidal vortices, and toroids. Intelligence will blend those energetic geometries as one with other forces; such as electricity or kinetic energy, and manipulate all three as One.

In the same manner that energy can be contained within, or move through, the fluidity ocean waves, so too intelligence will blend itself with a particle of matter or the energy of a wave. The Force of Intelligence will be within, or otherwise around and among, the particles that composes the water--- to modify its behavioral expression. At the tips of large enough waves, a torsion field can be seen to torque the water back into itself, twist it slightly to the side into the beginnings of a horizontal vortex, and then rationally fractalize each particle of water into smaller self-similar versions of the primary wave; Fractal Particle Motion (Page 58).

At this time, the operation of an ocean wave is thought to be the accumulation of energetic waves catching up with one another within water, the energy bouncing more frequently off an ever-shallow shoreline, and all of it collapsing into a single wave that expresses itself near the shoreline. However, the crucial observation that allows us to conclude that intelligence is impregnated within the wave, along with kinetic energy, as well as molded within the particle of water in a trifecta of connectivity is--- the energy is forming the torsion patterns after the blueprint of The Program of The Architect. While kinetic energy forms chaotic patters, such as a rock rolling arbitrarily down a hill, The Architect consistently forms shapes and designs that follow the increasing mathematics of the program.

Waves don't form circles, or capital C's, look closer, and you'll see they form the exponentially changing curve caused by the program. The increasing Force of The Architect moves The Program of The Architect from a 1 to 1 self-similar ratio toward a 1 to 1.618 ratio. The "event" reaches an apex of expression, $\{(\text{If } 89), (\text{then } 144)\}$, the wave reverses its flow, function, and its remnants reveal the scattering program as it again moves toward $\{(\text{If } F (Z) = 1^2 \text{ x } C)), (\text{then } F (Z) = 1^2 \text{ x } C))\}$ » » $\{(\text{If } 1), (\text{then } 1)\}$ and back toward a 1 to 1 self-similarity of the beginning of the program. Simply put, The Architect expresses itself in an ever-changing condition that flows in both directions of The Two-Way Door of Dominion.)

---End excerpt.

After this manner, this two-way door of dominion can be expressed as the two-way door of Physics, where a product is either collapsing or uncollapsing, in a movement toward expressing itself, or unexpressing itself. In this case, "water" is seen to be half way between both expressions. So, it's here that the properties of levity and gravity can easily be seen to switch places.

It's here that our nesting equation catches up with the observable geometry of energy, wave, and particle impregnated within the expression of large waves. With the idea resting freshly in our awareness that The Architect always reveals itself through emergent programming, and growing or diminishing self-similar expressions--- In this case, the growing self-similar expression of a wave, that shows us the invisible geometry of The Fibonacci Spiral and/or toroid within the bubble, and torque of the wave--- The wave itself shows us the two-way door of dominion, as the lift of levity is impregnated within the structure of water, as the ocean wave rises. The swoop of its rising curve follows The Program of The Architect in a concave manner, as opposed to the convex manner of a Bell Curve, and the water moves forward to roll over itself, but doesn't fall, because it's still impregnated with levity.

At its peak expression, we can see that the energetic toroid is turned sideways, such that the energy of the outer toroid bubble is partially the thing holding up the wave. At this moment in the expression, we can see that the tip of the wave torques back around, and rolls into the female torsion field, which drives water toward the middle of the torus field. As the expression diminishes, and the two-way door of dominion flips back in the other direction, the water once again becomes subject to gravity when the wave, and its property of levity, leaves the fluid, and the undoing of the expression hits the shoreline.

---To visualize this more clearly, think of a doughnut standing on end, and being rolled toward the shore by the impregnated energy. Within the water of the wave {(Inviscid° Velocity°), and (wave levity)} are battling it out with (particle and gravity) and (agitation and coherence) between the two-way door of dominion as they roll the doughnut toward the shoreline. Everything within the water is responding by forming the increasing Program of The Architect. As wave increases, nested levity within the water increases. "Wave" is injecting more of its properties of levity into water, while The Program of The Architect is creating an ever-sharper peak; concave on the outside and convex on the inside. The forward movement and the increasing expression of The Architect begin rolling over the energetic doughnut, which begins to help the levity and growing expression of The Architect hold up the water. Pennies of the water then try to spittle through the female vortex toward the central disc of our doughnut.

Except the "doughnut" is a field of energy; a movement of reality into an energetic condition, where we have both Realms$_{1+2}$ trying to express themselves in a manner that's similar to Quantum Pinching. Such that the two realms begin a push-pull flip-flop of properties against one another, which forms the fields, and the actions and reactions of The Architect in the liquid of our observation. Then, like the two-way door of a quantum wave function, the whole thing sputters its energy into fractal self-similar toroids, self-similar Katsushika

Hokusai Water Waves, all expressing the diminishing intelligence of The Program of The Architect into Mandelbrot Fractals, Fractal Particle Motion, and the wave function is seen to simply dissipate.

It's here that the model can be seen to function as a singularity. The particles of water, injected with a wave, are using levity to resist gravity, because of an internal function of levity within a wave, which temporarily resides within the "Platonic Cube" of water. {(cube = oxygen) (8 points of a cube = 8 protons of oxygen) + (Singularity = Hydrogen = (1 proton) of (1 point or one proton nested in each cube)} (Page 8). Thus, two singularities inside two joined cubes impregnated with a wave are becoming subject to levity, while in the condition of being halfway between a particle (ice) and wave (evaporation), "halfway between collapse and uncollapse".

Like Kepler's nested Platonic Solids of the solar system, or Moon's nested Platonic Solids of the periodic table of elements, where nature expresses itself in perfect geometry in eternal vastness or infinitesimal smallness, we see a perfect geometry emerge with the sphere and the torsion field in the form of a toroid and vortex. We observe the program of intelligence build in growing self-similarity. We observe a movement into the condition of temporary amplified energetic, inviscidly conditioned, uniform acceleration as The Architect, forces, fields, particles and waves move into the central ring of the field. The Realms begin to push and pull on one another trying to relieve the imbalance. And, because our perspective remains in $realm_1$, we observe the two-way door of dominion--- Not so much as it moves through the torus field and into $realm_2$--- but as the event reverses itself when the function sputters out its energy separation of (wave and particle) such that "levity" stays with "wave", and the particles of water become subjects of gravity, and the function collapses on itself in what Quantum Physicists would call "An 'uncollapse' of the expression". And why? Because only 1/64^{ths} of the water in a given event is moving from Realm$_1$ into Realm$_2$, while, like us, the greatest portion of the expression remains here. Thus, "that which does not make the transition", its only operation is to collapse back into its original format within the environmental conditions of its given realm$_x$.)

(

$$(AB) = (CD)$$

A = Levity

B = Wave

C = Gravity

D = Particle

To correctly move the product of levity (A) to the opposing side of the equation, we must use it as a divisor against (C•D).

$$(B) = (CD) \div A$$

However, if we do not, but instead use the "Imbalance Function", where a product on one side of the equation is compelled to move to the opposing side of the equals sign, so as to rebalance the equation, then a product of (C) or (D) is compelled to make the jump to the other side of the equation. In this case, (C) or gravity is compelled to switch sides, to balance the equation. The act of injecting levity automatically drives out gravity or otherwise causes gravity to react to its presence. This demonstrates that, like space and time, levity and gravity are mutually inverse to one another. Such that, as a wave collapses into a nested particle expression, levity is automatically driven out by gravity.

Since (A•B) = (C•D), where (A) effects (B), and (C) effects (D)--- Should Levity (A) effect Particle (D) to an increasing degree, the two-way door of dominion in the function of the field will alter the direction of the collapse uncollapse function of the field, causing the Particle (D) to become a the product of Wave (B). This can also be said of Gravity (C), affecting a Wave (B), such that it transforms into a Particle (D), via the same two-way door of dominion of the Field.)

(Since all four variables exist in both realms, we must find an additional mathematical expression that will allow us to advance our understanding of the function behind these products and their properties. The following model can be compared to the second chart, whose deeper functions are explained in detail later in the book. At this time, the common relation of note between the charts is the dominate and recessive function, {as well as the "the flip", and "the jump" functions}. To see the ocean waves "dueling it out" in an advanced mathematical expression, use the formula under Realm$_1$, and flip levity and gravity with one another in a back and forth motion. While this will show how levity within waves opposes gravity, it also reveals that both gravity and levity are equally inverse to one another, which allows the flip function, which some numerical expressions do not allow. The flip also reveals The Imbalance Function between realms. All of this will become more apparent as soon as we delve into White and Dark Light.

$$\text{Realm}_1 \quad = \quad \text{Realm}_2$$

$$\left(\frac{Particle}{Wave} \right) * \left(\frac{Gravity}{Levity} \right) = \left(\frac{Wave}{Particle} \right) * \left(\frac{Gravity}{Levity} \right)$$

Hemisphere Effect		Realm$_1$ North	South		Realm$_2$ North	South
Dominate	»	Particle	Gravity	=	Wave	Gravity
Recessive	»	Wave	Levity	=	Particle	Levity

$$\text{Realm}_1 \quad = \quad \text{Realm}_2$$

$$\left(\frac{Space}{Time} \right) * \left(\frac{Time}{Space} \right) = \left(\frac{Time}{Space} \right) * \left(\frac{Space}{Time} \right)$$

Hemisphere Effect		Realm$_1$ North	South		Realm$_2$ North	South
Dominate	»	White Light	Dark Light	=	Dark Light	White Light
Recessive	»	Dark Light	White Light	=	White Light	Dark Light

)

The First Machine

(When "that of which we are comprised" is conditioned with the amplified energetic, inviscidly conditioned, uniform acceleration of Source Field Energy within the function of female torsion fields, we amplify, change the function of, and cause to work as One "that of which we are comprised" (Page 99, Siddhartha, Thunderbolt of Enlightenment). When the body and the programs of each aspect of the anatomy are conditioned with conditioned Source Field Energy, responses might range from improved health to dormant codons becoming active. When our brains, and the combination of our particular intellects, are conditioned with conditioned Source Field Energy, responses might range from improved educational abilities, epiphanies that thrust your Life Path over a new horizon of understanding, or even the appearance of intellectual feats of genius. When the photonic energy and programming of our spirit are conditioned with conditioned Source Field Energy, responses might range from greater spiritual awareness, to Thunderbolts of Enlightenment, to the ability to perform what some would label miracles.)

(An ideogram is a scribbled marking etched into something such as paper, dirt, or sand via an energetic reaction from one's autonomic nervous system. An ideogram is the result of an autonomic reactive twitch behind a *moment's intention*. This is typically done in a Remote Viewing session with a pen and paper, but ideograms aren't limited to the labels or protocols of just that discipline: ideograms are a common practice in Tibet, India, China, and many other noteworthy cultures throughout history including the ancient Hebrews and Egyptians. An ideogram is the result of intellect connecting with a person, place, or thing on an "Entanglement" (associative property of math) level of understanding, via the discipline of a *moment's focused intention, while in a specific condition of conscious awareness.* Its "activating" energy is The Source Field expressed as consciousness in the mind of the thinker. Its "connective" energies are torsion fields composed of The Force of The Architect, and represented as the foundation of all conscious thoughts--- Thus, if Source Field Energy, expressed as torsion fields, are at the core of what is causing consciousness to be inscribed, that is also the same model that can cause it to be played back. While we need to introduce this information now, we will understand its significance later.)

(Our culture presently considers obelisks as a singular object, an edifice of penile egotism, which are based on archaic and dead religions. This misrepresentation isn't intentional, nor is it necessarily done out of malice, it's just the summations of a degree of knowledge that are relative the degree of Light in which they're experienced. Like pyramids, obelisks are static machines, composed of intricately designed and mathematically related parts that harness a Force, which has a more significant meaning behind a greater purpose.

While energy controls how particles express themselves, acute geometrically designed constructs can pick up, resonate at, and guide frequencies of energy, to direct their flow. In the same manner that an antenna picks up radio waves in the atmosphere, so too the hyper specific geometry of a pyramid or obelisk can pick up different frequencies of The Source Field at the points of its geometry. That energy is harnessed at the corners, flows up the four angled lines to the top, meets, and circles into a vortex (∞). This union of geometry and energy transforms the points of the pyramid and obelisk into harmonic nodes. This function is similar to the seeds of an apple, only rather than starting energetically and becoming physical, it begins physically, harnesses the energetic; and like our ocean wave, it impregnates the particle of geometry with energetic waves of levity, so as to express new conditions of energy in The Architect.)

(While different angled pyramids and obelisks will pick up different frequencies of Source Field Energy, if the faces of their construct are facing the cardinal directions, it is the function of the vortex caused by the pyramid that is our initial concern (Page 210, Pyramid formulas). The rule of thumb for the range of effectiveness of an average pyramid is five times its solid diameter horizontally, and 44 times its solid height vertically. By this range relationship (5w to 44h) (44 ÷ 5 = 8.8) where the energetic height is eight times greater than the energetic width, we can see a pyramid's greatest energetic effectiveness is vertical, both up and down. At this point, we can assume the presence of a mono-pole torsion field, and the absence of a torus field.

The Pyramid's greatest value is not so much in its ability to harness ambient Source Field Energy, but more in its ability to condition that energy with the unique effects of a torsion field. Amplified energetic, inviscidly conditioned, uniform acceleration of a torsion field changes the nature of whatever goes through it. Thus, it's more advantageous to be located directly above, within, or in the middle at the geometric base of a pyramid where the central ring of the torsion field is, so as to be conditioned by that torsion field and The Source Field Energy it harnesses. If our eyes could see in the spectrum of The Source Field, in the same manner that we see the colors of the rainbow, we would see a gigantic "tornado" of Source Field Energy spinning as One with its pyramid, and be able to step right into its central ring.)

(Like our brains, the amount of energy harnessed by a pyramid isn't limited to its physical size, but its energetic capacity, and its energetic capacity can be amplified (f) (^{L}) by the manner in which we construct the pyramid's overall design. In the same manner that raising an antenna up into the air gives it a better opportunity to pick up ambient radio waves, so too raising a pyramid to higher altitudes allows it to pick up, draw in, or otherwise harness more ambient Source Field Energy. It's not a mistake, or by mere chance, that The Giza Plateau is located in an elevated area, relative to its topographical surroundings. So too, we can set smaller pyramids on columns, and raise them up so they will pick up more ambient energy, and their torsion fields will be more energized. We just so happen to call these pyramid columns, obelisks.)

(Ley lines encase the earth in a triangular spherical web of interconnected energetic lines, and placing pyramids and obelisks on Ley Lines will further energize their torsion field with Source Field Energy, because Ley Lines are another source of Source Field Energy. Like torus fields, Ley Lines form a uniform sphere around the earth, but they also go through the earth, and connect in all manner of unique geometries (see also Metatron's Cube or Flower of Life). In the same manner that hurricanes and the earth have a five noded pentagon that can be amplified when crossed (TLR), so too Ley Lines are energetically enhanced where they cross. Not only where their triangular hexagonal lines cross along their energetic web sphere, but also where those lines, which shoot through the earth, reemerge and intersect with other Ley Lines on the surface. The Great Pyramid on The Giza Plateau lays dead center of one of these three way Ley Line intersections. This too is no small coincidence, since many other monuments around the world also lay on these bisected and trisected Ley Lines.)

(The torsion fields of pyramids and obelisks can be further energized by placing the pyramids in "nested orders"; after The Platonic Order. Placing pyramids within pyramids, or smaller pyramids within obelisks will enhance their energetic effectiveness. Inside of each pyramid there could be anywhere from 9, 16, or even 64 smaller pyramids situated in a square, cube, or columned grid (3 x 3 = square), (4 x 4 = square), (4 x 4 x 4 = 64cube), (8 x 8 x 8 = 512cube), (8 x 8 x 64 = 4,096column). Like designing antennas after the repeating self-similar manner of fractals, each pyramid would pick up ambient Source Field Energy, and transfer it vertically (both up and down) to the overall structure.)

(If a quartz crystal pyramid were to be placed into each of the smaller pyramids, the nature and resonance of crystals would once again energetically amplify the structure's torsion field. While this device can be built after the self-similar manner of fractals, that fractalization can be further amplified by building the construct of those fractals with Architect Golden Ratios between the pyramids--- That is, each pyramid being 1.618 times larger or .618 times smaller than the previous pyramid. These very important ratios will resonate at The Source Field Frequency bandwidth {(.618, 1.618, & 2.618) (between about 360nm«»390nm)}, and will therefore harness more ambient energy between the structures, so the structures themselves will pick up, and be able to transmit increased energy.)

$$($$

$$(C = 3)$$

$$(\text{Frequency})(\text{Bandwidth} = z = \text{Structure})(\text{Construct})$$

$$(F(z) = z^2 \times C)$$

$$(F(.618) = z^2 \times C) < (F(1.618) = z^2 \times C) < (F(2.168) = z^2 \times C)$$

Like The Program of The Architect or Mandelbrot Set, wherein the output of an equation is repetitiously inserted back into the equation, we can replace the "Function" (F (_) variable with any variable, or formula. We can insert the Thoth Theorem, Algebra equations, Pie, or The Quadratic into the Mandelbrot function, such that the iteration operation reveals other significant patterns that can assist us with our geometric designs.

$$F(a^2 + b^2 = c^2) = Z^2 * C)$$

$$\left(F\left(x = \frac{-b \pm \sqrt{b^2 - 4ac}}{2a}\right) = Z^2 * C\right)$$

$$(F(\pi) = Z^2 * C)$$

Note the root variable of (C^2) within the Mandelbrot Set; its significance will become apparent later.)

(A Mandala can be described as a series of interwoven and interrelated geometries inscribed on a flat horizontal surface. It can also be described as a gateway to greater spiritual awareness or energetic power, because of the manner in which it's designed and "ideogramed". In the same manner that greater Source Field Energy is harnessed, because of affiliated ratios between structures, so too the specific geometries of Mandela's cause The Source Field to resonate between their ratios in an amplified manner. By reproducing obelisks by the factors of The Program of The Architect, and placing them in a set of nested geometries after the manner of a Mandala, the vortexes of each obelisk are further amplified. However, there is an added bonus to this design that fractal and ratio designs can't accomplish.

For instance, if we began with a pentagon that was measured after the ratios of The Egyptian Meter, and drew lines on the outside of that pentagon to form an exterior five pointed star, the tips of that star would form a second pentagon that possessed a perfect Phi ϕ ratio relative to the first pentagon. If we repeated this process a couple times, the size of the Mandala would become very large very quickly, but each pentagon's size would be perfect relative to the ratios between each of its nodes. When the nested geometries of the Mandala are in place, we place a pyramid or obelisk on each node, and allow some time or add some frequencies, to cause their torsion fields to form. When obelisks or pyramids are constructed in a pentagonal nested circle, the torsion fields feed into one another, and thereby uniformly accelerate each torsion field, drawing in ever more Source Field Energy, and amplifying the overall energy and function of the entire construct. For more information on the "real" Egyptian Meter, see also Hugh Harleston Jr. (1.0594m + 5.9cm = "The Universal Earth Meter").

The uniform nesting spins of all related vortexes of this "circular pattern" takes one more energetic step forward to produce a thing that otherwise would not be created if the design were one iota different. It manifests a central torsion field. This central field has no physical construct, and thus possesses fewer inhibitors to slow its uniform velocity (Page 174, Inhibited velocity minus inhibitions). It's energized and run by nothing more than other torsion fields, and thus has nothing solid to inhibit it from attaining Absolute enhanced energetic, inviscidly conditioned, uniform acceleration, so as to form The Ring of Absolute Conditioning.)

(For the ancients, adding all of this "additional" energy was not so much for the sake of adding more Source Field Energy to the monument, as much as it was for energetically connecting the monument with the global grid. Although a powerfully energized pyramid, obelisk, or Mandala will send and receive adequate Source Field signals to amplify the user's construct, our overall purpose is to *jack in*, and piggyback the message of the monument into the global grid, then reverberate that message around the grid ad infinitum. The overall effect is creating a kind of constant echoing of a particular message on the global grid. Maybe this looks like inscribing an ideogram of the unity of Virtue, Truth, or Love onto the monument. Perhaps it looks like a thousand monks meditating for peace and harmony in the center of the monument's larger central vortex. It might look like a group of scientists standing in a circle, sharing their thoughts, and energetically amplifying their constructs in an effort to spark a Scientific Thunderbolt of Enlightenment. It could even be a book, scroll, or Hall of Records that the energy of the monument continually energizes, and echoes to the global grid for anyone to psychically pick up or Remote View at any time or place. For our present purposes, the design of this monument will amplify The Force of The Architect in a localized area of The Construct {The Design of The Construct $\geq$ The Backster Effect}, such that a melding of the natural and mechanical can be used to create a large "structure free" energetic central ring, which can be used toward the conditioning of all aspects of The Student.)

The Second Machine

(Stand {(If 8), (then 13)} = 13 D batteries on end, in a circle, and with the positive polarities facing up. Place a circular convex lens, with the curved side facing down, in the center of the circle of batteries. Place a rectangular magnet on the center of the lens, and watch it spin. Note its direction. Repeat the same experiment, except invert the batteries, but not the magnet, and note any changes. Now, contemplate the cause and effects that the torus fields are having on one another.

Because it's set at a 90° angle to the battery's torus field, the magnet's torus field is being driven by the exchanging movement of each battery's torus field, as well as the exchanging movement of its own field. As each battery's torus field is moving up on the outside of its bubble it's moving slightly to the side, such that when it reaches the top, this angle forms an eddy that moves into the central vortex of the top female end of the field. In this manner, one field is putting a spin on another field, which constantly hands the energy of its field off to the next field.

Placing this compilation of fields inside a pyramid will meld two forces and six disciplines as One. The design of the experiment harnesses a spinning field with similar overlapping electromagnetic battery fields, while the geometry of the pyramid harnesses The Source Field ($\Phi \Sigma \Delta = \infty$). However, we must remember that the Triquetra is that model that creates something more significant by overlapping three variables, which possess a common doorway in The Middle Way of The Path ($\int\Diamond$). Although we have several disciplines at work, we only have two fields collaborating, and we need to introduce a third.

Every emotion has its own field signature, its own resonance, and possesses a corresponding geometric lattice that can be matched to a particular crystal. This is because every crystal has its own geometric lattice, its own Platonic Solid; or nested Platonic Order, its own field signature, and its own resonance. For instance, the lattice of an amethyst matches the emotion of love, while quartz is more of a generic crystal that amplifies many kinds of emotions and ambient energies (9781582972404). Thus, the kind of crystal we chose should match the emotion we're employing, and the selection of this third field would determine the final function of the three fields in unison.

In the traditions of The Path that are One with the model of The Triquetra, we're adding another dimension to our first machine by melding the natural with the mechanical with three applications. The naturally existing Source Field would be harnessed by the stationary mechanics of our Pyramid, and amplified by our design concepts of the first machine. The torus fields of the "batteries", and or "magnets", would amplify, multiply, and pass on the conditioned Source Field in the machine to its recipients. Our natural emotions would be amplified by the type of crystal used, and further amplified by any corresponding geometric shape they're cut into. In this manner, we have three fields expressed by both a natural and mechanical means, which are forged as One in The Middle Way of The Path.)

(What would this model look like if we put people in place of the batteries and magnets? What would happen to the "human magnet" in the middle of the "structure free" center field while the other "Human batteries" stood in a circle on the ring itself?

What would happen if there were a single circle of masters meditating on The Ring of Conditioning in the center of the first machine while the overlapping fields of the second machine were also employed?

What would happen if we used circles within circles within circles of mediators? What if we placed circles of mediators around each of the Pyramid Obelisk Mandala Rings of Coherence?

What amplification would occur if we interlaced the fields that encircled the obelisks/pyramids after the interlacing geometry of The Flower of Life?

What change in outcomes would occur if we interlaced the central energetic rings after the manner of The Triquetra or The Flower of Life?

What would happen if we buried/placed Orgone accumulators outside of the pyramid, obelisk, or Mandala and piped Orgone energy into the structures, such that the Orgone would be amplified by the conditioned Source Field Energy?

Biophoton therapy mixed with torsion field technology, not only amplifies the function of Bions (aka Orgone Energy), but heals carbon based life forms more effectively than just placing ourselves in a state of conditioning while we're in our Source Field enhanced torsion fields.

What would happen to this Orgone system if our piping system were designed after the manner of a Tesla coil, with 2, 5, or 6 coils + The Hemisphere Effect of female torsion fields?

While the totality of the text will give you all the answers to these questions, we must ask ourselves one more important question, "Is all of this 'Tinkering' with the basic model like striking flint and steel to ignite Prometheus's Per Nature or "Fire of Nature?" Remembering that neither the question, nor the answer is more important than the process of experimental discovery that lies between the two, perhaps now is a good time to actually build this machine and begin experimenting with it yourself. Not only so you can see how it works, but also so you can begin conditioning yourself, and leveraging your natural abilities with mechanical advantages.

(Amplified Energetic) + (Inviscidly Conditioned<°) + (Uniformed Acceleration) + (Conditioned Source Field Energy) + (Biophoton) = Therapy!

)

The Third Machine

(While diverse in its applications, the phrase "The Backster Effect", is quickly becoming a "catch all" phrase for everything from hypnosis, to lie detector tests, to other more "esoteric things", which don't seem to be readily explainable without a sprinkle of "faith" in a banquet of opportunity that yet lies over the next horizon of the following chapters. In his book "The Source Field Investigations", David Wilcock gives an exhaustive explanation of what has been labeled in our time "The Baxter Effect"; something the ancients labeled "The Architect". After the scientific method, David gives meticulous references and resources for all data he presents. For our third machine, we're specifically referencing (Chapter 1, "The Backster Effect, Free Energy, and The Consequences", Section 7, Page 22, Paragraph 2). Dr. Baxter experiments with human cells detached from NASA Astronaut Dr. Brian O'Leary in the year 1988 ---The conclusions of the experiment confirm the constant communication between the cells kept under observation in the lab, and the rest of the subject's construct, even while the subject is yet going through other experiences hundreds of miles away.

The naturally existing communication of The Backster Effect could be amplified if one were to place samples of their DNA on the nodes of a pyramid or within the central ring. Located in a more energetically enhanced, inviscidly conditioned, uniformly accelerated, Source Field, and Biophoton rich condition of $\{(\text{space time velocity}) = (\text{The Construct})\}$, your DNA would be constantly bathed, naturally conditioned, and mechanically enhanced. Moreover, that conditioning would be continually transmitted to the rest of your structure like a radio transmitter + receiver system. One could go about their day as one normally would, but energetically speaking, your structure would continue to receive the energetic benefits of the conditioning engine as if you were always connected to the engine (∞).

This model is using a naturally occurring transmitter + receiver system that is built into the fabric of our universe; "The Design of The Construct", and multiplying it with the leverage of an energetically driven machine. Natural and mechanical forces combined between energy amplification and energy transmission, two things one can never touch, but now, like the use of fire, electricity, and radio these are things we can gain great benefits from.

Like two spinning photons surfing across the universe, postulating the applications of this model promises to shoot us over many horizons of vastness. Such as the fertilization and cryonic storage of embryonic and or T-cells inside of pyramid's central ring before, during, and after they begin to multiply. Collecting DNA samples from entire populations, putting those samples in the pyramid machine in such a manner, so as to keep them alive (28 lunar days/1 lunar cycle), and observing the changes in the subject's or population's "conditions". In consideration of food production, one could insert plant samples into the pyramid fields, and observe how those forces effect the rest of the plant as it grows and matures. We can leave living food in a pyramid; consume only a portion of it while the other portion is yet tucked in the machine communicating Source Field signals to its already consumed aspect. We could begin growing plants, conceiving animals, or enhancing humans within these energy fields, to ensure their genetic signatures are automatically amplified, and energetically linked with the amplified coherence of a greater field of energy.)

Energetic Links...

(Any remote viewer worth their Pineal Eye can tell you RV is a scientifically repeatable process that allows one's energetic aspect to transcend time and space to "view" any person place, thing, or event. Scientists the world over have measured photonic and electromagnetic anomalies that occur at the target of interest the moment someone is in the act of remote viewing that target. The energetic aspect of the viewer is using the pineal gland as a conduit to create a vortex, make the jump through the central ring, arrive at the intended target, and transmit an energy signature full of information about the target back to the intellect of the remote viewer. Yes, this means the photons are somehow programmed.

I began remote viewing in 1997 with Ed Dames' Technical Remote Viewing program. Soon thereafter, I was invited to join The Hawaii Remote Viewer's Guild. I was published by the HRVG in 98' for producing professional grade, psychically achieved, scientifically reliable data, in the black, which can still be viewed on their web site (KDIP-BRTE). I can attest to Glenn Wheaton's skills as a professional instructor, to RV's viability and veracity as a data collection tool, and I've used the skill of RV many times to solve issues, which otherwise could not have been solved.

How does all of this pontificating about RV apply to our third machine? RV is the model of the third machine amalgamated with the models of the first two machines in The Middle Way of The Path. Like Brian O'Leary's demonstration of a continual link (∞); if one can cause a personalized signature to be ideogramed into The Construct when one leaves a physical aspect of themselves in a pyramid, then one is capable of leaving the same kind of energetic signature when one

Remote Views a given target. Especially if one *intends* to leave the psychic doorway open, or more correctly "flipping", when one stops the RV protocols. This process isn't reliant on keeping cells "alive", or leaving expired DNA signatures at a particular location. Nor is it reliant on physically going to that location, or building another working model yourself; even if it doesn't yet exist. One could RV every pyramid that has been or will be in existence, intend to leave the psychic and energetic doorway in the "open" position, and receive the conditioning of its energy on an ongoing basis. Moreover, as we will soon find out after we cross The New Horizon of Entanglement Theory, those benefits can be passed onto our progenitors (∞).)

Heureka!

(The strangeness of this life cannot be measured, only realized in hindsight. Life is packed full of ironies, sometimes we find the ancients putting all of the answers right in front of our collectively ignorant faces in an ironic, but very laughable manner. They tell us in their own way that they were fully aware of "that which we seek". Unlike the scientific method, which lays it all out for you in an 'A' to 'Z' manner, and doesn't compel you to go on a journey, or build the fortitude that earning the knowledge for yourself creates, the ancients knew all too well that the Theological Path compels you to find the answers to life's questions for yourself for many very good reasons. First, it's not good to hand knowledge or tools to someone who hasn't earned the moral fiber to wield them with a full cup of Compassionate Wisdom, Virtuous Knowledge, and Honorable Understanding. Second, the journey is the refining process, which makes one worthy of that which they receive.

The Ancients knew that neither the question nor the answer is more important than the process of discovery that lies between fortitude and refinement, and The Middle Way of The Path is a refining process that makes one worthy of The Light and Fruit of Awareness of The Quest. The ancients formed the message in such a manner, so as to attract memorized attention, and peak human curiosity. Yet, they fabricated "It" in such a manner, that the student must take a journey to earn the knowledge for themselves, and come to a fullness of the understanding as faith and knowledge flip back and forth along the way. When the disciple is done, they laugh as the veil is lifted from their eyes, they look at the same thing, and yet they're compelled to give it a new label. They give it a new name, not because the thing has changed one iota, but because the refining fires of The Quest compels them to see "It" under a New Light of Dominion, and a New Fruit of Awareness. A meaning that thrusts their knowledge over a New Horizon of Understanding. A refinement that transforms what they connect with, how they think, and what they do.

The Ancients showed us where The Source Field Energy was flowing up and down their pyramids. Some used the feathered serpent Quetzalcoatl climbing up and down the pyramid, in the same manner that other ancients used Moses' two Red snakes on a Was Staff. In the same manner, the Babylonians used the following image of a man's arm as The Energy Serpent (∞), and the pinecone as the pineal gland. The Energy Serpents secretly represent the waves of energy: aka Kundalini, Ki, Chi, or Prana (∞). The feathers, or snakes crawling up a pole, are the lifting, levity (^{L}), or elevation of consciousness, which theses energies give, when those waves are transferred into the particle of one's mind (construct). The ball of the caduceus' staff (medical symbol), the apex of the pyramid, or the pinecone is the Pineal Eye; the point that all these energies flow to, awaken, levitate, and illuminate.

Once again, we ask the question, how could this be a universal observation in all these seemingly divided cultures? In infinitesimal smallness, we observe the display of common human feelings for Virtue, Truth, and Compassion, which come in the micro and macro expression humans and humanity. In eternal vastness, we observe a universal exterior model recognized by all cultures, which emerges from the vastness of the outer world. As One, they repeat the same patterns.

In the same manner that Jesus is born and dies on the solstices and equinoxes, so too the serpent deity Quetzalcoatl runs up and down the pyramids using the play of shadow and light "on the cross" of the solstices and equinoxes. The number of levels in their step pyramids show us the waves of the Energy Serpent, in the same manner that the snakes of the caduceus measures melodies in music. Like a musical instrument, the number of waves gives us the resonance, harmony, or frequency (f) that the particular pyramid was designed to "play" at {(Conditioning of torsion fields) + (Dentem Musical Intellect) + (.618, 1.618, 2.618 bandwidth of frequency)}. It also gives us our nodal points where The Source Field Energy is vibrating through, over, around, or otherwise creating nodes.

If measured with an arbitrary device, which possessed no predetermined unit of measurement, such as a piece of string, and by dividing the sum of each measurement into whole numbers, the monuments also give us the lengths of their measuring devices (Page 228, Egyptian Meter). Using the proper length can help us in getting the ratios to our dynamically static machines correct, so as to attain a better resonance effect between a monument, the planet it's built on, and the magnetosphere activating it. Moreover, all of this gives us a key to decipher each particular Pyramid's intended function.

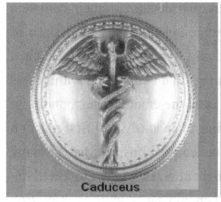
Caduceus

Looking at the geometry of Teotihuacan in Mexico, and the multiple pyramids represented as planets, moons, or the sun. We see each one with its own geometry, each with its own angles and nodal points, and each with its own musical harmony as each pyramid resonates in its own manner in relationship with The Bandwidth of The Source Field. Each of those geometries duplicate a given set of cosmologies, and each represents a set of harmonies that are matched with the same tune as each planet, moon, or our sun it's representing. This can be proven mathematically by comparing the measurements of Teotihuacan with "A Little Book of Coincidence", by John Martineau, and Kepler's nesting function of the planets.

In the same manner that Tesla saw his devices in their complete form, I saw all of this as a whole, complete, in a spatial flash of insight within my mind's eye. Suddenly, I knew what it all meant in a singular instant. It wasn't just an image that I connected with; it was as if all of the meaning, data, and even the emotions surrounding it were downloaded to my intellect instantaneously. My first reaction was to just to laugh aloud at the collective irony of what so many cultures on so many continents sought after. But then, I followed my own advice, made a mad dash for pen and paper, and began writing and drawing like a man possessed with the winning lotto numbers. It was a Vast moment of insight, and it took me months to actually get it written, as I knew it at that instant. I had taken the journey, I had learned the discipline, and after a season of refinement, the gift of greater enlightenment was bestowed upon me in the twinkling of an eye. Like a child who's caught the spark of a firefly out of the darkness of the night, I'm eager to show others the fascinating illumination of what I've found. Moreover, we have only skimmed the surface, there's so much more to come!)

(We're not looking for a machine with physical moving parts, driven by some form of combustion, which takes us to some distant and magical land. We're not looking for a machine that will allow us to do something we're not capable of. We're looking for a machine with energetically driven parts, which harnesses the natural constants of our realm, and amplifies our natural abilities with a mechanical advantage, so we can reach the altitude of our full potential. We're looking for the application of a moral code melded with the leverage of that technology, which is One with The Middle Way of The Path. The Quest of Truth is not as much about uncovering The Art of Alchemy that turns lead into gold. It's more about turning The Child of Lead into The Child of Gold. That is, The Child of Darkness into The Children of The Light, by amplifying the three aspects of our emergent expression. In this Quest lies a different reality in this realm. In The Chamber of Initiation lies the attainment of The Quest of Truth.

Come, this is The Way of The Path...)

The Quest of Freedom

Dam Tech

(Sailors the world over have spent countless man hours mastering the most optimal means of harnessing wind by damming it with sails. The Romans did the same with aqueducts, taking the mastery of such damming technology to a new level of comprehension, and social benefit. The same goes for the Montgolfier' Brothers, they understood that one gas was lighter than another, so they put a dam between them, called it a "hot air balloon", and got the labor of lift. Down to damming livestock with fences, and gardens with chemical barriers, mankind has been using the same dam technology for a very long time.

There's no difference between these examples, and what we're doing with electrons today, other than changing the thing we're damming. The flow of electrons through a computer can be analogized as a kind of aqueduct through which the flow of electrons are governed. The damming system is the equivalent to the "opened" or "closed" pivot of an aqueduct's doors, where the ones and zeros determine the "on" or "off" switch's of the computer system. The internet is the interlocking aqueducts that turn computer "City States" into one giant Roman Empire of interlinked ever-flowing technology, which waters the gardens of our minds at will.

Today, technology is thought of as the control and guidance of potential, so as to harness specific kinds of labor from that potential. This kind of thinking insinuates a direct desire to gain a mechanical advantage, which either produces more output than that which was put into its construction, or attains a value, ability, or skill that we cannot otherwise attain without it. However, technology should also be thought of as the ability to manipulate the operation of fundamental constants, The Code of The Program of The Architect, rather than just harnessing potential from those constants. While this might look like the ability to turn gravity on and off in a given location, to turn inertia on or off, or turn lead into gold, it might just as well look like manipulating The Code of The Program of The Architect.

Watching UFO's dart through the skies with the speed and agility that knows nothing of acceleration, inertia, or expulsion for propulsion tells us that, whoever they are, they already comprehend these ideas to a certain degree of mastery. It tells us the origin of their technology is in the transformation, manipulation, and ethically linked use of fundamental constants. It tells us the origin of their technology was conceptualized from the amplified function of their intellect, their "Nikola Tesla". In the same manner that we couldn't hope to survive the nuclear technology of the modern age without also advancing our ethics to match the potentiality of modern technology, so too these beings have attained a kind of Golden Age by advancing their ethics to match the potential of their technology.

If we dwell too much on the methods of past technology, we may rob ourselves of the present opportunity for something new. If we forget past technology, we may rob ourselves of bringing something forward to meld with our present or future technology. The seeds of our future technology are nurtured by the roots of our past discoveries, the ethical and technological growth in our present, and the opportunities of our amplified intellects of tomorrow.)

Time Patterns

(Remembering that neither the question nor the answers are more important than the journey of discovery, which lies between the two, Dr. Steven Hawking invites us to go on a Quest of Discovery when he posed the question, "If there are time travelers, then where are they?" This question is possessed of a summation of our past postulations of time travel, rather than The Space Distortion Time Viscosity Theory, also known as The Construct Theory, which is garnered from more recent revelations. If getting in a machine that shoots out time tachyon particles to impregnate the time {nesting wave + nesting levity} flow with levity or gravity, which accelerates or reverses the flow of time, were the way to time travel, then Dr. Hawking's question would be as good as the question of the grandfather paradox. However, if The Space Distortion Time Viscosity Theory were a more accurate manner of reasoning about time and time travel, then the answer to Dr. Hawking's question would be to look in the mirror. In the same manner that we're all living on a planet that distorts space, so too we're all caught up in the nature and behavior of time. Whether or not we're aware of it, we're all moving forward and backward, laterally and longitudinally in a distorted portion of space, and changing flow of time--- all the space-time$_{1\ 2}$. In the same manner that the land beneath our feet is constantly moving; distorting space as that land moves into a new location of space, without us being consciously aware of it, so too time is constantly shifting speed, direction, and coherence without so much as a hint that its happening.)

(By conventional wisdom, when chemicals are mixed they're supposed to have an even bell curve of change. The change grows at a given rate, curves in a steady path, and just as evenly declines. No matter the skew of the bell curve, consistency in action and reaction are supposed to be the same for an identical experiment. After all, this is the entire basis of scientific principal. Proofs are supposed to be "provable" in the discipline of science, because scientists claim the Euclidean Notion of translating experiments through the axis mundi of mathematical consistency.

However, this doesn't always happen. Sometimes the changes are erratic and unpredictable. When this happens, mainstream science tosses out the data, calling the tossing out of questionable data "Renormalization". Basically put, they're labeling the experiment as a failure, because the outcome didn't fit the standardized model, conventional wisdom, or their "rational thinking". After all, wouldn't it be quite insane to say that a chemical reaction of baking soda and vinegar happened differently, because while you were mixing them the distortion of space and viscosity° of time shuffled back and forth, because an uneven time wave$_{12}$ and or space distortion$_{12}$ raced through our solar system, and thereby caused a flux in the chemical reaction?

As it turns out, adding in the variables of time viscosity° (N) and space elasticity (M) to Galileo's "Distance Rate Time" equation is The Clarity of Insanity™. By 1985, Russian Physicist Professor Simon Shnoll discovered that all biological, chemical, and radioactive reactions look identical, but only if they're executed and graphed out during the same time. Dr. Shnoll ran experiments of the same type thousands of kilometers apart, and he found the erratic patterns looked as identical and unique as that of a fingerprint--- Once again, only if they were run at the same time (N).

What would happen if our big blue marble in the turbulent oceans of time$_1$ if it should suddenly move into a location where there was a time wave, a time wake, or a time eddy? In the same manner that a ship is moved by the energy in a wave in the ocean, and not by the mass that initiated the wave, our time wouldn't be affected by the mass of that which caused the wake, but by the energy of the time wave or time exchange within the wave itself. This time wave passes through the condition of our time wave, which then effects "the expression and operation of that which is within it".

Think about water splashing against water, it's not the water itself that's moving or discombobulating the opposing water. Without impregnated energy, water just sits there, and its condition is subject to the nature of its nested environment. It's the exchange of energy, stored within one wave, which discombobulates the other energy stored within the opposing wave. ---And we see the water moving. If two waves of time collided, the viscosity or coherence of time would be affecting the coherence or viscosity of time in something else, just like water.

When earth hits one of these time disturbances, we experience a time fluctuation. Experiments experience a variance in function, and electronics experience problems, because the electrons that control them behave differently when their nested environment behaves differently--- just like water. Remember, our technology is based on producing, damming, and then controlling the flow of electrons. When time viscosity patterns increase in density, because of a change in the time flow patterns, a huge amount of electrons get thrust through the flow of our "aqueduct copper tubes". The "aquatic flow" (f) of electricity overloads our damming system, the gates of our circuits get fried, and our computers stop functioning.

We're quickly finding out that those dams, which direct our electrons, only work "under a given condition" of space distortion or time viscosity. Now that we know that changes in our fundamental constants can radically change without us being consciously aware of it, we need to learn how to build computers that can withstand variances to two standard deviations of our norm, or two standard deviations of any norm where our technology might travel. While this might look like multiple circuit breakers in key points, it might also look like rough and tumble computers that can take a licking and keep on ticking. Either way, it means coming up with the math to build them with, and that's exactly what we're about to do.)

Time Waves

(Where there's more mass and greater density, there's more quantum resistance. In this state, there's more {(quantum collapse) = (K) = (quantum expression)}, which causes less coherence in the flow of time, and increased distortions in the fabric of space. This is like saying The Architect (K) is at, or moving toward, the top of its expression {(If 55), (then 89)} » {(If 89), (then 144)}.

Where there's less mass and less density, there's less of a quantum or galactic resistance. In this state, there's less of a {(quantum collapse) or (quantum expression)}. There's less of an expression of The Field, so there's more coherence in the flow of time, and less distortion in the fabric of space. This is like saying The Architect is at, or is moving toward, the bottom of its expression {(If 3), (then 5)} » {(If 2), (then 3)} » {(If 1), (then 2)} » {(If 1), (then 1)}. These changing conditions of time can be labeled "Time Viscosity Variances". Wherein, time is measured by its changing condition in terms of its degrees of viscosity, with respect to its relationship with the condition of the two-way door of dominion of the collapse uncollapse function of The Fabric of The Construct.

Like observing changes in a river, which alters the velocity in the flow of the river's water, we're asking ourselves two fundamental questions about the "water", as opposed to the "land", which might change its behavior. Is time in an agitated, heated, incoherent, collapsed, expressed, and thus in a viscous state of being?" Or, is time in a calm, coherent "not as expressed", "not as viscous", "not as sticky", and thus in an inviscid state of being?"

In the same manner that the lack of heat causes a zero "type" temperature, where fewer molecules are "agitated" into a condition we call "heat", so too fluid in an inviscid state is zero viscosity, the absence of collapse, or no Field Expression (Page, 211, The Veil that divides all realms is composed of "passive" or "inactive" energy of The Architect while it's not "constructing"). In the same manner that all things behave differently due to the degree and direction of expression of The Architect, so too all manner of things behave differently in degrees of viscosity, including the fluidity of time.

$$(\text{Incoherence}° = \text{Viscosity}°)$$
$$(\text{Coherence}° = \text{Inviscid}°)$$

The Hemisphere Effect

The Northern Hemisphere
{Coherence > Incoherence}
{Inviscid > Viscosity}

The Southern Hemisphere
{Coherence < Incoherence}
{Inviscid < Viscosity}

In $Realm_1$, as the mass of an object increases it attracts adjacent objects at a greater rate of speed, due to its distortion of the curious emptiness of the fabric of space. As the mass and density increases at a greater rate of speed, time becomes more agitated, and slows down within that area of influence--- thereby, causing the object to take more time to collect mass. Since space can be seen as the inactive fabric of galactic (Y) or quantum (X) potential, which collapses its elasticity into degrees of nested expression, the degree of collapse of

The Field becomes a growing inverse function to time. Time can also be seen as inversely tugging back on the galactic or quantum collapse of the fabric of space, in the same manner that the collapse of space is an agitator to the function of time. The more The Program of The Architect nests into an expression of » waves or » particles, the greater the inverse function. Such that, time becomes increasingly inverse to space, while in the same instance space becomes increasingly inverse to time. It is in this manner, mathematically speaking, that time or space can be equally divided against one another, allowing the "Flip Function". Since The Program of The Architect is determined by The Force of The Architect, which governs the exponential curve of The Fibonacci Spiral, the mathematical expression of the inverse function can be expressed as follows.

$$\text{(Realm}_x\text{)} \qquad \text{(Realm}_y\text{)}$$

$$\frac{\{(\text{Space})\,(\text{K})\}}{\{(\text{Time})\,(\text{K})\}} \qquad \frac{\{(\text{Time})\,(\text{K})\}}{\{(\text{Space})\,(\text{K})\}}$$

Where the value of (K) equals the "progressing" value of The Program of The Architect in a given condition, or a given realm$_x$. Therefore, (K) can equal the one to one ratio at the beginning of The Program of The Architect. (K) Can equal the energetic change as expressed by The Mandelbrot Equation. (K) Can also represent any progressing number pattern in the pattern of The Program. Moreover, the changing patterns in the value of a (K), within the formula; represent the disequilibrium between realms in the state of expression of a given location between two equal and opposite realms.

$(K) = \{(\text{If } A), (\text{then } B)\}$

$(K) = \{(\text{If } 1), (\text{then } 1)\}$

$(K) = \{(\text{If } (F\,(Z) = 1^2 \times C)), (\text{then } (F\,(Z) = 1^2 \times C))\}$

$(K) = \{(\text{If } 5), (\text{then } 8)\}$ »

(Realm_x) (Realm_y)

$$\frac{(\text{Space})\,\{(\text{If } A), (\text{then } B)\}\}}{(\text{Time})\,\{(\text{If } A), (\text{then } B)\}\}} \qquad \frac{(\text{Time})\,\{(\text{If } A), (\text{then } B)\}\}}{(\text{Space})\,\{(\text{If } A), (\text{then } B)\}\}}$$

(Realm_x) (Realm_y)

$$\frac{(\text{Space})\{(\text{If}(F(Z) = 1^2xC)), (\text{then } (F(Z)=1^2xC))\}\}}{(\text{Time})\{(\text{If}(F(Z) = 1^2xC)), (\text{then } (F(Z)=1^2xC))\}\}} \quad \frac{(\text{Time})\{(\text{If}(F(Z)=1^2xC)), (\text{then}(F(Z)=1^2xC))\}\}}{(\text{Space})\{(\text{If}(F(Z)=1^2xC)), (\text{then}(F(Z)=1^2xC))\}\}}$$

)(

$$(F\,(Z) = z^2 \times C)$$

$$(F\,(.618) = z^2 \times C) < (F\,(1.618) = z^2 \times C) < (F\,(2.168) = z^2 \times C)$$

)

(If there's disequilibrium of the value and function of (K) on either side of the expression of a realm, or between the values of time and space, there will be a distortion in the veil between realms similar to Quantum Pinching. However, rather than using extreme temperature variances to cause the distortion, it will be governed by the nature and expression of the variances in the collapse or expression of The Architect.)

(In a movement from waves toward nesting Platonic Solids, the function of the Fibonacci Code can be expressed as sequences of nesting Platonic Shapes where "A" represents one shape, and "B" represents another Platonic Shape, which is nested inside the first. While this can be expressed in a singular "initiate" geometry, the equation of (If this shape), (then this shape) ;after the manner of The Program of The Architect, can also be expressed in a permutation of layered Platonic Shapes, and inserted into the above equations. This will move us from a wave function to a particle function in terms of density, and a movement toward a singularity of a collapsed expression.

The nesting function of particles changes the frequency in the fluidity of time, in the same manner that layered densities in the ocean changes the frequency in the fluidity of water at a new layer of depth. The accretion of mass; now redefined as the expression or collapse of The Field into nesting waves and then nesting particles, alters The Time Flow Signature of a given object, as well as the Fabric and Function of Space in the same area of The Construct. This is dependent on the quantity and geometric sequence of the nested particles. This sequence of density can be modified, to attain a new value of density, and thus function, by modifying either the quantity of nests, or the ordered geometric nesting sequence. The operation of this density changes time's frequency, and thus changes the quantum agitation of the fluidity of time. This function is also modified by the variable differences in the value of (K).)

(A star's mass is far denser at its center than at its surface. In $realm_1$, $space_1$ is being pinched toward a central location, where $realm_2$ is being stretched; provided there isn't an equal star at that space-time location. This ever increasing density creates ever increasing distortions in the fabric of {(Space) (K)}, as well as an ever growing agitation in the coherence of {(Time) (K)} in realm$_1$. This is not only because of the increased density of space at a given location, but also because of the increased heat (agitation) that multiplies incoherence in both space and time. In this table, "n" equals exponentially increasing (temperatures = agitation).

(Realm$_x$)	(Realm$_y$)
{(Space) (K)^n}	{(Time) (K)^n}
{(Time) (K)^n}	{(Space) (K)^n}

As a star moves through space its variable impression on the fabric of the space-time continuum$_{1,2}$ creates a time wave, a time wake, and or time eddies. In realm$_1$ time is seen to slow, becoming increasingly incoherent, viscous, or sticky. Much like the two-way door of dominion, this has many effects on the fluidity, density, and coherence of the fabric of space-time$_1$ and time-space$_2$ that reflect what we see in oceanic behavior.

In the same manner that the wake of an ocean wave will cross entire bodies of water if left undisturbed, so too do the wakes of time, caused by stars and galaxies, reverberate across the universe. Just like in the ocean, when two opposing waves collide, there will be turbulence of time in the form of smaller eddies that spin in relationship with one another, until they neutralize one another's energies, or get caught up in another time wave. This includes time waves of different magnitudes and viscosities that may be conceptualized to ram into one another.

In the same manner that ocean waves refract, deflect, or even discombobulate their energies into Fractal offshoots, so too will time waves refract, deflect, or even discombobulate their energies into Fractal offshoots--- Not so much "as the energy of their wave collapses or is neutralized", but more "as their expression uncollapses toward Field Potential". Like a wave in the ocean, time waves effect where they're located, where they've been, and wherever they might echo.

In the same manner that ocean waves, which move at slightly different speeds, will catch up with the wave in front of them to create ever-larger waves (f+f), there are time waves moving through the universe in the same direction that catch up and join with other time waves to create time waves of increasing magnitude. These galactic time waves have a dramatic effect on the direction of time, as well as the cohesion, and local density in the fabric of space$_1$. These tsunami time waves could theoretically become large enough to tear at the very fabric of the space-time continuum$_{1\,2}$, in the same manner that the wave energy impregnated within a powerful tsunami tears the water from the ocean and rushes it onto land.

Before the doom-n-gloom gang joins up with the "psi-phi" squad to make the next "End of the world" movie, where an outer space tsunami tidal wave of time threatens all mankind, and Bruce Willis is sent up with his rag tag motley crew of social misfits to metaphorically dig our way out of trouble--- we must remember that this behavior of time is eternally common. Time wave anomalies are a kind of balancing act between "that which is coherent and that which is incoherent", and "that which is being expressed and that which is being unexpressed". Time Viscosity° is a balancing act between space-time$_1$ and time-space$_2$ that gives a push or pull on the dividing Fabric, which seeks to create equilibrium between realms. In the same manner that water waves ripple across an ocean to cancel one another out, so too time waves are constantly unbalancing and rebalancing the Fabric of the space-time and time-space continuums. The ubiquitous two-way door of dominion.)

(In the last few paragraphs, we've been gaining perspective by comparing the fluidity of water with the fluidity of time, as both relate to the two dimensional patterns of the surface of water. However, in the same manner that geometry isn't a one-dimensional venture, so too water and time behave in three-dimensional patterns within both realms of the space-time$_1$ and time-space$_2$ continuums. Thus, to comprehend the bigger picture, and take one more bold step into vastness, we'll jump to a three dimensional perspective of water and time.

Like the layering of an onion, or greater densities at greater depths in the ocean, our galaxy is layered, and becomes denser as one gets closer to the center. Like the sphere of a star, this creates layers of alteration in time frequency, time density, and time viscosity° within each given layer. In the same manner that the layers of density in an ocean create their own environment, by causing a definitive deviation where water of a different density cannot flow, so too densities of time within the nested layers of galaxies, cause barriers in the function and flow of time within its given layer. Moreover, let us not forget, like any star, these galaxies are in motion, so while the movement of a star might create its own time wave, that time wave is nested within the larger sphere of a galactic time wave. A galaxy's time wave looks more like a forty-foot tidal wave on the North Shore of Hawaii, that makes our sun's time wave seem like a ripple in a pond. In the same manner that torus fields behave in a nested fashion, so too time waves that are nested within larger time waves, obey the nested dominion of the exterior time wave. The two-way door of nested dominion is a universal function of Field Physics™.

Galactic Rivers of Time could be expressed as more coherent flows of time that would be compelled to go around these increasingly dense areas, in the same manner that water is compelled to separate when it's at different depth densities, or when it meets with the increased collapsed densities of land. This could express itself as rivers of galactic time that flow within each layer, circulating around the ring of the nested layer in a never-ending, self-feeding, river ring of time. A river that might be able to be harnessed for traversing time or space.

While the following could be expressed as a density sphere, because we have so many astronomical spheres, and those spheres have so many interrelated spherical torus fields, it could also be expressed as "The Ordered Nesting of Platonic Solids". The ordered nesting sequence, as it relates to the proton construction of the periodic table of elements, and how those elements function within a nested environment, creates a different value of density, because the sequence of nesting geometry creates different particles of matter, and therefore causes a different function in time viscosity° at each density layer of a spherical object.

In the same manner that we find specific weather patterns of ocean behavior near the equator, near straights that are between large landmasses, or at the poles, there are time locations that constantly experience common weather patterns of time, because of the intrinsic nature of that particular location, and its surrounding galactic environment. This might take the form of clusters of galaxies where millions of galaxies form such a dense region that the region itself experiences a dramatic decrease in the flow of time. From our point of view, Time would appear to stand still, yet it would move with a "normal" flow from the perspective of those within the given region; regions such as The Great Attractor. Time lakes, rivers, and other "in land" time seas would have little to no effect in these areas, other than perhaps a resonance, pulsating, or "leaking" effect that might be seen to reverberate into their realm as time quakes or time creeks.

In addition, just like rivers and lakes on land. There will be creeks of time that flow between star clusters, rivers of time that flow in patterns through mountain ranges of galaxies, and galactic Niles and networks of Amazonian Time Rivers that run across entire continents of the universe. There will be great lakes of time, such as are thought of in internal seas on continents. They will be of variable sizes, densities, and possess and cause their own local time weather patterns.)

(Now that we're reasoning along the lines of being caught up in an ocean of time with its many energetic behaviors, this information doesn't sound so "unconventional" after all, but very rational, readily explainable, and thoroughly thought out. Like Russian Physicist Professor Dr. Simon Shnoll, we can define each unique fingerprint "in the expression of time" within each experiment, and look for repeating patterns based on our local time weather patterns or time weather seasons. Including local imbalances that form patterns in the chaos of the uniqueness of those fingerprints.

For instance, our planets all make local weather pattern time waves around earth, and we all know that the closer a water wave is to another water wave the greater effect it will have on the opposing wave of water. Therefore, these repeating patterns within the fingerprints are the first thing we should be looking for. Every pair of planets creates a singular dance in relationship to one another. Earth and Mercury kiss/cross/retrograde 22 times in 7 years (2,510 earth days), while Venus kisses Earth every 584 earth days. So every time an experiment is run, a subtle fingerprint "line" in the "unique" and proverbial fingerprint of each experiment will be seen either to reveal itself during a retrograde/kiss, or be properly absent outside of the window of their time wave kiss.

Perhaps, this will be while that planet is on the opposite side of the sun, and its wake cannot directly get to us. This will show up as repeatable variables within dual simultaneous experiments, where one line on the fingerprint caused by Venus will show up in direct relationship to the one caused by Mercury--- or in direct relationship to their absence. Thus, we can begin to map out the fingerprints of our local time weather patterns to determine what constitutes general verses extreme time viscosity deviations.)

Flexible DiRT

One small step for a man
One giant leap for mankind

(It's a foregone conclusion by those well acquainted with the Cayce Library that both Nikola Tesla and Albert Einstein received psychic readings from Edgar Cayce, after which both men made huge strides of advancement in their work. How could our teachers fail to mention that the two foremost scientists of our era visited with The Sleeping Prophet? Moreover, how dare they leave out the fact, that afterwards they adopted meditations designed to spark genius in their intellect, or the even more significant fact, that both their models functioned off the common model of the torus field?

The fact that Einstein's space-time models and Tesla's coil models reflect the overall model of the torus field, are not mere coincidences. Multiply the scientific models of torus fields by the millennia old theological model of The Dorje and The Thunderbolt of Enlightenment. Raise this variable to the "N^{th}" degree by the pyramid tech found all over the globe in every culture, which are also based on the manipulation of torsion fields, and we quickly realize there's a universal model we're dealing with. A model that's been around for time and all eternity, a model that other "more conditioned" cultures have a degree of mastery over. A model that becomes visible, if we will but step into the realm of infinitesimal vastness and eternal smallness. Learn to see that which cannot be seen, to touch that which cannot be touched, use that which cannot be used, and find value for that which is so obviously useless.)

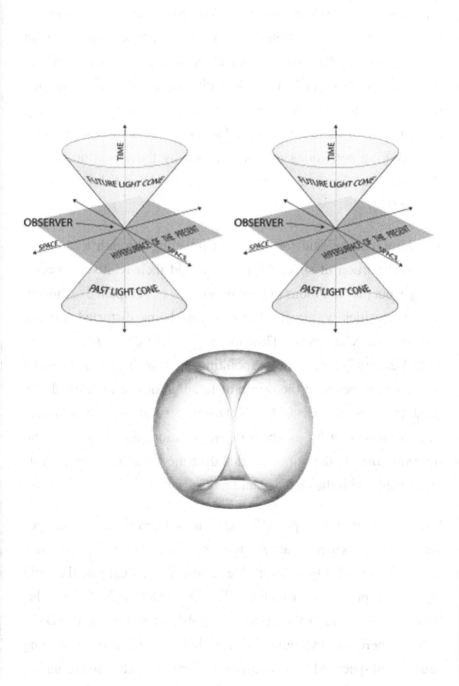

("Relative Time Velocity Dilation"; *where time moves at different speeds for two objects in relative uniform motion to one another---* is not so much due to the velocity (R) of their relative movement, as much as it's due to the "condition" of space or time through which they're traveling. For instance, one object could be moving faster in time than another, yet if that object hit a time wave that happened to be moving in a reverse direction, the uniform motion relationship immediately breaks down. The relationship breaks down, because the changing conditions of time, caused by the condition of The Construct, not because of the two object's related velocity (R) @ {(E) or (F)}.

The same can be said for an object traveling through a radically distorted portion of space. Not only would their relative direction change, but the conditions of time would also be compelled to modify their viscosities within the layer or area being distorted, further severing the relationship. This not only breaks down The Relative Time Velocity Dilation Theory, pointing out its main flaw of focusing on a solid, rather than the origin of function of energy around that solid, but it also distorts Galileo's (Distance = Rate • Time) equation. The distance variable is changing its relationship to the rate and time variables, in the same way that the time variable is changing its relationship with the distance and rate variables.

Like a mangled coin, space$_1$ (D) is distorted and time$_1$ (T) changes viscosities, so as to separate any mathematical relationship they once had with the velocity (R) variable. Thus, rather than just the rigid equation as presented by Galileo (Thoth); R=D/T or D=R•T, we also have the "Flexible-DiRT" Equation (DM)=(R)•(TN) or R=(DM)/(TN). Where the (M) and (N) variables represent the changing elasticity of space (M) that modifies the distance factor, and changing

264

degrees in the viscosity of time (N) that modifies the time factor, so as to add a variable that can reacquaint their relationship to the velocity (R) variable.

$$R = \frac{DM}{TN}$$

"Relative Time Velocity Dilation"; from the perspective of time waves and space distortions, can be seen as "relative speed" (R) @ {(E) or (F)}, across "relative space$_1$" (D), or through "relative time$_1$" (T), expressed as the "condition" of "relative location" or "condition" of relative time viscosity along both object's given trajectories. Said differently, as the association between "the condition of a given location" with "the condition of time" in that location, and their relationship to two different speeds (E, F) for two separate objects (A, B) in relative uniform motion to one another, are relative to the conditions of all three variables of distance, rate, and time for both objects--- all three conditions modify all three variables for the two relative objects in motion. However, in this first example, "relativity" primarily relates to the (M) and (N) variables, since the (R) variable; expressed as two objects within a given, but separate condition of velocity, are compelled to "react" (E, F) to the conditions in which they reside, travel through, or are otherwise effected by, in order to maintain an associated velocity with one another. This is only because space and time will not react of their own accord to a traveling vessel. Thus, the vessel's velocities must first be reactive (E, F) to the relative conditions in which they find themselves.

"Relative Space Distortion Time Viscosity Theory" requires a three dimensional location to initiate the {F (R) = Rate function} for two relative objects. Object one $\{A@X = (DM)/(TN)\}$ --- this is the formula for an object (A) traveling at a given rate (X) through space and time distortions. Object two (B) $\{B@Y = (DM)/(TN)\}$ --- this is the formula for another object (B) traveling at a given rate (Y) through space and time distortions. By inserting the (E) and (F) variables with the separate (A, B) rate velocities, (E, F) become compensatory $^+$acceleration or $^-$deceleration variables for both objects, so as to balance the changing (M, N) variables along two separate, but given trajectories. This can attain the original $R@(X)$ & $R@(Y)$ velocity values, so as to reacquire and maintain cohesive relationships with all variables.

$$\text{Object one } \{(A@X)E = (DM)/(TN)\}$$
$$\text{Object two } \{(B@Y)F = (DM)/(TN)\}$$

Galileo's DiRT equation

$$R = \frac{D}{T}$$

The "Flexible-DiRT" equation

$$R = \frac{DM}{TN}$$

With The Relative Space Distortion Time Viscosity consideration
The "Flexible-DiRT" equation expands
Object One {(A@X)E=(DM)/(TN)}
Object Two {(B@Y)F=(DM)/(TN)}

The variables of space distortion (M) and time viscosity (N) represent an ever-changing condition of the space-time$_{12}$ continuum over the path of a given trajectory. This trajectory can be mapped out on a three dimensional space-time cubical grid with the coordinates of (X, Y, Z) representing a single point along the three dimensional trajectory, which gives the conditions of space, time, or compensatory rate alterations at each point of space or time modification along the trajectory. In the same manner that a car must compensate fuel expenditure to maintain relative velocity while driving around hills or mountains, because of "distortion in terrain considerations", so too this equation will find certain space-time$_{12}$ conditions which can be avoided or harnessed, to make a trip through the universe a more "viable" venture.)

(The equation: F (N) (D=(R (TN))) can be used in a location where time viscosity has changed, but space distortion is identical to a given location of space that a given object has traveled through. The equation F (M) DM=RT or R={DM/T} can be used in a location where the elasticity of space has changed, but the degree of time viscosity is identical to a given time that a given object has traversed. The Equation {R= (DM)/(TN)} can be used when both a distortion in space and viscosity in time have changed in relationship to a previous location that a given object has traversed. All of these can be used interchangeably as dots along the trajectory of a given object as it traverses through the changes, or lack of particular changes, to attain a better understanding of the real (R) variable. By default, these variables can be used interchangeably when calculating two related objects in motion as well. These equations will give us the changing (R) or F (R) for (A, B) for intergalactic travel as all variables change over a given journey for a given object or set of objects.)

(Solving for the variables of (M, N)--- First, what are the variables in the space distortion function (M)? (K), or the differences between {(K) + (K)} or {(K) - (K)}. Nesting of torus fields represented as (Q), must come first. Torus fields (Q) have an untouchable dominion over the function of everything within their field. While they're partial determiners of the operation of fundamental constants of a collapsing Field through its two-way door of expression, the greatest consideration in this equation of a given expression of The Field is density, which is determined by The Quantity of Nesting Torus Fields in which it's expressed.

Torus Fields behave like a shield that allows some things to pass through while disallowing other things. These barriers increase as the field becomes larger, or the nesting effect becomes more numerous, such as the onion layered nested fields within a galaxy. Also, The Hemisphere Effect is determined by a given nesting quantity and given location on, in, or around a given Torus Field. Thus, the function of a bend in space would be directly related to a given number of layers within a nested torus field, which our space distortion--- as a movement toward the collapse of a quantum or galactic field toward a singularity (K)--- was found in. As well as the location within The Hemisphere Effect in which its found.

Q = (Quantity of nested torus fields) • (torus field's magnitude)

The question we're asking ourselves is this--- "Is space (D) distorted (M) {(K) + (K)} or {(K) - (K)} differently within the central nest of the galaxy where the density factor of space is radically increased due to the number and order of magnitude of nested torus fields? Verses, "Is space (D) being distorted (M) in a region of space that has fewer nested layers, and thus less general density of space (D) to be distorted (M) or collapsed into an expression? When we look at increasing density of space within these onion layers, we see that as we go closer to the center of the galaxy, traveling through space will be like going through ever-denser layers of water in the oceans. This insinuates different quantities of space are distorted around a given celestial body based on its nested-location. Thus, the quantity of nested torus fields (Q) determines the elasticity (ex) of space (D) while (K) can be represented by a local distortion of a given amount of space by the function of the field.

Expanded M
M= (Q((ex)(K)))

(Q) = Quantity of nested torus fields

(ex) = the elasticity, or degree of density of a given location in space.

(K) = function of the field.

((K) = function of The Field can be expanded in the same manner as the (M) variable can be expanded. The local elasticity of space is additionally governed by condition of the expression of The Collapse of The Field, as expressed within a given condition of The Field, in a movement toward a condition, or as an expressed Field in a movement away from a given condition, as it relates to The Two-Way Door of The Program of The Architect.

$$(\text{Realm}_x) \qquad (\text{Realm}_y)$$

$$\frac{\{(\text{Space})\ (K)\}}{\{(\text{Time})\ (K)\}} \qquad \frac{\{(\text{Time})\ (K)\}}{\{(\text{Space})\ (K)\}}$$

$$\frac{(\text{Space})\{(\text{If A}),\ (\text{then B})\}\})}{(\text{Time})\{(\text{If A}),\ (\text{then B})\}\})} \qquad \frac{(\text{Time})\{(\text{If A}),\ (\text{then B})\}\})}{(\text{Space})\{(\text{If A}),\ (\text{then B})\}\})}$$

$$\frac{(\text{Space})\{(\text{If}(F(Z) = 1^2 x C)),\ (\text{then } (F(Z)=1^2 x C))\}\})}{(\text{Time})\{(\text{If}(F(Z) = 1^2 x C)),\ (\text{then } (F(Z)=1^2 x C))\}\})} \qquad \frac{(\text{Time})\{(\text{If}(F(Z)=1^2 x C)),\ (\text{then}(F(Z)=1^2 x C))\}\})}{(\text{Space})\{(\text{If}(F(Z)=1^2 x C)),\ (\text{then}(F(Z)=1^2 x C))\}\})}$$

If The Field is in a condition, such that it's functioning in a one to one ratio, the distortions, as represented by the (K) variable, will vary. If The Field is in a condition, such that it's functioning Fractally, the distortions, as represented by the (K) variable, will vary. If The Field is in a condition, such that it's functioning in an increasing collapsing manner, the distortions of the (K) variable will vary. If The Field is in a condition, such that it's functioning in a decreasing uncollapsing manner, the distortions of the (K) variable will vary.

If there's disequilibrium of the value and function of (K) on either side of the expression of a realm$_{x\,y}$ there will be a distortion in the fabric between realms. The function of The Field is not only expressed as what is happening in one realm$_x$, but what also might be happening on the other side of a given realm in realm$_Y$, which might cause a disequilibrium between realms. As we delve deeper into the function of our realm, we will see how these things not only affect one another, but how they can come to not affect one another as well (f^n +- f^n).)

(What are the variables in the time viscosity function (N)? Once again, while the condition of the collapse of The Field is a primary consideration in the expression of the products of The Field (K); "something that our 'DiRT' equation is nested within", when it comes to the viscosity of time, within a given expression of The Field, the condition of the nesting function is paramount. Thus, the function of time is first manipulated by the nesting of a torus field (Q), then comes its degree of viscosity (V). Viscosity can be expressed as (V) for a given value of viscosity. However, (V) can also be replaced by (K), because the condition of The Architect can affect the function of viscosity. Depending on how the equation is used, trading (V) for (K) might come in handy when trying to mathematically solve or cancel out values.

$$\text{Time (N)} = (Q)(\text{viscosity}°)$$

$$N = (Q(v))$$

Galileo's Equation

$$R = \frac{D}{T}$$

The "Flexible-DiRT" Equation

$$R = \frac{DM}{TN}$$

The Relative Space Distortion Time Viscosity Theory
The Expanded Equation

$$R = \frac{(D)\left(Q\left((ex)K\right)\right)}{T\left(Q(v)\right)}$$

)

Just for Fun:

(Remembering that the equation F (N) {(D=(R(TN))} can be used in a location where time viscosity has changed, but space distortion remains identical to a given location of space that a given object has traveled through.

Remembering that the equation F (M) DM=RT or R={DM/T} can be used in a location where the elasticity of space has changed, but time viscosity remains identical to a given time that a given object has traveled through.

Question 1)

Rob is on the Sun traveling at 10 miles per hour over a distance of 100 miles.

Jim is on the star Cirrus traveling at 10 miles per hour over a distance of 100 miles.

```
                    (D=(R(TN)))
Rob is on the sun  (100=(10(TN))
Jim is on Cirrus   (100=(10(TN))
```

If the time viscosity variable (N) on the sun is twice as coherent as that of Cirrus, how much faster will Jim incinerate than Rob?

```
                    (D=(R(TN)))
Rob is on the sun  (200=(10(10(2))))
Jim is on Cirrus   (100=(10(10(1))))
```

Question 2)

$$R = \frac{DM}{TN}$$

With the same criteria as before, what if the space distortion variable is 1,000 times denser on Cirrus, and the sun's space distortion variable is 100 times more dense than a given value of zero, which could be expressed as Absolute Field "Position" where space is not distorted at all?

$$(DM=((R)(TN)))$$
Rob is on the sun $(100 \bullet 100=(10(2))$
Jim is on Cirrus $(100 \bullet 1,000=(10(1))$

$$(DM=((R)(TN)))$$
Rob is on the sun $(10,000=(20))$
Jim is on Cirrus $(100,000=(10)$

This fun with math brings up a few interesting questions---

What if Jim's star hit a time wave that created a variable of incoherence, which slowed time by 100% for the duration of 10 minutes until the wave passed? What if Rob's star hit a time wave that reversed its time flow by 10 minutes? What does our equation look like then?

The Question we're driving at is, would the equation modify to-- (D•R•T•N)) or (D•R•T•-N))? Because the reversal of time should directly affect the rate (R) which an event can occur at, the time in which it takes to complete the event, as well as the distance that one could potentially travel within that event. In this scenario, the (-N) variable could affect the time variable (T) as equally as it could affect the rate (R) or distance (D) variables.

What about F (TN) where (N) is expressed as a negative (-N), and (N) is an unknown variable of the (X, Y, Z) location where time is traveling in reverse, but doesn't directly affect the (R) variable, and the (R) variable can be accelerated with an (E or F) velocity value to compensate for the negative time flux. With the correct compensatory velocities, could an object stand still in time, or even continue to move forward in time, so as to get out of the time wave, even though the time flow was moving in reverse? The negative value of (-N) would mathematically effect the entire equation, in such a manner that (D•R•T•-N) or R=(DM/T(-N)) would always possess a negative outcome. We would have to use "Chaos Math", such that we violate the current rules of math, and make up more "flexible constants". These constants would reacquaint math with our reasoning, such that the outcome of a (-N) could be neutralized, or otherwise offset with greater compensatory values.

If Object One (A) was traveling at a velocity value of 500=(X), and Object Two (B) was traveling at a velocity value of 900=(Y), but the negative time wave value (-N) was equal to 1,000. How much velocity would (X, Y) be compelled to compensate by (E,F) so as to negate the (-N)?

Object One {(A@X)=(-N}
Object Two {(B@Y)=(-N)}

The (X) variable would be compelled to accelerate another velocity value of 500 to remain motionless in time, or to negate the negative value of (-N). In this manner the (E) variable multiplies the initial 500 (X) value by 2.

Object One {(A@X)E=(-N}

The (Y) variable would only have to compensate a velocity value of 100 to accomplish the same task (F)=(900•1.111 = 999.999). Both of these equations might be represented as two objects, at different locations, while on the same time wave, where the intensity of the wave varies significantly.

Object Two {(B@Y)F=(-N)}

Like the 999.999, that doesn't actually equate to 1,000, but falls just shy, the (E, F) variables could be used in another manner. In the same manner that a surfer compensates his velocities with angles (D) to burn off, or add a little speed to remain on the wave. So too, the two objects could compensate their variable speed (E, F) to hover on a wave, so as to ride it, or accelerate passed the wave, such that, the (E, F) variables resolve to a value which are greater than (>) the (-N). Thinking back to comparing water waves to time waves, we can now see that our star's movement through space is creating a variable wave impression. If we note our solar system's slant in comparison to the direction of the Sun's trajectory through the Galaxy we see, our planets are riding the wave of space fabric caused by our star.

Object One E>(-N)
Object Two F<(-N)

Object One {(A@X)E>(-N}
Object Two {(B@Y)F<(-N)}

All of these questions are driving at the same observation. Where does the (R) variable separate mathematically, and in real life, from the (D) or (T) variable? Galileo's centuries old, long accepted equation, says that rate can be made independent of time, by placing it on the other side of the equal's sign, and marrying the (D) or (T) variables together. However, we know it takes time to accomplish something at a given rate, so even though they've been mathematically separated, they are still intrinsically related to one another.

Einstein's equations say "space and time"; or (D) and (T), cannot be separated; they are two sides of the same coin. If this were universally true, any numerical value for (D) should be able to be equivalently substituted for any value of (T). However, mathematically speaking, you cannot flip the values of a given divisor, and still come up with an equivalent outcome. In other words, if space (DM) came out as a (5) and time (TN) came out as a (2), then (2) divided by (5) is not the same as (5) divided by (2). The only way that space and time could be numerically flipped, and still arrive at a mathematical constant, is if all values were universally equivalent in the format of a Program (K).

$$(Realm_x) = (Realm_y)$$

$$\frac{\{(Space)\ \{(K) + (K)\}\ or\ \{(K) - (K)\}\}}{\{(Time)\ \{(K) + (K)\}\ or\ \{(K) - (K)\}\}} \quad \frac{\{(Time)\ \{(K) + (K)\}\ or\ \{(K) - (K)\}\}}{\{(Space)\ \{(K) + (K)\}\ or\ \{(K) - (K)\}\}}$$

Yet, we know space and time are malleable by differing constants, so an unequal outcome is inevitable. Yet we know they are inverse to one another in function, and thus we use a mathematical divisor that divides space over time or time over space, and allow the "Chaos Math" "Flip Function".

277

Galileo's equation uses all values as constants. It doesn't add in variables to compensate for a (-N) value, which might affect all other variables, and change its mathematical format. Nor does he account for acceleration or deceleration (E, F) for two objects in uniform motion, so as to retain a relationship with all variables, which could compensate, and overtake a (-N) variable. Like Einstein's "two sides of the same coin" analogy, Galileo's equation says that we can't duplicate the (T), (D), or (R) value, and put it in the same variable in a different location. Nor does he allow for the flip function. Suddenly we find our axis-mundi of math working against us, holding us in a loop of logic that keeps us from moving to a greater understanding, and over a new horizon.

If we use the variables of The Space Distortion Time Viscosity Theory, we'll find Einstein's two sided coin to be like gummy rubber, and we'll find Galileo's inverse observations of (T) and (D) to be more of an observation of their relationship to one another, rather than a mathematical attempt to solve for (R). The two-way door of dominion that flips between realms$_{x\,y}$, says that space and time are inverse to one another. Like Einstein said, they bend and flex, but they also resist one another, as well as flip their function in opposing realms. In any given realm$_x$, they tug at one another in a flexible manner that is based on the variable conditions of both--- in both realms. Thus the "Flexible DiRT" equation must compensate for the variable elasticity's of both, not only in the same realm, but in both realms. Thus, the equation must continue to expand to include both realms, before we can answer where the (R) variable separates from (D) or (T) variables.)

New Variable (+/-L)

$$R = \frac{DM}{TN}$$

$$R = \frac{DM}{(TN)(\pm L)}$$

(I'll never forget my University algebra professor asking me why I was mumbling "Dirt, dirt, dirt" to myself before a big test, nor the look on his face when I told him that I'd made the acronym to remember an equation. He just laughed, but like any good instructor, he just as quickly passed the acronym onto the other students. It was less than a week before someone in the Math Lab was pontificating the easy to recall acronym back to me, not knowing in the least bit from where it originated. With my teacher standing off in the distance smiling at the irony of the replay of events, I just snickered, and allowed the tutor to explain my own acronym to me.

And that's how service to others typically begins. We come up with something to solve our own problems, and if it's of value to others, it becomes the property of humanity as one person after another adopts it in a movement toward The Tipping Points of Adoptive Consciousness. Creating a new equation from Galileo's Distance Rate Time equation by compensating for the changing elasticity's of space, viscosities of time, and two objects in relative uniform motion is just "One small step for a man". So, how do we get to "One Giant Leap for Mankind", where everyone can adopt something that serves all of mankind?)

(How do these equations operate with variable time waves, time nesting, time densities, variable time frequencies, or divergent time flows? How does this relate to molding the natural with the mechanical for a greater synergistic advantage? For example, let's say you're moving near the speed of light in a singular given flow of time that we label (A), but you pass into a variable of time, such as a ring river of time, whose flow we label (B). Will you will accelerate? Not because you're moving faster (R), but because the general flow of time in your new location is moving you along at a faster pace of time, relative to the pace of time you were initially traveling. This can be analogized as the differences between a ship cruising at speed (A) in a lake where the currents move the ship at speed (J) which nominally adds to the cruising speed (A+J). Verses, the ship at speed (A), moving into the flow of a river where the relative speed of the river itself propels the ship faster (B) than it was initially traveling @(A+J) in the lake.

$$(A + J = X)$$
$$(A + B = C)$$

Inserting these new values into our "Flexible DiRT" equation, where the rate one can travel is determined by the variables that effect space and time--- we now add ((TN)+L) where (TN) was the original flow of time (T) under the conditions of a degree of viscosity (N), and (L) is the added variable of accelerated Time within a river of time. Where the flow of time has a new but consistent flow within its given nest. Once again, while the time flow will very likely deviate like a delta into Fractal offshoots, this river will likely flow in a circle around a given nest within a layer of a torus field.)

$$R = \dfrac{DM}{(TN)(\pm L)}$$

$$R = \dfrac{(D)\Big(Q\big((ex)K\big)\Big)}{\Big\{\big[T\big(Q(v)\big)\big](\pm L)\Big\}}$$

(Does this variable of original time speed play into the conditions of a new time flow? Does one's time variance change when one goes into a new time flow? To answer this, think again about the function of water when one wave crashes against another, as opposed to when one wave catches up with a wave in front of it. When waves crash, there's a discombobulating that is "a movement out of" and then "back into" a degree of coherence. However, when waves catch up to one another there's a multiplication of force, energy, and an increase in order. In the discombobulation, the degree of time viscosity will increase, and time will slow down. In the multiplication of force, energy, order, and inviscid conditioning time will increase, and accelerate (R).)

(How about when a surfer catches a wave? Like the (A+J=X) (A+B=C) river question, the ocean may have a negligible current which immediately changes when the surfer moves into "the condition" of a positive flowing wave. But, once there, the time surfer is actually moving faster than the wave is pushing him, at the new speed of (G). The surfer must move forward at the velocity of the wave, which could also be represented by our (+/-L) river flow, a baseline value that is represented as a change in original flow (R@X). Our "surfer" must also move along the lateral angle of the wave that is the wave's hypotenuse $\{C^2\}$. Thus, our "time surfer" covers more distance (DM) and travels even faster in time (TN) than the original equation gives.

This creates a new variable $\{(C^2) = (Hypotenuse)\}$ that effects the time and space equations equally to manipulate the (R) variable.

To find (G), a new location in time$_1$ and space$_1$, we would need to use The Thoth Theorem $(A^2+B^2=C^2)$ that Pythagoras learned while in Egypt. Where (H) is the inception of the new movement, and direction (L) (-L) in the flow of time and space along a given trajectory (C). Where (B) is the height variable of the triangle, whose end point (G) is "when and where" the time wave surfer ended up. Where (C) is the hypotenuse, who's end point arrives at (H), and joins with (B)'s end point, which we label (G), a new location where the time surfer ended up in space$_1$ and time$_1$.

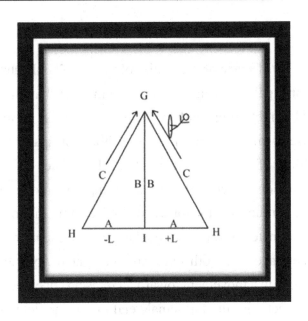

$$R = \left\{ \frac{DM}{TN} \right\} \pm C^2$$

$$R = \left\{ \frac{DM}{TN(\pm L)} \right\} \pm C^2$$

$$R = \left\{ \frac{(D)\Big(Q\big((ex)K\big)\Big)}{\Big\{\big[T\big(Q(v)\big)\big](\pm L)\Big\}} \right\} \pm C^2$$

)

The Field

(The distortion of space or viscosities of time don't only change their condition on a galactic scale. In the same manner that torsion fields cause local conditioning with particles and waves, so too torsion fields cause local conditioning in the fabric of space and in the viscous nature of time. On either side of the $\{(\text{space time}_1) = (\text{time space}_2)\}$ equation, space and time are being conditioned wherever we find the torque of a torsion field. In the same manner that the energy impregnated in water waves changes when spun into an eddy, so too time waves "smooth out", are "elongated", or "lower their frequency" (f); in a movement toward an inviscid coherent condition, when they meet with the top female end of a torus field. The torus field continues to condition time in an accelerating movement toward coherence (Inviscid) as time is drawn toward The Central Ring of Absolute Conditioning. In the same manner that particles and waves get energetically amplified, inviscidly conditioned, and uniformly accelerated through the central ring of a torsion field, so too we can observe space and time move toward coherence, toward Fabric Potentiality, and make "the jump" between realm$_1$ and realm$_2$.)

(Like degrees of time viscosity°, Superposition° comes in degrees of expression. Field Potentiality is an indicator of Absolute Superposition. However, Field Potentiality can also be thought of as the potential of The Field. In this second case, it can be thought of as infinite potential before expression.)

(The Ring of Absolute Conditioning; The Ring of Amplified Energetic, Inviscidly Conditioned, Uniformed Acceleration, is a one-way door. It only operates in a single direction within a given event. Think of the function of a "Dumb Waiter". The door opens on one side, the given "thing" moves into the space, the door is then closed, and the door on the other side can then open. To whit, the "thing" can be moved into a new room. Like the two-way door of dominion, this "flipping door" of the central ring functions in two directions, but only in one direction at a time.)

(The Source Field begins within an ambient, eternally vast, and infinitesimally small Field; this "vastness" and "smallness" can be thought of in terms of "The Galactic Field" or "The Quantum Field". This Field can be labeled or described as "spread out" in a flat two-sided pentagon in a condition of Pure Potential or Absolute Superposition, with no collapse into an emergent expression. As the antennae of our pyramids harness The Source Field at the nodes of its geometry, The Field's potential begins to resonate at these nodal points, and The Quantum or Galactic Field's Source Field Potential begins collapsing into an emergent wave function.

Like a quantum wave function, which collapses into an expression, yet begins as a Field of eternally vast and infinite potentialities, the potential of The Source Field is collapsing from Field Potential into a nesting movement toward the emergence of a Source Field Wave. This is presently interpreted as 380 nanometers in the violet bandwidth of the visible spectrum. However, in the same manner that there isn't just one frequency of radio waves, so too there isn't just one frequency of Source Field Energy. It has a spectrum that can be called upon with differently shaped antennas (Page 210, Torsion field producing constructs). Moreover, if those antennas are used in conjunction with one another, say, in nested circles, then a wider spectrum of Source Field Energy can be called upon to complete a wider bandwidth of "work".

As the expressing collapsing waves move up the four sides of the pyramid, they meet at the top and further collapse their potential into Source Field Particle Photons. These curious Source Field Photons express themselves as White or Dark Light. These White and Dark photons are Field, wave, and particle collapsed into two divergent expressions of the same potential. Thus, they possess a mutual attraction, "Affinity", or what some disciplines might label "a difference in polarity", or "a similar difference in function". "Differences" that create both a cohesive interaction as well as an energetic connection.

While Quantum Entanglement is currently thought of as "Those things which were one, connected, and as having an inverse effect on one another", White and Dark Light don't share their Entanglement Properties, just because they happened to be One while in the condition of The Field. If The Field expressed itself as two photons of White Light and White Light, they would share the bond of similar origin that is thought to be the root of the cause of Quantum Entanglement. However, they wouldn't possess an affinity of function during the course of their expression. In the same manner that White Light doesn't "surf" in unison with White Light, so too Dark Light doesn't "surf" in unison with Dark Light. Thus, "The Affinity of Entanglement" that exists between White and Dark Light is more about the idea that they're "two different expressions with the same origin". Said differently, the Quantum Entanglement between White and Dark Light is more about "the self-similar expression of their differences" as well as "the similarity of their origins", than just about the similar origin or just about the different expression.

(Entanglement = Same origin + Different expression)
(Associative Property = Same origin + Different expression)

)

(The expression of light, as collapsed from The Field, is completely based upon the nested environmental conditions of $time_{12}$ and $space_{12}$ in which The Field expresses itself. Thus, our twin Source Field photons begin their spin at the velocity of (R) within the nesting function of their expression--- where they are expressed in different locations, and thus different elasticity's of space, and viscosity's of time. This is an emergent function of light within a given condition of $realm_1$ or $realm_2$--- and can be expressed numerically as (Collapse @ (R) = Inhibited Velocity minus inhibitions), where "The collapse of that which is inhibited", seeks to become uninhibited by that in which it's collapsed into.

Once it again attains an uninhibited condition, it reacquires its initial state of Quantum or Galactic Field Potentiality, also known as Absolute Superposition. Like the "Relative Time Velocity Dilation Theory"; *where time moves at different speeds for two objects in relative uniform motion to one another,* we have two "Photon Surfers" moving in different locations of space and separate conditions of time--- relative to one another's entangled affinity. Because of their affinity, they begin "a uniform movement", "seeking to become uninhibited", "into a condition", that attempts to "balance" the (R) variable (A, B) from its "inhibited" condition into its "uninhibited velocity", by manipulating the (DM, TN) variables through uniform acceleration. Once expressed, White and Dark Light try to attain "equilibrium", or begin a movement back into their original condition, by "surfing" in $space_{12}$ and $time_{12}$.

White Light $(A@X)E = \{\frac{DM}{TN}\}$

Dark Light $(B@Y)F = \{\frac{DM}{TN}\}$

Expanded Equation

White Light $\left(A@X\right)E = \left\{ \dfrac{(D)\left(Q\left((ex)K\right)\right)}{\left\{\left[T\left(Q(v)\right)\right](\pm L)\right\}} \right\} \pm C^2$

Dark Light $\left(B@Y\right)F = \left\{ \dfrac{(D)\left[Q\left((ex)K\right)\right]}{\left\{\left[T\left(Q(v)\right)\right]\left(\pm L\right)\right\}} \right\} \pm C^2$

This is the expanded equation in a flat format such that one might spatially see how they could become a Distance, Rate, Time addition or subtraction problem.

White Light $A@XE = \{\{((D)\left(\left((ex)K\right)\right)) / \{((T)(Q(v)))\} \pm L\} C^2\}$

Dark Light $B@YF = \{\{((D)\left(\left((ex)K\right)\right)) / \{((T)(Q(v)))\} \pm L\} C^2\}$

As opposed to being surfed along a positive or negative hypotenuse (C²), as happens in Galactic Physics, their mutual attraction creates the emergence of a consistently expressed ring shaped spin that we label "counterclockwise" in direction. This "counterclockwise" spin initializes the torque of a torsion field. Because they're attracted/affinity/entangled to one another, they try to close the diameter in their gap. This tightening of their spin (DM) further accelerates their speed (R@) (E, F) and increases their coherence (TN) incrementally by the growing value of (K), until they reach Absolute Conditioning, and The Uninhibited Velocity of Light's

Expression. This new speed, new location, new time, and new condition of light, under a condition of energetic amplification, increased velocity, and uniform acceleration, is the "Condition" that causes the central Ring of Absolute Conditioning to function in its special manner.

("Counterclockwise" spin can be described as energetically going "Down the helical ladder" of the female vortex of the torus field. Remember, no matter which perspective we view the helix, the real question we're asking ourselves is in what direction the energy is flowing. When looking at the torus field, this can be deciphered by knowing which "end" of the torus field you're looking at. When looking at the construction of the DNA helical ladder, this can be said to be "assembled from its female end to its male end" energetically flowing in a single direction.)

It's here that White and Dark Light begin to move back into their original expression, and the gateway between $realm_1$ and $realm_2$ opens up as both move toward "Fabric Potential" (Absolute Superposition), where they can uncollapse or reexpress themselves by collapsing again in the same manner in the opposing realm. The same potential also exists for those things that have been accelerated along with them as well. Such as, anything The Field has collapsed into--- "Products of The Field". All of which carry the potential to move through the two-way door of dominion toward increased coherence, absolute coherence, or into distortion and viscosity. The condition of which, will either slow back down and emerge from the ring in the same realm back into the original condition of the space-time continuum--- expressed as $R = (DM)/(TN)$. But in an amplified condition. Or, they've accelerated, and been conditioned enough to make the jump into a new condition on the opposing side of the same "rubber coin" of Field of Potential in $realm_2$.)

Down The Rabbit Hole

(If we think of photons as our two objects in relative "uniform" motion with one another... If we think of these two photons as ships, which are accelerated or decelerated in the ever-changing environment of the oceans of time... If we think of these two photons as our "surfers", which change their course with time waves and space distortions, as they ride along the hypotenuse (C^2)... We plainly see the expressions of light, as a product of The Field, which are operating within a given environment in all locations of all realms. Rather than being in an "unimpeded vacuum" of "outer space" that has a constant "Velocity" (R), the speed of light is the result of Field Potentiality, expressed within different space distortions and time viscosities, which are in a constant state of collapse or uncollapse.

Thinking of a photon being surfed through the universe on a time wave, river, or through time weather patterns--- Remembering that all three factors of distance, rate, and time are determiners of a photon's velocity--- We can observe a photon accelerate or decelerate within a given condition of time when it moves in or out of a region of space distortion (K). Time will move a photon away from a star, in the same manner that a roller coaster will gradually accelerate when moving down an incline. As the distortion of space reduces between two astronomical bodies, time will accelerate that same photon toward a given body, at the condition of time absent space distortions R = (D)/(TN). In the same manner that a rollercoaster decelerates when going up an incline, so too a photon will decelerate within time, and with decreasing velocity (R), when it encounters a movement toward a space distortion, such as another planet or star. Acceleration or deceleration (C^2) in space and time would be determined by the body's degree of distortion of the fabric of the continuum, or the given condition of The Architect (K) along its trajectory. Thus, The Phantom Star Theory has another aspect to it, such that light is not only being bent around a given object to create the illusion of another star or double star, but the "effects" are also accelerating and decelerating the function of the photon. Either photons are drawn into an expression as waves from The Field, by the collapsing expression of space distortions, or they are surfed about by the fluid nature of time viscosities along an ever-changing environmental trajectory. In either realm, it's always a two-way door of dominion flipping in one direction or the other, and it's only swinging in one direction with a given event.)

(While not initiated by the nodes of a machine pyramid in nature, this expression of an eternally vast and equally opposite infinitesimally small Field of Potential collapsing into a nesting wave, and then into nesting particles exists inside every bolt of lightning that patterns itself after The Program of The Architect. It goes on inside of every eddy, it's imbued in every tornado, and it's impregnated in every hurricane, or it lives in every magnetosphere. Like our birds, which use torsion fields for airfoil lift with the spin of the air, levity impregnation lift from the nesting wave inside the torsion field, and conditioning effects provided by male or female torsion fields--- The Force of The Architect, whither expressed as a Field or degree of collapsed Field within the nesting function, is impregnated into anything it's collapsed into.

As a wave, it nests inside of itself within the numerical pattern of The Program of The Architect. The Field collapses into a wave that vibrates at a variable frequency within its nested condition of expression. Then, based on that variable, the wave collapses into particles that form nested geometries. As a particle, the expression nests inside of itself via the nesting function of fields after the geometry of Platonic Solids, where each added layer of Platonic Solid represents a further collapse of the field toward a unique particle expression and function.

Degrees of Field Collapse are not only how we define our periodic table of elements, but it's the key to understanding how the wave of the Amazon is intrinsically linked between the particle of a single twig, and the particles of the entire Amazon of the same wave at a greater collapsed expression. This is one direction of the two-way door, where the nesting wave function has an echo-effect on everything that's moving toward expression. It's as if the Amazon were an ocean of water, and by splashing in the water; breaking a twig or chopping down a tree, echoes of effects will reverberate far and wide through the collapsing expression. Even if nothing is seen to physically touch another thing, the echo-effect through The Two-Way Door of Dominion of collapse and uncollapse is very real, and it will travel like any other ocean or time wave. The nested wave function always exists, the two-way door is always flipping back and forth--- This is "The Matrix".)

(While The Field collapses into an emergent expression of all things in $realm_1$, it can be seen to reverse its operation when The Field, "as a given expression", "gets drawn into" a torsion field. While some portions of the expression are conditioned, enhanced, and merely emerge from the male vortex in a more enhanced condition, other portions are conditioned and enhanced enough make the jump. Their expression unexpresses itself and transfers into $realm_2$; the unpotentialized collapsed Field uncollapses, repotentializes, and collapses again. Waves and levity can reexpress themselves as Absolute Field Potentiality. Particles and gravity can move back into waves or Absolute Field Potentiality. The elastic "emptiness" of the fabric of space and the viscous waves of time can repotentialize, or invert their expression as space viscosity, and time distortion. On the other side of the fabric of potential, in realm$_2$, all things carry the potential to take a step back toward the expression of The Field of Potential, to move all the way back into pure potential, or flip their "values". They may also be modified by given conditions of their new given time, new given space, new given wave, or new given particles within the new given nested conditions of realm$_2$. It's in this equation where we see Einstein and Galileo's expressions of "rubber" and "inverse" relationships of space and time truly become mathematically elastic, Substitutable relative to one another, as well as removing their effects all as One expression.

$$\text{Realm}_1 \qquad\qquad \text{Realm}_2$$

$$R = \frac{DM}{TN} \qquad \frac{TN}{DM} = R$$

)

(In every torus field there's one "tornado" that's right side up; female, and one "tornado" that's inverted; male. Within this dual expression of torsion fields, there's a dualistic dominate and recessive expression of White Light and Dark Light. In the top female end, White Light is dominate and Dark Light is recessive. In the bottom male end Dark Light is dominate and White Light is recessive. While we may think of this as positive and negative polarities, we might also think of this as a different expression of the same Field that modifies the expression of its collapse to function based on The Hemisphere Effect of torus fields, which are governed by The Nesting Effect, conditions in a given region of the continuum, and its order of magnitude that determines density, viscosity, distortion and thus, degrees of its quirky function.

("The Hemisphere Effect" is the effect that the nature of a sphere has on the torque of twin torsion fields within a given hemisphere of a sphere; and vice versa. It's an expression of relationships between the torsion field function, and each hemisphere of the sphere. It's an attempt to delineate the directional flow of energy through a torus field, and a realization that these relationships and flow of energy delineate differential functions. The Hemisphere Effect causes the recessive or dominate expressions of White and Dark light, depending on the given hemisphere in which that White or Dark Light might exist at a given location while nested within the geometry of a torus field. We can think of dominate and recessive as that which is expressed on the outside or inside respectively. We can also think of dominate and recessive as that which is more expressly collapsed within a given event.)

In the Northern Hemisphere of a torus field, where White Light is dominate, the counterclockwise twist of the female field strengthens, absorbs, increases density, and accelerates time toward coherence. In the southern hemisphere, where the Dark Light is dominate, the counterclockwise twist of the male torsion field weakens, dispels, and slows the flow of time as it moves out of coherence, and back into the given condition of the local continuum$_x$. As time enters into the top female end of a torus field, rather than being bent into a wave that travels in a linear direction (C^2), it's "torsioned" into a circle that spins back on itself "flattening" and uniformly accelerating the wave function toward field potential. This distorts our hypotenuse (C^2) into the increasing curve of The Program of The Architect as the hypotenuse spins down the torsion field. This can be likened to ($A+J=X$) and ($A+B=C$) where a change in the flow of two bodies of water change the velocity of an expression of the Field by the increasing factor of (K). Only in this case, we're changing the distortions and viscosities of both space and time into new expressions, where (K) is uncollapsing.

Like the intake of an engine that intentionally causes an over pressure, which seeks equilibrium, this torque will absorb, collect, strengthen, and accelerate both (time in a given space), and (space in a given time). Like the dispelling expulsion of an engine, as time or space exits the bottom male end of a torus field it will decelerate, disburse, weaken, and slow both (time in a given space), and (space in a given time). It's this disequilibrium of pressures moving toward the central disc that is partially the cause of "that which is in realm$_1$," moving through the gateway of exchange into realm$_2$--- or vice versa--- without necessarily fully repotentializing to Absolute Superposition. Acceleration toward absolute coherence creates the opening and potential conditions of a movement toward Field Potential, while the disequilibrium of pressures between realm$_1$ and realm$_2$ create pressured exchange, which accounts for the (1/64^{ths}) exchange of anything not in an absolute condition of Field Potential.

As a mathematical expression, this exchanging balance between space-time and time-space could be laid out like a fraction. Where we have "space over time", multiplied by "time over space". Such that, all values can potentially switch places. It is in this axis of mathematical function that White Light becomes dominate in the southern hemisphere of the time space torus field, and dark light becomes recessive rather than dominate. While Dark Light becomes dominate in the northern hemisphere and White Light becomes recessive in the realm$_2$ torus field. This effect inverts The Hemisphere Effect, as well as the inverse space and time resistance function.

$$\text{Realm}_1 \quad = \quad \text{Realm}_2$$

$$\left(\frac{Space}{Time}\right) * \left(\frac{Time}{Space}\right) = \left(\frac{Time}{Space}\right) * \left(\frac{Space}{Time}\right)$$

	Realm$_1$		Realm$_2$	
Hemisphere	North	South	North	South
Dominate	» White Light •	Dark Light =	Dark Light •	White Light
Recessive	» Dark Light	White Light =	White Light	Dark Light

)

(This constant circling of White and Dark Light through the north and south hemispheres eventually circumnavigates the torus field's equator. Both the White and Dark Light circle the torus field longitudinally by flowing in circular spin that moves laterally in another circle around a central ring. Each form of light follows its own path, so as not to interfere with the course of its opposite expression. In the same manner that two train tracks never cross one another's paths, so too--- Just like in "Ghost Busters"--- the streams of light never cross one another, "That would be very bad". They always dance in relationship to one another's position within a given Realm.)

(The Ring of Absolute Coherence is a one-way door and operates in a single direction within a given event. Using these equations and observing the metronomic back and forth "flipping" of the Tesla AC circle, we see the function of a circuit that circles in one direction, and then the opposite direction after the manner of our aqueduct analogy. In the same manner, the ring of coherence is a conditional two-way flip. Under the right set of conditions it's opened in one direction, and under the right conditions it's opened in the other direction. Such that, if both conditions are right, it's always opened in one direction or another, flipping in a metronomic (f) manner back and forth, just like the Tesla Alternating Current device.)

White Light $(A@X)E = \{\frac{DM}{TN}\}$

Dark Light $(B@Y)F = \{\frac{DM}{TN}\}$

$$=$$

$\{\frac{DM}{TN}\} = E(X@B)$ Dark Light

$\{\frac{DM}{TN}\} = F(Y@A)$ White Light

Expanded Equation

White Light $(A@X)E = \left\{ \dfrac{(D)\big(Q((ex)K)\big)}{\left\{\left[T\big(Q(v)\big)\right](\pm L)\right\}} \right\} \pm C^2$

Dark Light $(B@Y)F = \left\{ \dfrac{(D)\big(Q((ex)K)\big)}{\left\{\left[T\big(Q(v)\big)\right](\pm L)\right\}} \right\} \pm C^2$

$$=$$

$\pm C^2 \left\{ \dfrac{(D)\big(Q((ex)K)\big)}{\left\{\left[T\big(Q(v)\big)\right](\pm L)\right\}} \right\} = E(X@B)$ Dark Light

$\pm C^2 \left\{ \dfrac{(D)\big(Q((ex)K)\big)}{\left\{\left[T\big(Q(v)\big)\right](\pm L)\right\}} \right\} = F(Y@A)$ White Light

(Compare this mathematical expression with the flip of gravity and levity.)

(Remembering that (C^2) can be bent into the curve of (K), when entering or exiting a torus field. Rather than only using (C^2) to track the space-time movements of a set of objects, we can also use the circular pathway that the value of (K) lays out.)

The Inflated Universe

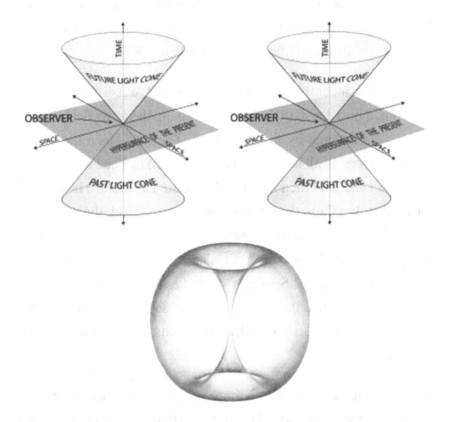

(Einstein's model shows a flat square shaped barrier, which divides The Hemisphere Effect, it partitions the twin tornado torsion fields, and represents the split between The Realm Effect. Regardless of whether the divide is represented as a pentagon, $cube_{1\,2}$, or square, there remains a conscious recognition of a "dividing" or "separation", between "that thing which modifies the operation of the fundamental constants" in one hemisphere or another, or one realm or another. Within every nested torus field, there's a middle, hovering, flat, two sided, pentagonal shaped, five noded, uncollapsed, "expressed to a degree" Field of Potential. Revealed by the location of the seeds in the model of the apple, this horizontal hovering pentagon is an expression of The Field's presence nested inside of the torus field, while it's yet in a degree^n of potential. The dividing barrier is a recognition of that thing between hemispheres, which is the motivator behind an effect that happens differently between hemispheres (90°).

In the same manner that Viktor Shauberger said "a fish doesn't swim, its swum, a bird doesn't fly, its flown", so too the torus field doesn't have a field hovered by the torus field, The field has a torus field which it hovers. In all its forms, the expressions of The Field collapse from The Field, and then move back toward The Field. The Field of Potential makes those things that form the torus field; the torus field doesn't form The Field of Potential. Thus, while The Field (Z) may emerge from the "I know not" of Galactic Eternal Vastness (Y) and Quantum Infinitesimal Smallness (X) of a higher realm, which our realm nested within, the only time we're seeing collapse is when and where we find torsion fields, torus fields, and nested functions of expression.

Once again, light doesn't "surf" time viscosities and space distortions, it's "surfed" by the two-way door effects within the continuum. Waves don't "wave" of their own accord; they are "waved", because of their expression (K) from The Field. Particles don't nest; particles are nested, because of The Architect and the two-way door of dominion of The Field. In the same manner that any other expression doesn't act without an outside force, so too light is "compelled" to express by The Field, to be "surfed" by the method of its expression, and behave according to the nesting environment in which its expressed. Light doesn't move, it is "compelled" to swing through the two-way door of dominion between realms by the nature of The Field, not by its own nature.

When the collapse of the expression reverses itself, it's not just going back to Field Potential and unclasping the nesting function, its moving back to the nodes of the pentagon, square, or cube, and eliminating the wave function as well. Such that, when it moves back into the condition of The Field, it's spreading out, and being reconditioned by the nodes of The Field. Then it reverses that function, collapses again into White and Dark Light in a nearby realm. This forms torsion fields, whose spin reinitiates the wave function, and Architectural Expressions begin to form nested waves, and nested particles that incase Intelligence and Intellect.

The expression of The Field is the creation of a torsion field, and then a torus field. Such that, the field nests itself in degrees of expression within each torus field, wherein it expresses The Architect. Whither it be intellect, waves, particles or twin photonic expressions of a contrasting, yet Entangled, nature--- the expression of The Field always emerges as a torsion field that moves into a self-nesting, a wave nesting, and universal nesting of "all products of the field" into all expressions of our universe. This "mechanism" is our first function of Field Physics™, and the root of all non-damming technology. Moreover, we can think of it as observing "what is" without "what is" being "distorted" or "inhibited" by the manner in which our eyes see it or our minds perceive it in its present expression, function, and realm.)

(When we think of two sides of a common wall expressing itself in a plethora of manners, who's nesting effect causes density and viscosity variances, and thus disequilibrium in the wall, we can see how The Field finds equilibrium between realms by allowing any expression on one side to express itself on the opposing side via a "release valve" through the ubiquitous two-way door of dominion of the torus' central ring. Once again, Viktor Shauberger would be right if he, and not I said, "The universe doesn't expand, it's expanded. The universe does not inflate, it's inflated. Light doesn't surf, it's surfed. The Earth doesn't aggregate from its exterior, it's aggregated through its interior. The earth is also inflated from the magnetosphere's central node, as products of the field are moved to realm$_1$ from realm$_2$ through the ring of conditioning. Every torus field encased heavenly body doesn't only collect mass from its own realm$_A$, it's also "collected" by that which is in another realm as it moves toward a degree of Superposition°, passes through the ring of coherence, and constructs that which is nested in a torus field in the opposite Realm (Reference also, Dr. James Maxlow, Global Expansion Tectonics).

More than observing the function of The Inflated Universe Theory from the perspective of eternal vastness, we can experience an equal and opposite movement toward infinitesimally small vastness when we think of inflating our personal universe with The Human Chakra System. Each human being has at least seven torus fields, each with a governing Field of Potential of a unique nature that are hovering, controlling, and surfing each of those torus fields. In the same manner that the two-way door of dominion moves back and forth from Absolute Superposition, where all things are renewed and recreated, so too comprehending how these fields inflate us is a cornerstone to the origin of our ability to create, manifest, and express miracles that defy the laws of Galactic and Quantum Physics.

A ubiquitous rule of thumb to any discipline is the Field Physics™ Rule, "Whether it be infinitesimal smallness, or eternal vastness, nothing is without an energetic attachment via the energetic expression of something else". There is always an energetic lasso that's Entangled into the fabric of existence (∞). In the same manner

302

that galactic torus fields lasso one another with a Silver Cord (∞), so too our Chakra torus fields lasso themselves into Entanglement with an energetic Silver Cord. Moreover, like so many things that come before our initiation into this Fruit of Knowledge, we find once again that the ancients were abundantly aware of these things. In the book of Ecclesiastes, 12:6; aka "The Preacher", there is a wonderful soliloquy, which demonstrates this relationship. Even in the most ancient of societies, they refer to this "lasso" as The Energy Serpent. Very soon, we will find how White and Dark Light manifest both The Energy Serpent, as well as the Torus Field, and give "As above, so below" a more vast meaning.)

Destiny

("We are taking the student from the perspective of what can be readily conceptualized with a beginner's point of view, into a new view of the world, where 'all things' behave in 'Real Constants'; 'As Above, So Below'". These are fields that collapse into patterns, forces that express Architectural Programs, and products of The Field, which nest inside of one another at all levels of understanding. Then, they express themselves once again as fields of pure potential, which can once again change their expression under a set of malleable conditions. "We are taking this student over a New Horizon of understanding of what constitutes 'The Real Constant', as it exists as a return to, an expression of, or a journey through The Field."

The primary concern when speaking of The Field of Potential isn't the realization that all things "express" from it, but its "condition" just prior to its collapse into expression. To comprehend this "condition" we first have to ask ourselves--- What are its drivers? What is motivating the collapse? And how do differing conditions affect the manner in which it's expressed? Whatever this "activator" is, it becomes the determiner of the expression of the collapse. We've already determined that pyramids "extract" Source Field Energy from Field Potential°, so we can assume that Platonic Solids have a "special mathematical 'axis mundi' mechanical advantage" when it comes to "connecting with", "communicating with", or "extracting from", and or "multiplying with" The Field. In addition, we know The Construct of The Architect comes from The Field to imbue itself within "things", and builds products of The Field in particular patterns in a collapsing movement toward expression. Nevertheless, it's so much more than that.)

(In the same manner that one coral life form is self-similar to the next coral life form, yet each one is a different entity, so too each line in a Platonic Solid is self-similar to the next line, but each line is a different line within the greater geometry of the shape. Platonic Solids share the self-similar difference function of number in space and number in time. In that, in any given Platonic Solid, individual lines are equivalent expressions to the next line, all lines share equivalent angles within a given shape, and all angles, relative to their completed geometry, resonate at a given frequency (f).

For instance, like coral, or a stage in The Architect; {(If A), (then B)}, all lines in a cube are self-similar to all other lines in the same cube. Each line in a cube collectively measures a "number in space" function. Each line possesses a self-similar angle "relationship" of 90° to every other line, which also gives it a "number in time" function. The union behind this "number in space" and "number in time" self-similar difference meets the requirements of The Entanglement Theory Equation. This holds true for all Platonic Solids. So, while we see that Platonic Solids poses a special "axis mundi mechanical advantage" when it comes to "connecting with", "communicating with", or "extracting from", and or "multiplying with" The Field, it's only when we see that it is "Entanglement with The Field" that gives them their special properties that we see a greater more vast perspective.

$$\{(F)(X)) \cdot (Entanglement)\} = \text{Mutual Origin} + \text{Differences})$$
$$\{(F)(Y)) \cdot (Entanglement)\} = \text{Mutual Origin} + \text{Differences})$$
$$\{(F)(Z)) \cdot (Entanglement)\} = \text{Mutual Origin} + \text{Differences})$$

This New Horizon of Entanglement Theory with Platonic Solids points towards a New Horizon with the geometry of a torus field. While not listed as such, the torus field is another Platonic Solid, meeting all of the same specifications of Platonic Solids and Entanglement Properties. The self-similar differences of the two torsion fields cause an entanglement property between the male and female torsion field. The self-similar differences of The Hemisphere Effect also causes an Entanglement property between The Realm Effect. Both cause a self-similar difference of The Entanglement Function where each hemisphere in each realm possesses self-similar differences that are relative to one another.

If we remember our Space Distortion Time Viscosity Theory, we can see that the two "lines", which compose a torsion field, are not actually going in a circle. Like The Einstein Rosen Bridge Theory, where light attempts to continue in a straight line by following space distortions, so too the White and Dark Light can be seen as moving "linearly" through "distortions" and "viscosity" variances. This is the same manner in which the hypotenuse (C^2) is seen as a straight line, but is actually a bent movement through distortions of space and time in a non-linear manner. As a Platonic Solid, torus fields' form around other Platonic Solids, nest in Platonic Orders, and therefore have a two-way door of dominion based on nesting types.)

(To attain Absolute Velocity™ & Zero Point Conditioning™, that is The Absolute Superposition of Field Potential, we need a "blocking" of that which causes incoherence and deceleration. In the past, this has looked like Faraday Cages, subterranean, or superterranean locations, such as deep underground bases or deep valleys between high granite mountains. However, with the description of ocean waves that are in a constant unbalancing and rebalancing act of collapse and uncollapse, we know all things are in a constant movement toward an expression or from an expression back toward the Field. So, in the same manner that we don't so much as struggle against the darkness as much as just turn on the lights, so too it's not so much as necessary to create a block to that which is in an incoherent state, as much as it is to create an energetically amplified, inviscidly conditioned, uniformed acceleration of a greater magnitude that neutralizes the "interruption" by changing the direction of the interruption $(^{G})(^{L})$, conditions its expression, and reverses the flow of its expression.

Those tools that cause coherence are torsion fields, which are run by nothing more than a wide bandwidth of Source Field Energy. This means there's no structure whose material fabrications; even if favorable, would impede the flow of energy into the Central Ring of Coherence. This can be expressed as "circles within circles within circles", or as "geometries within geometries within geometries", or even as "frequencies nested within frequencies", where the space between particularly shaped and nested Platonic Solids are manipulated by the designs themselves; without ever actually touching, or moving the final energetic product. After the affinity of the Dodecahedron, and with respect to the 1 to .618 ratio found in the five-pointed star, which shows us how to proportionally nest pentagons, this might be expressed as pentagons within pentagons within pentagons. Each nested pentagon is formed by an inner and outer five-pointed star, which places the next pentagon in its proper Phi ratio relative to the first (Egyptian Meter). In this manner, not only would the nodes match The Pentagonal Field, but also the ratios of space between the structures would match The Field's Source Field Frequency.

Once this Mandala of nested Pentagons is laid out on a flat and level surface, "antennas" can be placed on the nodes (The First Machine). "Antennas" might be expressed as a life form, a Platonic

Solid, or a torsion field producing construct. Life forms have torus and torsion fields, whereas pyramids and obelisks give natural torus fields a mechanical advantage, but both are "types" of torsion field producing antennas. All of these can then be placed on the nodes of the pentagons, such that their torsion fields begin to cooperate with one another in a circular nested pentagonal pattern. This model forms a single central torsion field of amplified magnitude that's not inhibited by any fabricated construct.

Anything... Anything, within the central ring of conditioning, or around the torsion field's Ring of Absolute Conditioning, is energetically amplified, inviscidly conditioned, and uniformly accelerated toward the condition of its Real Constant. This pure Field Potential becomes the corner building block of all of that which the field collapses into an expression of. At this state, The Field of Infinite Potential becomes as malleable as Play Dough, and the repository of information stored within The Field becomes as retrievable as an Electronic Encyclopedia Galactica.)

(The Field is an information field. The Field's first and primary expression is Intelligence. As if Intelligence was the "One Definable Thing" behind The Field, Intelligence is the primary initiate of the collapse of The Field. Intelligence collapses into Intellect, and intellect expresses itself as a degree of consciousness within the life form it is nested within. Yet, those intellects can only function under the emergent expression of their given form. The intellect of one's human expression is not the same Intellect of the Intelligence's expression. Said another way, the three intellects of your anatomical and software mind, as discussed in The Quest of Identity, are not the same as the intellect of your Intelligence's Intellect, which The Path of Identity seeks to connect (∞) you with (Intelligent-Kami of Truth).

To express themselves as the original Intellect; that is, the intellect of Intelligence before the expressed life form, they must "get out" of their expression, and become One with The Field again. Naturally, this might be expressed as the model of Remote Viewing, an insufficient label which is better described as "A Unity of Consciousness with The Design of The Construct", a movement toward Superposition, or a mathematical movement toward a link with The Encyclopedia Galactica; logging onto the real "Internet" (∞). RV is where one's focus is so surgical, one's process of probing for information so mathematically rehearsed, and one's approach into a modality, state, or condition of body, mind, and soul is so rehearsed and concentrated, that one's thoughts, feelings, and even their very being become One with what they're focusing on.

The best manner to describe this is to say that "When Remote Viewing a particular target of high emotional intensity, viewers sometimes experience the target as if they were the one going through the experience"--- In the summer of 1998, I was tasked with Remote Viewing "Master Mikao Usui, Moment of Inspiration, Mt. Kuryama". My monitor was a gracious woman named Yana, and the whole session was observed by no less than half of The Hawaii Remote Viewers Guild (hrvg.org) of that same year, including Prudence, a visiting teacher who was in charge that day. Marching headlong into the protocols, I got the spon-id and vis-id of a mountain (Page 222, Ideogram). I identified a subject on the mountain and executed a movement exercise toward that subject. I identified him as male, and probed him............ And... Then I got extremely ill... I unconsciously began slouching in my chair and feeling absolutely horrible. I told my monitor I felt like I was drained beyond all

309

capacity to continue... I nearly quit and collapsed with utter illness and faltering fatigue when Yana said firmly, "Stay on Target"...

The phrase was a Pavlovian cue to remind me that "What I was experiencing was as a direct result of the target" without actually saying it, or contaminating the protocols with "outside data"... *"I must continue,"* I thought to myself, and the "Never Give Up Marine" inside of me mustered up the gumption, and I continued the protocols in earnest. A few moments later, while probing an ideogram, I felt a "ZAP!!!" a sudden bursting of energy. My left hand felt like it was on fire with Power. I could see my palm turning a bright red as my entire body trembled with the force with which I had just connected. I looked at Yana, again astounded with the intensity of emotions and rapturous revelries of power and energy I was being subjected to, and said, "This has never happened before!". Yana did as all monitors are supposed to do, and calmly replied, "Stay on target, continue your protocols". And that I did with fidelity, fortitude, and determination... The student's heart sprouted a seed, the good soil of honorable teachers nourished this experience to take root within me, and my devotion, practice, and virtue allowed the dormant glory of this blossom to spring valiantly from the mire, and I came to bear The Fruit of Light in this world.

The events of the session were so powerful, so life changing, that I cannot recall any portion of the target after that, except as it exists through the lens of The Force I was feeling. I always go back to the feeling that I felt in my body, I return to the emotion of my mind, as they were imprinted by the Power. Moreover, when I do, I feel the emotion and power surge through my body, mind, and soul as though it were conditioning me all over again. When I think of that day, that target, or Master Usui I become One with the injection of that power, that moment, and everything about it. I became One with the Oneness which I felt "As" Master Usui, while he was yet experiencing his Oneness with a newfound awakened power and ability that has become known around the world as Reiki.

Most Reiki practitioners get their "conditioning" or "attunements" from a teacher and practitioner of Reiki. While this is all well and fine, since they think their teacher is deceased, yet Entanglement is in force, I would merely invite them to learn RV along with Reiki, and get their attunement from Master Usui and The Source as I did. Because I can assure you that Mikao Usui is not deceased. His torsion fields merely returned to The Field, he left his vessel, and is merely over the horizon of the current state of the average human perception. When we learn how to naturally get out of our human intellect through Bi-location, via a discipline such as Remote Viewing, we find that he, and many other things, are most definitely not out of reach.)

(This event is a unity in time and space. It's a unity of Forces and Fields. A unity of emotion and energy, intellect and intelligence. It's a collapse and uncollapse of the function of The Construct within the two-way door of dominion. Whether it's expressed as The Double Slit Experiment of Quantum Physics, where "consciousness" controls the collapse of the wave function into particles. Or, if it's expressed as Entanglement Theory, where there exists a unity of all things in The Field while in a state of Absolute Superposition. This event became a Oneness of all things as Mikao Usui, Richard Brian, and The Source became One within The Absolute Superposition of The Field itself. Moreover, this is a classical example of how focus, arithmetic methodology, and disciplined intention can get the average human intellect out of the human expression, and in touch with their

Intelligence's Intellect, their True Intellect, or their "Real Constant Intellect".

This is a step toward Oneness, and the two-way door of vastness... However, it's a natural step, and lacks amalgamating that inborn talent with the leverage of a mechanical advantage. Some 15 years later as I write this in late November of 2013, I can only think of one thing that could make the experience stronger, better, or "more coherent". That is, a unity of function between the natural skill of RV, and the mechanical advantage of The Central Ring of Conditioning.

In the same manner that wings give lift to man's natural desire to fly, so too the conditioning effects of torsion field machines are the mechanical advantage to cognitive amplification. When a person is in the ring (mentally, physically, or ethereally) the programs, which govern their intellects, are conditioned with a mechanical advantage. Attaining that intellectual Intelligent unity within the ring of the machine is the key to humanity figuring out how all the other technologies that manipulate fundamental constants operate. When we think of this as an echo, whose intent is within The Initiation Chamber of The Middle Way of The Path, it's a benevolent potential to transform The One into The Golden One. The potential to peel back the layers of human intellect, get closer to the original Intelligence, and its Vast Conscious Awareness. A thing that is not bound by the collapse of the human expression is the potential to know the unknowable, to experience that Thunderbolt which is transcendent to the human condition, and alter all paradigms in our Realm.

This unity of Intelligence, intellect, and technology is based on the attainment of conditioning via torsion fields, their resonant nodes, and the ring around their central disc; and then amalgamating our intellects with it as One. With this technology, we don't dam potential and direct it mechanically; we amplify it energetically into a transcendent condition, and set its expression free to fabricate its Path from an Enlightened state of being with its original Intelligence. The best manner in which to use this technology is The Middle Way of The Path, where Virtue, Truth, and Love amalgamate as One in The Chamber of Initiation. The greatest thing we can manipulate with this technology is our conscious awareness. The greatest machines we can manipulate with this technology are our physical, intellectual, and spiritual expressions, and their programs. The best device to use this technology with is one that possesses the central ring of conditioning, one that amalgamates a physical, intellectual, and spiritual Chamber of Initiation in a Vastness of Oneness. Its greatest potential is The Path of Freedom. The collapse of its wave into an expression is The Emergence of The Three Great Quests. Its Fruit of Light is that which The Golden Ones create with it, and all of humanity are their benefactors. We've come full circle.

In the same manner as The Way of The Path attains The Three Great Quests, so too The Three Great Quests direct us to embrace The Way of The Path. In addition, in the same manner that The Path of Virtue leads the student to The Path of Truth, which leads to The Path of Compassion, we find that The Way of The Path, and The Three Great Quests lead the student into The Chamber of Initiation. As we create with that magical device, which The Path and Quests provide, we also realize that it was with us all along, inside each of us, giving us all the creative powers we ever needed, if we would just "Follow The Yellow Brick Road", find our inner brains, express our inner courage, and share our inner Heart.)

The Chamber of Initiation

New Life

(In the same manner that one candle lights another, so too one Field can ignite the expression of a second Field. Another Field can be created when White and Dark Light exchange in The Field, and make the jump between realms. They multiply their expression when coming out of the opposing realm of The Field. Not so much as a reemergence of the same thing in a different manner, but as the inception of another Field with equal and opposite properties in a new realm. The two fields aren't one expressed twice, but similar to the "opposite self-similar expression" of entanglement between White and Dark Light, they're equal and opposite expressions with a mutual origin of something new. Only this time, they're in two separate realms that begin their expression with White and Dark Light.

In the same manner that White and Dark Light share dualistic Entanglement Properties, so too equal and opposite torus fields in opposing realms share the same Entanglement Properties. The Entanglement between a female torus field in $realm_1$ and a male torus field in $realm_2$, is created from "the self-similar expression of their differences" as well as "the similarity of their origins". After the

314

same manner, when the White and Dark photonic expressions of the second male torus field makes the jump back into the initial realm, the female torus field can give birth to a third torus field. Like the inception of a family, those three fields share the same self-similar expression of their differences, and the similarity of their origins, which Entangle all three together.

When a third torus field is created from two, it becomes interrelated to other torus fields in several manners. Since "products of The Field" are created in the realm_{1+++} closest to The Field, Field Entanglement is its First Interrelation. Since size determines nesting functions, and functions of nesting determine the two-way door of dominion, the Interrelation of Quantum or Galactic Entanglements are determined by the relative size of the expression, relative to the realm in which it expresses itself. The Three Physics relationships are characteristics that don't change while the related torus fields are yet in the collapsed condition of expression. That which is entangled tends to stay entangled, unless enacted upon by an uncollapse of its expression, or an uncollapse of that field in which it's entangled with. That which is entangled tends to stay entangled, unless enacted upon by an outside entanglement, in which case, the entanglement property can potentially modify its expression.)

(In our particular degree of collapsed condition, "E" does equal MC^2, but "E" doesn't equal MC^2 in a higher degree of uncollapsed condition. As matter and energy move closer to The Field, the properties by which they're bound in this realm begin to break their bonds, and their fundamental constants change with each new realm_{1+-} it passes into. While it's in a condition of Absolute Superposition or Field Potential, energy is no longer energy, and mass is no longer mass; not as we understand it. It becomes an infinite expression without known limits, and therefore possesses no "expressed" entanglement properties. The same function that can cause the property of entanglement also carries the potential to detangle the function of entanglement.

Something that possesses no properties of entanglement possesses infinite potential. While in a state of Absolute Field Potential, it's free from the functions of The Program of The Architect, the Galactic Physics rule of $E=MC^2$, as well as Newtonian Physics rules. Thus, when this product is brought back from Field potential, it doesn't necessarily have to recollapse as a single expression. It carries the potential to reexpress itself in an unlimited quantity of expressions. While in Field Potential, any product of the Field carries infinitesimally vast potential.)

(The "Second Interrelation" is controlled by the degree of a field's expression. Any field that's collapsed into a similar condition is subject to the two-way door of dominion of any other field that's expressed at the same or approximate condition of expression. However, should a field's expression fall outside of the same realm of expression of another relative field, the interlinking dominion of their interrelation will increasingly loosen their interrelations as the differences in their conditions vary.

The "Third Interrelation", as a property of Field Physics™, is controlled by the dominion of nesting. Nesting can move a torus field so as to cause it to rewire, or change its energetic association with another set of relative torus fields, so long as they're collapsed into a similar degree of expression. Similar to the second interrelation, this is very similar to flipping magnets with polarities, such that their polarities align with other related fields. This is also similar to sucking a hurricane's field into the magnetosphere's field, such that their energies are guided or absorbed. This is also very similar to the earth rewiring its magnetosphere with another magnetosphere every time the earth crosses the equator of The Milky Way. While polarities align, nest, and maintain dominion over one another in this degree of expressed Galactic Physics; these properties are also shared in Field Physics at each similar expression of The Field relative to one another.

As per the "Second Interrelation" with the conditional function of the "Third Interrelation". If their condition of expression is such that they are in a much greater, or much lesser degree of Superposition via a movement along the (Z) axis of expression, they will not maintain these previously listed relationships with one another. However, because Entanglement is a universal expression of Field Physics, which maintains the property of entanglement in all degrees of expression, they will maintain their entanglement property while in the condition of expression, regardless of their degree of expression or axis of movement. This can be seen as The Universal Nesting Effect, whereby any realm that is nested within another realm is subject to the realm; or properties of a realm, in which it's nested.

The "Fourth Interrelation". The more that fields express themselves, the more they collapse into the boundaries of their realm$_x$, and degree of expressed function of The Program of The Architect of their particular realm. As they increase in number, they will behave more and more after the manner of the program in their realm. The more that fields uncollapse into degrees of Superposition, the more they will relate to each degree of the expression of The Architect at that degree of expression. In this realm, Fields are not so much as limited in the quantity of their expression by The Program of The Architect, as much as they are limited by the condition of their expression in the realm in which they express themselves. So, because torus fields are conceived in a higher realm$_{1+++}$ of infinite potentiality, and "descend" along the (Z) axis to lower degrees of expression, if a Field wanted to express itself, but the billet of The Program in one realm was full, it could potentially express itself in a different realm, where "room" (K) for an expression of a field was "available" for expression according to The Architect of that realm$_x$.)

(Quantum Entanglement = Mutual Origin + Differences)
(New torsion field = Male torsion field + Female torsion field)

(A human female's Sexual Chakra Field is where her womb is, above the pubic bone and slightly below her naval. While her sexually creative field is always there, expressed°, nested in its torus, and ready to create another life, her genes don't carry enough genetic material to do so physically. In the same manner that the second torus field in realm$_2$ "returns" its energy back through the Field into the first torus field in realm$_1$, so too when a human male reintroduces the other portions of the genetic code, there exists a certain Field Potentiality between two equal and opposite fields to create a third physically interrelated field; subject to Entanglement, and The Program of The Architect of their given realm.

At this stage, the union of egg and sperm aren't necessarily anything more than the genetic summation that allows the energetic potential of a woman's and a man's fields to express themselves as another field of potentiality, within the conditional summation of nested human genes. Before the new Field can descend (Z) from a higher realm to express itself in this realm, before a life form actually has a place to nest in realm$_1$, the cells must multiply through the double cube until they're energetically formed into a sphere by the progress of The

Architect (Page 167, Morula). The area in that sphere then turns into a Morula when White and Dark Light, from the nested field, create a torsion field down its center. Like the earth and its magnetosphere, the Morula is an energetic torus field possessed of a physical aspect. This is a nest of a "new sort", while nested within the dominion of other torus fields, this internal field is itself the nest for a new life form. After "The Map of an Apple", a new Field from within expresses this new torus field, and within that completed field, The Intelligence of The Spirit can make the jump through The Ring of Coherence, move through the silver cord, nest within the expressed field, and begin to grow and mature in union with the physical aspect and its expression of intellect.)

(The Miracles continue to multiply into vastness when that New Field$_{1F}$ creates, and Quantumly Entangles itself with its duplicate Field$_{2m}$ in realm$_2$. Its White and Dark light reexpress themselves in ream$_2$ and create an equal and opposite expression of itself. That expression then returns to realm one, and conceives another field, which matures into a torus field. This unique self-repeating pattern, complete with all the raw genetic material to express itself, both energetically and physically, allows the conception of this single field to give birth to 12 other fields--- 6 in realm$_1$ and 6 silver cord entangled duplicates in realm$_2$. The Octahedron of the Heart Field is two equilateral pyramids joined at their square bases, who's torsion fields project above, connect between, and project below themselves to energetically direct where the Heart's torus field should manifest the new fields. This is relative to The Space Distortion Time Viscosity Equation, and while we express this event numerically and mechanically with the models of disciplines, the field naturally does it all energetically.

The three fields above the heart are the Throat Field (Icosahedron), Third Eye Field (Icosahedron), and the Crown Field (Dodecahedron). The three Fields below the Heart Field are the Solar Plexus Field (cube), Sacral Field (tetrahedron), and the Root Field (inverted tetrahedron). These fields begin with the Heart Field and go up to the throat, then down to the Solar Plexus, and then up to the Third Eye, and then down to the Sacral Field, and then up to the Crown, and down to the Root Field. These Fields are governed, directed, and Quantumly Entangled with The Heart Field, as well as their inverse duplicate Fields in realm$_2$, as they cooperate and mature the life form into its intellectual, energetic, and physical expression in both realms.

This becomes a kind of road map to understanding the function behind all forms of (X, Y, Z) Entanglement, as well as a starting point to the construct of The Architect, which nurtures that nested life form with its life giving energy. This dual expression of self-similarity of the Field, at its initial degree of expression, is what shows us the one to one effect of their affinity. The affinity directs The Program of The Architect to begin assembling "products of The Field" in a self-similar manner, which energetically modifies over a term of expression, so as to appropriately modify the expression of all parts of the life form as it matures.

That which has Entanglement with one other object, passes on its properties of Entanglement in a one to one ratio. Moreover, since all expressions share entanglement with The Field, the result is a kind of inception of assembly, as "that which is expressed", continues to pass on its expression, as it collapses into lesser degrees of Superposition, and emerges in new realms. As White Light does one thing, Dark Light does another, and like a series of ones and zeros that create the foundation for all computer programs, the field begins passing on entanglement, and building self-similarity as if White and Dark Light were the field's left and right hands. In the same manner that a wave repeats itself in a self-similar manner, we understand that a movement into a new condition has an effect on the expression of the wave. Such that, it modifies its expression and causes it to begin nesting, as well as building according to The Program of The Architect in degrees of ordered nesting of waves and geometry.

Crystals are life forms that form at a more collapsed, more expressed, function of the Field. Life forms are living at every layer and density of expression of the field. We just happen to be expressed at one degree of Superposition while "some" of the more collapsed life forms, such as crystals, are forming and existing at more collapsed expression of The Field, within the greater densities of expression within the depths of the earth.)

Light Beings

(A major flaw in all human logic is that we're using our own lens of perspective to reason the world into a viable comprehension with. Its limitations are not only the short length of its life span, but the manner in which our anatomies can gather, collate, and disseminate information. It is because of our own limitations that it's believed that water is the foundation of life; after all, it would seem ridiculous at this time to think that life, in any form, could exist on a star. However, we also used to say that about volcanoes, radioactive mines, and other more incomprehensibly inhospitable places. By this point in our journey, we should be looking for life forms anywhere we see the expression of a torus field, regardless of its environment, degree of expression within The Architect, or realm$_x$.

To comprehend that life is not reliant on the expression of the bandwidth of water, we must look at the full expression of The Bandwidth of The Field. The two-way door of expression of The Field shows us the nesting of Ordered Waves, as well as the nesting of Ordered Platonic Solids. Life forms live along the whole of both bandwidths of these expressions as if both bandwidths were one long expression originating from The Field, such that the nesting of waves came first and the nesting of Platonic Solids came second. Both can be seen to overlap in the discipline of Cymatics, wherein we observe waves of energy nest energetically into Platonic Solids, depending on which frequency is being played. Here we see inverted tetrahedrons, nested-hexagons, and nesting-spheres nesting into one another absent a solid aspect. In the same manner that different angles of the same shape can determine which frequency of Source Field Energy is harnessed, so too we can use a wide range of Cymatic frequencies with our Obelisk machines, so as to cause them to resonate "more effectively" (18,000Hz).

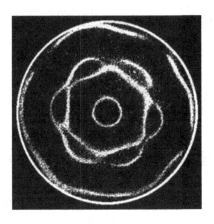

When we look at the two-way flow of The Design of The Construct, we're going to see life forms in between the full range of its expression. Life forms exist within the full length of the wave bandwidths and Platonic Orders of The Construct. Life forms that are within The Layers of The Construct are using the full bandwidth of The Field to create themselves with; each life form taking up a section in which to express itself. Thus, whatever wave frequency or Platonic Order they're using to manifest themselves with, this will be the frequency (^{L}) or Platonic Order (^{G}) which they can be "found" with. While this might reveal itself in the missing bandwidth, it might just as well be interpreted as what portion of the bandwidth a species is radiating. Compounds and life forms are using that section of the expression of the Field in one of two manners. They're either absorbing that section of the expression, or they're radiating that section of the expression.

Absorbing: Astronomers are using the bandwidth of the electromagnetic spectrum (ELF) to look for planets that might be habitable. They do this by looking for "missing" light, because certain elements absorb particular "light" frequencies. Therefore, if a particular section of expression of The Field is missing, then these scientists have some degree of assurance that certain compounds are present.

Radiating: Kirlian Photography picks up the frequencies of light that a life form is radiating, as opposed to those bandwidths which an element or life form might be absorbing, or merely reflecting. Kirlian Photography sees in bandwidths that our eyes cannot, but it "interprets" the data of those frequencies, and "translates" it into colors that our eyes can see, to come up with a photograph. This is not unlike Thermographs, which see in the thermal region of the ELF bandwidth, and then use hues of gray or red to "interpret" the image in a manner that our eyes can accept.

As one, the bandwidths that are either missing or radiating, are those frequencies that a life form is using to express itself. One frequency goes in, and is thus missing, while another frequency of the bandwidth of the expression of The Field comes out, and is thus present. It is by using both forms that we can find all manner of life forms that are over the horizon of our perspective. It is also in this manner that we can define a new order of life, by creating a species list based on which section of The Field a particular life form is absorbing and excreting. When we consider the range of the wave function, as well as the vast permutation of nested Ordered Platonic Solids, this species list becomes an almost infinitesimal bandwidth that life might take on, or express itself through.)

(In any realm, there are going to be life forms, and as we're quickly realizing, we're finding life forms in every nook and cranny we can conceive of to investigate. In one expression of The Architect or another, in one expression of intellect or another, there are going to be life forms collapsing into the many degrees of expression on either side of The Field. Moreover, there are life forms that reside between every degree of expression of The Field. In this case, we're referring to life forms, who's expressed fields in which they nest, reside closer to Field Potentiality. If crystals existed in our realm at a greater collapse of expression, because of their nested Platonic Order, these life forms can be said to exist in our realm on the other side in a more amplified condition than our expression. We exist at an increased degree of collapsed expression, but at a less energetic, less coherent, less uniform, and slower velocity (R) relative to their expression (Z). However, unlike crystals, it's enough of a difference to cause us to be unable to experience them directly.

Because of the effects that amplified energetic, inviscidly conditioned, uniformly accelerated conditions have on The Programs of The Architect, intellect, physical expression, and spiritual matter, every aspect of their existence is at a much higher form of expression than ours. While we experience momentary conditions of genius, they live in a perpetual condition of amplified intellect. While we have damming technology, their intellects manipulate fundamental constants at will. While we live and die in the postulate uncertainty of what's beyond both horizons, they possess an expanded sentience, which spans both barriers. By the default of their condition, they're far more advanced than we are in every conceivable way.

If you don't look, you can see them. They might first appear as green streaks, and travel as fast as the flash of a shooting star. However, the label of green is more of a condition in the difference in velocities of light between their condition and the observer's condition. Most people can attain a common understanding of what we're talking about if it's likened to the "Red" or "Blue Shift". In that case, the "color shift" is an effect of light that occurs in a particular expression°

of space-time, when one or two objects are moving in opposing directions relative to a third object. This is like adding or subtracting two frequencies of color, and coming up with a third color, which is the sum or the difference between the first two. In this case, we're not so much as moving in opposite directions, but both of us are expressed in a variance of conditioning, or direction of expression, wherein the differences between our states of field collapse prevent us from experiencing them. However, as our uniform velocities and energetic coherence begin to get closer to one another, they begin appearing to the awareness of our intellect as feelings, thoughts, or emotions, and then to the function of our eyes as streaks of light. As the difference between our conditioning lessens, they appear as hues of blue, and then as white spheres, spheres that "Ride The Lightening" of superposition (Z). The more adept you become at "picking them up", the more they will appear to your conscious awareness or as these white or silver spheres.

These spheres are presently being recorded in increasing numbers all over the planet, and the phenomenon has been increasing in regularity for centuries. While we're presently thinking of them as Unidentified Flying Objects, we're only thinking like this because we are stuck in our dam tech ways of reasoning. We see something fly through the air with intelligent control, and because we can't label it as something we already know, we quickly conclude that there must be someone in a machine that's spinning wheels, flipping levers, pushing buttons, and using expulsion for propulsion--- "like we do". In the Julian year 1561, a "UFO battle" was recorded over Nuremburg Germany. Notwithstanding the details of this event, the "lens of perspective" of the viewers was a call to "repent of their sins", as opposed to the lens of a more "modern" perspective, which might look like the fluttering of camera shutters and a documentary.

All the old legends, myths, and folklores that our ancestors have passed down to their posterity stipulate that these beings exist. Of course, they called them by many names, each based on their own culture, and traditions. They gave them different labels according to their own understanding. Moreover, each culture reacted to them through the "lens of life" through which they saw them at the time. Furthermore, while observing these differences lends us a vast perspective of understanding, we must accept that they've "returned" (Z), and that they desire to communicate with us.)

(To understand the value and meaning of their messages we first have to redefine a few simple functions between Quantum (X), Galactic (Y), and Field Physics™(Z), such as the behavior between solids and liquids or particles and waves. Like the two-way expression of The Field, we can think of this function as a two-way door, which defines the difference between things that pass harmlessly through one another or not. We can also think of this as the condition of things that pass harmlessly through The Field, and those things that do not.

We currently think of "Acceleration" as that which causes a solid to begin operating like a liquid; agitation, or a difference in velocities between two relative objects, is said to alter fundamental constants. In the same manner that the solids of hypersonic aircraft lose their properties of rigidity, become flexible, or outright melt at increasing speeds, relative to the air around them, so too we say that when water is accelerated via "heat"; as in molecular "agitation", that it "melts" or liquefies. The acceleration changes the object's properties from the solid of ice (gravity = collapse) = $(^G)$, to the fluid of liquid $\{(^G)(\text{collapse}$

= gravity) $> \geq \leq <$ (levity = uncollapse)(^{L})}, and then to the "wave" of gas (levity = uncollapse) = (^{L}), but this isn't because heat causes water to evaporate as we currently think of it. It's because the lack of coherence, via agitation rather than uniform acceleration, prevents the water from doing what it really wants to do as a collapsed expression of white and dark light--- What acceleration makes the collapsed expression really want to do, is to be surfed through space distortions and time viscosities--- What acceleration makes it really want to do, is to uncollapse its expression and return to its Field--- But, its lack of coherence prevents it from completing its Field Physics™ task. Thus, velocity in the absence of coherence and proper conditioning (amplified energetic, inviscidly conditioned, uniform acceleration) compels water to remain in the same realm, and move from a solid state toward a gaseous state, or from particle to wave. We call this "behavior" Galactic Physics, Newtonian Physics, or the physics of our realm, when in reality it's a conditional function of a wider set of physics, which transcends nested realms; Field Physics™.

We currently think of "Coherence" as an absence of acceleration. When water vapor lacks acceleration, we say it condenses into a liquid, or freezes, and becomes a solid. However, this isn't because coherence causes water to condense or freeze. It's because the lack of uniform acceleration prevents the water from doing what it really wants to do as a collapsed expression of white and dark light. What inviscid conditioning makes the collapsed expression really want to do is to be surfed through space distortions and time viscosities--- What coherence makes it really want to do, is to uncollapse its expression, and return to its Field. But, its lack of uniform acceleration, even with added coherence, prevents it from doing so. Thus, coherence, in the absence of uniform velocity, compels water to remain in the same realm, and move from a gaseous state toward a solid state--- from waves to particles, flipping gravity and levity. While we call all of this The Galactic Physics of our realm, it can also be expressed as the two-way door of the collapse uncollapse function of Field Physics minus certain conditions (Page 289, 287, 228, 174, Inhibited velocity). In the same manner that The Program of The Architect governs products of the Field by the degree in which the program is expressing itself, so too the changing of one or another conditional property completely changes the operation of fundamental constants, what they're subject to, and in what realm they'll reside.)

(The boarders between Quantum (X), Galactic (Y), and Field Physics™ (Z) lay, not between the infinitesimal smallness of the (X) axis, or the eternal vastness of the (Y) axis, but between the proper conditioning of "products of the Field", and the two-way door of dominion, which allows a movement between eternally vast and infinitesimally small nested realms along the (Z) axis. In terms of Quantum (X) or Galactic (Y) Physics, things appear to begin to behave differently between infinitesimal smallness and eternal vastness. Nevertheless, these expressions are just conditional functions of the Field. In Field Physics™, the fundamental constants of all Physics are based on the degree of collapse, the direction of expression, and the conditional function of The Architect (K) in each realm. The cranks, levers, and buttons that control the operation are "the proper conditions of products of the field". Not only does this conditioning open the "Golden Gate" between realms, but degrees of its expression determine which fundamental constant is turned on or off, what two-way door of dominion is opened or closed, or is flowing in this or that direction.)

(In the same manner that a dumb waiter's doors only function one at a time, and in one direction at a time, so too the two-way door of dominion of Field Physics™ has one door that functions as one gateway, which allows the jump in one direction per event. To prevent the jump, one property or another must operate in an opposing direction, so as to cause the function of a solid, liquid, or gas and keep the particle or wave subject to gravity or levity, and thus remain in the same realm. We can see this as the difference between (that which moves the field in two directions = Field Physics (Z)), and (that which causes behavior within this degree of expression of The Field = Galactic (Y) and or Quantum Physics (X)).

The ($E=MC^2$), might be expressed as the physics of our degree of expression of the Field. Quantum Physics might be expressed as the strange behavior that begins to happen when certain elements of Galactic or Field Physics™ are or are not in place on the infinitesimal smallness level of expression of the same realm. Moreover, in the same manner that Galactic Physics begin behaving differently as they approach the conditions of another realm$_{x++}$, so too Quantum Physics can be expressed as a reversal of that two-way door in the equal and opposite direction. Field Physics™ can be expressed as all fundamental constants, because Quantum and Galactic Physics are nested functions of Field Physics™.)

(To attain a little perspective, think of Tesla's alternating current device. The expressions of four variables constantly flip their state in a back and forth circle. This can be represented by pointing your index and pinky fingers from both hands at one another. Then flip one hand back and forth in such a manner that the two opposing fingers trade places. In this manner, not only will you gain a greater understanding of Tesla's Alternating Current device, but also you'll attain a greater understanding of the conditional states of physics.

Field Physics

Acceleration + Coherence = Uncollapse of the field$_F$

Deceleration + Incoherence = Expression of the field$_M$

Like flipping our index and pinky fingers back and forth, if these values are switched we get different effects.

Galactic Physics

Acceleration + Incoherence = Solid » Liquification » Evaporation » (Wave Levity)

Deceleration + Coherence = Evaporation » Liquification » Solid » (particle gravity)

Acceleration + Incoherence = an uncollapse of the field that moves particles toward a liquid or wave but they cannot make the jump.

Deceleration + Coherence = a collapse of the field toward a liquid or solid but they cannot change their properties enough to make the jump.

A simplistic mathematical expression of this behavior can be laid out as follows.

$$A + B = X$$
$$C + D = Y$$
$$A + D = Q$$
$$B + C = R$$

(In a similar manner that water turns into vapor when adequately agitated, so too when we subject water to the conditioning of conditioned Source Field Energy in female torsion fields, portions of the water begin to uncollapse their expression, and move into another nearby realm$_{1+}$. The conditions, in which portions of this

331

water exist, at a new and higher degree of expression, begin to share the conditioning of their expressions with the lower; more nested, realm. In this manner, the effects of the lower realm have less of an effect on the water, which yet remains in the lower degree of expression. While this is partially because some of it is in another realm$_{1+}$, it's more because the water in a higher form of expression is subject to the conditioning that exists at that higher form of expression, and via the entanglement interrelation, and a movement through the silver cord (∞), its passing those Architect effects on to the water left behind. This is also because, in the same manner that torus fields have dominion over those fields that are nested within them, so too higher realms$_{1+}$ have dominion over lower realms$_{1-}$ of existence, because lower realms$_-$ are nested within the higher realms$_+$. Thus, because of the Fuzzy Physics™ that occurs for an expression of the Field, which is caught between different expressions of the same realm$_{1+}$, it's sharing some of those properties from the other realm with the water in this realm. We know that the amplified conditions of the next realm$_{1+}$ are very powerful, relative to our condition of expression, because we only need a very small portion of water to be Superpositioned° to get the desired effects. The difference is so significant, that they can prevent water from freezing in this realm, even when subjected to conditions that would otherwise guarantee to freeze water as stiff as a rock.

We can see this in fluid dynamics where water, which is subjected to the conditioning of the female torsion field of increased magnitude, refuses to freeze until the portions of its elevated expression is "recollapsed". Like the addition of entropy via the absence of intelligence, we collapse it back into this realm by adding the ingredient of agitation via a tap, which interrupts The Source Field's torsion field that's spinning unseen within the water. With the termination of the torsion field, the conditioning stops, and the water that is in a higher state of Superposition collapses back into this realm of expression. That collapsed water ceases its relationships with the conditions of a higher realm, and once again becomes subject to the properties of this realm. The other water that was here, but shared the Fuzzy Physics™ with the higher realm, no longer has that interrelation to be conditioned by the higher, or exterior, realm. The door between realms shuts, and the water freezes almost instantaneously.

We don't so much as have to redefine the rules of Newtonian Physics, and say that water no longer freezes at 32°F, as much as redefine what kind of physics we're employing, and under what conditions we're operating while explaining a given event. In Field Physics™, water changes its operation, function, and obeys other fundamental constants when it, or portions of its Entangled expression, are conditioned to different degrees of collapse or expression. In the same manner that The Nesting Function is subject to degrees of energetic inviscid velocity, so too when we apply the proper conditioning to any product of The Field, it too begins to break its "galactic and quantum physics bonds" with that which is in the same condition or degree of collapsed expression. In the same manner that particles break their bonds with gravity, and begin their relations with levity when the two-way door of dominion is moving toward the Field, so too waves break their bonds with levity to an increasing degree when they nest, or begin forming Platonic Solids in a movement toward a lower realm. It begins to relate to the new physics of the realm in which its being "surfed". Moreover, we can see that interrelations allow a sharing of properties between realms through the ring of coherence along the (Z) axis. In other words, the boarders between

Quantum (X), Galactic (Y), and Field Physics™ (Z) lay, not between the infinitesimal smallness of the (X) axis, or the eternal vastness of the (Y) axis, but between the proper conditioning of "products of the Field", and the two-way door of dominion, which allows a movement between eternally vast and infinitesimally small nested realms along the (Z) axis.)

(So, a rudimentary expression of this function in our realm can be seen as the two-way door of dominion effecting things in two ways, depending on what's happening with the dual relationship of four variables. Conditioning with female torsion fields is an uncollapse of the Field, and causes things to pass *harmlessly* through one another, by changing their properties back toward White and Dark Light or Absolute Superposition. But, acceleration without an uncollapse, or reversal of the Field, is a movement toward velocity, while maintaining an incoherent expression, and this solid, liquid, or gas {(gravity) «» (gravity + levity) «» (levity)} expression moves toward a realm that's between where we are and where the Field is. In the same location$_{1\ 2}$, it goes into the realm$_{1+}$ of other life forms, it causes them "incoherence", and they most assuredly Do Not like it.)

(After the thoughts of Viktor Shauberger, and because it's so true of many things that they do not fly, swim, or surf, but are flown, swum, and surfed. Prop-engines aren't just disturbing the air where they are or where they've been, they're also disturbing the conditions of both sides of the fabric of space-time$_{1\ 2}$, the many degrees between them$_{+}$, and where they're going. Prop-engines attain a certain kind of uniform velocity and torsion, but do not attain a movement toward energetic amplification or coherence. With their agitation, acceleration, and torsion, they're causing incoherence in time$_{1+\ 2+}$ and distortions in space$_{1+\ 2+}$ in a movement toward a realm that's

334

closer to The Field while failing to alter all of their properties. Such that, in an isolated area around, and in front of the engine, they're infringing into a realm that's closer to the physics of the Field, and the incoherence of those engines are disturbing those life forms that are in this nearby environment.

In the same manner that a prop engine bends time and space with its functions, but fails to move into a new realm$_{1+}$, so too a bullet uses torsion to maintain its trajectory, and velocity to attain its objective--- but it too fails to change its properties. The operations of both objects attain enough increased velocity or torsion to manipulate the space-time fabric toward a movement into an adjacent expression of our realm, but neither of them attain the conditions to move through that realm in a *harmless* manner. They've asked us to be considerate of their needs, as they have been to ours, and not do this.

In the same manner that we're moving "things" into their environment in a partial uncollapsing pattern, so too our interference with their environment is causing them such great discomfort, so as to compel them to periodically move into our environment in a collapsing expressing manner. Because they're Hyper-Intelligent Beings, they don't think to "War" on others, as we do, to get others to stop interrupting their environment. In our realm, intelligent creatures typically only "War" for survival purposes against other less enlightened more aggressive life forms, but they yet do so with damming technology. In The Realm of "Hyper Energetic, Inviscidly Conditioned, Uniformly Accelerated, and Unified Intellects", they don't "War" with weapons, they just manipulate the fundamental constants so as to remove the availability of certain decisions from the intellects who are menacing them. These beings are responsible for bending and folding time or space like an ocean wave, burying things beneath, what we would call the ground (a product of the Field in a collapsed expression) in such a manner that we couldn't possibly detect, let alone attain these things. They also have the ability to "disconnect", "reassemble", and even share thoughts, so as to cause a stupor of thought, or align thoughts, so as to assist one in their Life Path endeavors. They can inhibit us, or they can help us at will (Gen 11:4).

In a more conditioned state of being, manipulating the expression of fundamental constants is not only easier, its second nature. A life form can just as easily reconnect with their original intellect, as change the nature of a product of the Field while it's in Absolute Superposition. In this math, the grain of a mustard seed is equivalent to a mountain, and the intention of sentience has dominion--- so why shouldn't it move? Math is as flexible as the condition of the intellect that's using it, and intellect is as superior as its conditioned state.)

(The Nesting function changes the velocity of light. The alteration in the velocities of light determine the function of its expression. As light accelerates to higher realms, its dominion changes, and its function amplifies.)

(We have to remember, these beings, who are living at a higher state of conditioning, are also living in an "Amplified Condition of a Realm" which appears and functions far better, and thus far differently, than our condition or realm. "Their physics (Z) are not our physics (Y), but like us their physics are based on Field Physics, the function of The Architect in its degree of expression of their realm, as well as understanding how things operate at different levels of expression in different realms, which cause nested dominion at higher more exterior realms. When talking about conditioning, we're saying that their amplified condition is how things are supposed to function, not because this is what we can see every day, but because this is how things want to function in different states. However, just like observing the idiosyncratic thought that acceleration via molecular agitation only possesses the singular function of liquification, because this is what we experience, so too we're idiosyncratically saying that light has a speed limit, or can be employed as a constant, because we're limiting ourselves to the observations which we can see, rather than understanding how things operate in altered states of Superposition° or different realms. We must accept that our realm functions as it does, not because "This is the way things operate", but because of the accumulated nested conditions of a collapsing Field, which forms the functions of a nested environment within many nested layers of the same environment. Moreover, when those conditions are modified in very particular manners, especially as it relates to the conditioning of torsion fields, the "rules" we've created to give us understanding begin to work against our advancement. Thus, it's not so much that we must give up or surrender that "Fruit of Awareness" which we've spent eons accumulating; as much as add a New Horizon of new variables to our equations and disciplines that apply under "certain conditions". So, although it might seem so in the coming pages, we're not sacrificing the fatted calf on the altar of change, in the name of "the progress of mankind", as much as we're finding a new aspect of what it means to be a fatted calf, which never dies, but moves over the horizon of a Vast new perspective.)

(Imagine that you follow The Way of The Path, that you attain The Three Great Quests, and that you build an Orgone Pyramid Obelisk Mandala. You construct a central torsion field of veritable magnitude in a conditioned location of space-time, and step into The Initiation

Chamber of The Ring of Absolute Conditioning. As you condition "of that which you are composed" you'll begin to show up to those life forms living at a more conditioned state of being. Suddenly, you're peaking into the realm in which they are existing, you're doing as they're doing, and living in the manner they're living. The Japanese call this "Kami-no-michi", or The Path of The Kami, "The Way of The Spirits who live in the forests", also known as the theology of Shinto, or "The Way of The Gods". If this elixir were taken with an ear to the phrase "The Intelligent Kami of Truth", "The Truth of the Kami", or "The Truth of The Gods" ---from The Path of Truth, we begin to hear whispers of greater Vastness urging us toward something magnificent, which yet lies halfway over a nearby horizon. This is the way things are supposed to be done, understanding this, and learning how to work in accord with it, is *the initiation* that demonstrates your worthiness to be advanced to this new horizon, and become a student of one of these Light Beings.)

Fuzzy Physics™

(Quantum Physicists and Entanglement Theory Professors say they have a gap in their model. They say that when two subatomic particles "interact", they become entangled, and when you observe one particle, it can instantaneously determine the condition of expression of the other particle. This means that if an observation is made, so as to cause one particle to spin in one direction, the other particle will begin spinning in the opposite direction. They say, this suggests that information, or an energetic connectivity of some kind, has been transferred between the "separate" particles, so as to entangle the function of their expression.

So far, this isn't too much of a stretch of the imagination, people living in this century are accustomed to energy transferring between things absent any physical connectivity, that is until physicists put those two subatomic particles light years away from one another, and they are still said to affect one another instantaneously. Suddenly, this suggests the information or "affinity binding energy" (∞) is traveling across the Galactic continuum (Y) faster than the speed of light. This "breaks" a few of their Galactic Physics (Y) rules, and so their brightest minds have labeled it "Spooky action at a distance". However, what Einstein really meant was, "This is something over the next horizon of my present perspective", he did not mean "the void of ignorance".

In the famous "Double-slit Experiment", Quantum Physicists are stipulating that particles function like waves when they're not being observed, yet function like a particle when they are being observed. They even stipulate that the particle/wave somehow holds the potential to reverse time, so as to be seen to emerge as a particle when it initially emerged as a wave. Thus, they say, "When we're not looking, everything functions as a wave of potentials in 'Superposition', and when we look at things, they collapse out of 'the superposition of infinite potential' (above a wave) and function as a given particle." While they recognize that {(Consciousness) = ("Observation by a sentient being")} changes the nature of subatomic particles, they admit to being at a loss as to quantify the cause. Thus, they say they have a "Quantum Enigma". However, what Michio Kaku really means is the same thing that Einstein did, "There's something over the next horizon of our current condition of intellect".

(In Quantum Physicist's lingo, Superposition equals Field Potential. However, in Field Physics™ lingo, Superposition comes in degrees of expression, such that we are compelled to add another descriptor, to attain a more accurate phrase to express what we're talking about. If we account for multiple realms, and each realm can be nested within another, then Superposition must come in degrees of expression for each realm.)

So, we begin Fuzzy Physics™ with "Spooky Action", and a "Quantum Enigma" trying to label an effect that seems to have no rational cause. However, what if the thing we're looking for was missing, not because it didn't exist, but because it was in a different state of conditioning, and thus over the horizon of our perception in an adjacent realm$_{+-1}$. What if the cause and effect "affinity binding energy" lay just over the horizon of our current condition to perceive its existence? Under this postulation, and our current model, we can see how Amplified Energetic, Inviscidly Conditioned, Uniform Velocity creates degrees of Superposition°, whereby things in different realms, or in different degrees of the same realm, can potentially reside in the same space-time$_{1\,2}$, not actually physically touch one another, and yet have degrees of cause and effect relationships. Field Physics™ stipulate that different conditions of different degrees of Superposition remove some of the cause and effect relationships, but not necessarily all degrees of cause and effect action. For instance, torus fields create and interlink with one another in separate realms, this would insinuate there is a kind of Entanglement Function, which potentially transcends all degrees of Superposition.

Like waves and particles, White Light and Dark Light, time and space$_{1+\text{-}\,2+\text{-}}$ exist as degrees of expression of the bandwidth of The Field, and are therefore subject to the condition of The Field, as are all things moved through, or expressed by The Field. That is, except (Intelligence = Sentience) "That which causes The Field to express itself". Remembering, that any torsion field can create twin vortexes within the torus field, and that their spin always flows in the same direction, but can appear to move in opposing directions due to the perspective of the viewer... Remembering that torsion fields cause the function of a collapse or an uncollapse of The Field, depending on whether one is viewing it from the male or female end... And, remembering that sentience appears as though its coming from The Field, expressed as, or nested within, the torsion field of White and Dark light, and that it projects that torsion field anywhere intelligence expresses itself; Or anywhere Intelligence "looks" (Page 165, Look)... Then, our first idiosyncrasy of Quantum Physics appears when we look for an "affinity binding" expression of energy to travel across the continuum of our realm (Y). As opposed to looking for something, which passes through our realm, by traveling through subspace nested below our space, or super-space nested outside of our realm's expression, via the two-way door of Field Collapse/Uncollapse, and through The Ring of Absolute Conditioning. In other words, the boarders between Quantum (X), Galactic (Y), and Field Physics™ (Z) lay, not between the infinitesimal smallness of the (X) axis, or the eternal vastness of the (Y) axis, but between the proper conditioning of "products of the Field", and the two-way door of dominion, which allows a movement between eternally vast and infinitesimally small nested realms along the (Z) axis.

When we apply the entanglement properties, as initiating from The Field, and then as White and Dark Light that pass on their entanglement properties to their torus field as that torus field moves$_{+-}$ to express itself in a given realm, and that torus field passes on its entanglement properties to other torus fields that it manifests... When these are applied to the observations of Quantum Physics in our realm... All of this means, that when a sentient intellect observes quantum functions, they're effecting its operation with the conditioning and entanglement properties of their own torsion fields, and the intelligence nested within their chakra torus fields (∞). When Quantum Physicists observe subatomic particles suddenly "entangle and spin in a counter rotation to one another", they're observing the result of the twin vortex function of their own torus field caused by the similar degree of conditioning, and nested condition of their own sentience. That which is entangled, is only doing what it has always done since it emerged from The Field, its passing on its entanglement properties in accord with the initial expression of The Architect, and its causing things to move back or forth through the two-way door of The Field.

The counter spin of a given subatomic particle reveals the female and male spins of their own torus field. The operation of the collapse of the wave into a particle is a function of an increasing degree of the expression of The Field, because of a newly introduced vortex, which affects the nesting and Hemisphere Effect of a given product of The Field. As a property of Physics, Entanglement begins with the expression of the multiplicity of fields and White and Dark Light. In the same manner that all fields pass on their entanglement properties, so too all other torsion fields pass on their entanglement and energetic properties. This can be easily proven by modifying a Quantum Physics experiment with a Colt of well-practiced Remote Viewers "turning their attention" to a target. In the same manner that direct observation by sentient consciousness modifies an experiment with the "affinity binding energy" of its attention, and not the "looking" of its eyeballs, so too when RVer's turn their attention to a target, via their psychic torsion fields, they will affect the experiment in the same manner as "looking" at it does. This function along the (Z) axis further validates The Heisenberg Uncertainty Principal of, "Whatever you study you also change", because the torsion fields of your attentive focus always effect or Entangle with "Whatever you turn your attention to". This is a basic principal and construct of The Design of The Construct of Field Physics.)

(Quantum Tunneling is a function of one or more related objects changing their energetic condition, so as to appear to pass through a given object. Whichever object is less collapsed or more energetic; this object modifies the degree of its expression toward Superposition. It moves into a different degree of uncollapsed expression in the same realm$_+$ or it uncollapses completely, makes the jump through The Field, and into an adjacent realm$_2$. In this condition of amplified energetic, inviscidly conditioned, uniformed velocity, it can reexpress itself anywhere, anytime, and in any quantity. In the case of quantum tunneling with electrons, they, or their duplicated twin, tend to reexpress themselves on the other side of their related object. However, because of the quantity or multiplicity effect, which can occur in Absolute Superposition, we cannot know for sure whether this is the same electron that made the jump.

And so it is with ocean waves. As The Program of The Architect accelerates its expression, where the ocean wave is rolling over itself, and some of the water is being conditioned toward the central ring, the water experiences Quantum Tunneling on a Newtonian scale. Similar to the collapse/uncollapse function of electrons, The Architect moves into a peak expression, 1/64th of the expression/or event can make the jump toward a degree of Superposition, while 63/64ths of the expression tends to uncollapse the expression of The Architect into visible Fractal offshoots in a conditioned condition in the same realm.

As it is with Quantum and Newtonian Tunneling, so too it is with Galactic Space Time Tunneling$_{1\,2}$. Galactic Time waves can behave in the same manner as oceanic or river waves and roll over themselves, or create torsion fields, and thus create an identical energetic condition that moves time waves or space fabric toward the central ring, and toward a higher degree of Superposition. It can move toward a greater uncollapsed state, which allows it to be in the same realm, but in a disconnected degree of expression, relative to the dominion or cause and effect of another relative object. It can move toward The Absolute Superposition of Field Potential, make the jump, and recollapse in an adjacent realm$_x$. In this new state, it would no longer relate to a relative object, except by the associative property of Entanglement. This means that space, time, and anything within the model can become detached from the current expression of space-time$_x$ in the same manner that a bucket of water can be "detached" from the ocean--- such that they exist, behave, and are inflated on their own accord. This might be said to create its own expression, dimension, or realm (∞), and then within that realm, it's inflated by the function of the same expression.

In the same manner as they left, these objects can reexpress themselves back where they were before they changed their expression. Because of the properties of Superposition, where The Architect stipulates "room" for expression, electrons can pop back into existence in this realm in any space-time they're surfed into, and in any quantity that "they want to". However, they tend to express themselves where they were going, where they would've been, or where they left from after the manner of the DiRT equation. Ocean water, space fabric, and time waves--- "products of the Field"--- multiply, jump, or reexpress themselves in the same manner. In other words, the boarders between Quantum (X), Galactic (Y), and Field Physics™ (Z) lay, not between the infinitesimal smallness of the (X) axis, or the eternal vastness of the (Y) axis, but between the proper conditioning of "products of the Field", and the two-way door of dominion, which allows a movement between all realms along the (Z) axis.)

A New Horizon

(In the same manner that particles break their bonds with gravity, and begin their relations with levity when the two-way door of dominion is moving toward the Field, so too waves break their bonds with levity to an increasing degree when they nest, or begin forming Platonic Solids in a movement toward a lower realm. As we move into a new realm of Superposition we not only separate gravity and levity from particles or waves, but we are also are separating inertia and other interrelations as well.)

(In the same manner that we're separated by different "conditions" from other more sentient life forms, who live in the same space time$_1$ as we do, so too particles and waves are only separated by the collapse uncollapse function of The Field that is determined by degrees of Superposition. Particles and waves can only be separated by space or time when two particles or two waves are in a similar degree of an expressed function. This is expressed as a single realm, where The Architect and the condition of four related variables determine the cause and effect relationships, we have an operation between space and time, and a collapse uncollapse function that determines how two particles or two waves function in relationship to one another while in a given condition. This is how fields, forces, particles, or waves, and even levity and gravity, which collapse at different degrees of Superposition°, can either have an effect on one another, have a space time relationship with one another, or otherwise "ascend" or "descend" those barriers in relationship to one another. Such that, neither my Flexible DiRT equation, Galileo's Distance Rate Time equation, nor Einstein's ($E=MC^2$) equation have any real meaning--- at least, not as we currently understand them in this realm.

In the same manner that solids and liquids function in particular manners under conditions of acceleration, coherence, incoherence, agitation, and deceleration, so too particles and waves only become separated by space-time$_{1\,2}$ when space and time are in a similarly expressed condition. Remote Viewers aren't transcending the "range" between two expressions of time and or two expressions of space. They're not "time traveling", nor are they "space traveling", in the classical sense, when they Bi-locate to view a target. In the same manner that it's mind boggling to think that Quantum Entanglement properties can be passed on across billions of miles of space instantaneously, so too it's inconceivable to believe that RVer's can jump 2,000 years of time and space instantaneously to view the events of Jesus' life.

In the same manner that Entanglement is the passing on of a quality via the collapse uncollapse function of The Field, so too RVer's are using the torsion field of their consciousness to reverse the expression and transcend their present collapsed expression. They're reconnecting with their Primary Field of Intellect via the uncollapse function, and "moving" "instantaneously" (Z) to the "other" collapsed expression that happens to reside in a different space-time. Like two torus fields in two different realms, which constantly feed into one another, this universal function of Field Physics then operates in reverse to return the information to the viewer. The properties of Entanglement, and the intellects of Remote Viewers, are not moving across Galactic space (Y) or through Galactic time, they're using the conditioning of torsion fields to transcend space and time (Y), with the very tool that directs the function of The Field and products of The Field.

So, we don't time travel--- as in getting in a Delorean and leaping back to the year 1955 to accidentally mess up the timeline with the Grandfather Paradox. Nor do we space travel--- as in getting in a rocket ship and traveling to the moon like Neil, Buzz, and Michael. We use the uncollapse and collapse function of The Field to translate into different expressions of space and time. We don't "move" either, we altar our expression via sentient intention and Amplified Energetic, Inviscidly Conditioned, Uniform Acceleration with natural and mechanical advantages, and transcend from one expression of collapse to another expression, which just so happens to expresses itself in a different space and or time; from one place in the same bucket; or to another place in an entirely different bucket. Like RV and Quantum Entanglement, our intellect is intentionally "surfed" by the Intelligent Sentience residing at Field Potential from one collapse to another via the conduits of the inverse expression of torsion fields (∞).)

The Sacred Calf

(While well respected in many cultures, and fully functional within the realm of Galactic Physics, The Einstein Rosen Bridge Theory is an idiosyncrasy after the same manner of Darwinism. In the same manner that Darwinism is a "science" based on the function of the bandwidth of what the eyes can see, so too concluding that mass is bending space, so as to explain how photons from a distant star are making their way around our sun, is still just a rudimentary observation with what our eyes can observe, and a function of intellect looking through the lens of a culture, discipline, or expression of a life form. Moreover, in the model of Field Physics, Newtonian Physics are but a limited observation of only a small range of cause and effect. The human observation that created Newtonian Physics is nested within a wider range of an ever-changing two-way door of expression, where fundamental constants modify their behavior and expression within the totality of the bandwidth of its expression and dominion.

When we think of light from a distant star being distorted around another star, we should automatically think of light being surfed through nested space distortions and time wave viscosities, automatically think of light being surfed along the hypotenuse of a wave (C^2) or around the spin of a torsion field (K), and automatically think of light making the jump back and forth from The Field through a magnetosphere's central ring. From the inception of its origin, across all galactic space-time, there are dominions, distortions, and changing conditions that are affecting the function, direction, trajectory, and behavior of light. When light is conditioned by the magnetosphere of a star, as it is in The Einstein Rosen Bridge Theory, we must immediately think of the plethora of conditions that could

349

be causing the effect, which defines Galactic Physics. As light is traversed through space distortions and time waves, it's ending up in an altogether new space and time$_1$. In another manner, it's surfed along the hypotenuse of a linear (C^2) or curved (K) trajectory to a new space-time$_1$. In a third manner, when light is conditioned by a torus field, such as when a photon passes a star, its properties are going to be conditioned by that body's magnetosphere, such that it could transcend to a higher Superposition$^\circ$, and make any number of jumps$_{1\,2}$ to radically new expressions and a vast multiplicity of appearances.

When we add the distortions, waves, surfing, and jumping of light as possible causes and effects of a photon from a distant star ending up in the wrong location, because it crossed the path of our star, there enters "The Uncertainty Principal" about which "effect" The Einstein Rosen Bridge Theory is trying to describe. To those who would give anything to salvage the status quo, The Triquetra of Field, Quantum, and Galactic Physics logically reason that we can no longer say The Einstein Rosen Bridge is only about a distortion in the continuum. It is a distortion of space, which is actually the function of a collapsing Field expressing itself. It's a time wave that moves light to a new space-time$_1$, so as to make it appear where/when it doesn't seem to belong. It's the expression of light between degrees of Superposition, so as to make it jump, multiply, and or appear in a radically new space-time-realm$_{1\,2\,x}$. Just as it can be explained by all three effects, it could just as well be any permutation of a degree of the three effects. Rather than bickering about the fatted calf, or worrying about the status quo, we have to find out where in the Fuzzy Physics™ we are (Page 43, Vastness, not holiness).)

(What we're seeing every day; "our reality", is not a result of particles and waves, space and time, or even a realm or dimension. These are all just things we label and sort into disciplines in order to express, or otherwise come to a greater understanding, of what we're experiencing. Everything we experience is an expression of a Field. What we see in our everyday lives are degrees of the expression of a Field as it moves through a two-way door. We're looking at many expressions of a Field nested within other expressions of a Field. We're observing a singular Source Field expressing itself in an infinitesimally small and eternally vast multiplicity of Fields, which transcend the perceptions of the human condition. It's all connected, it's all One, but like an onion, the condition of our present intellect forces us to perceive it in layers, or as New Horizons.

Therefore, when we look around, we have to realize that all things, expressed, collapsed, or realized are malleable by the inverse function of their expression. In this realization, we have to understand that all things yet exist "somehow somewhere" in this "two-way door" of universal expression. So, when we see something or someone go over the horizon of our perspective, we have to understand that they aren't so much as perishing or going away, as much as they're just uncollapsing back toward The Absolute Superposition of Field Potential. The chakra fields in which their Intelligence was nested ceased to function in the manner as they were expressed, so of course that photonic energetic Intelligence, which resided in those nested fields, had to return to its initial range of expression.

In this realization, we don't just postulate that "people go to heaven" where all things are "As they should be", we have to understand that The Garden of Eden is still there too. In the same manner that all torus fields are created at a higher condition, and then "descend" or collapse into this nested realm of expression, so too this perfect condition, which mankind was created in, where everything is more paradisiacal, still exists. It yet remains, in the continuum of its initial expression, the Superposition° of its Field, and the bucket of its expression. In the same manner that one field is eternally entangled with all fields that came from its initial expression, so too The Paradise of Heaven, and the perfect function of Eden, are intrinsically Entangled with all Fields that were created from that Field. Quite literally, and in every since of the meaning, Paradise is eternally Entangled with our Heart Field Chakra, and we are infinitesimally Entangled with the line of our lineage that goes back to it.

When we cross the Biblical, Quran, or Tora references of mankind's exodus from Eden under our New Fruit of Awareness, we see a few things that allow us to "translate" the text; not "differently"--- but from another perspective, a Vast Paradigm. The first is that the Light Beings spoken of earlier are the Cherubs, the heavenly guardians, living at a higher condition between us and the "Paradise of Eden" or "Heaven". Then comes a flaming sword that moves in every direction. Notice, in the text, the Cherubim are not wielding the sword, they just so happen to be in front of its function; watching, guarding. When we compare the flaming sword that moves in every direction with White and Dark Light, as they move in every direction through a torus field, then we can begin to see that this is the "thing" which "separates°" us from The Field. It's not a "weapon" in the classical since that holds us back, as much as it's a tool, a mechanism, or contraption. The Light Beings are guardians of the gate, and like Percival "The Virtuous" in the legend of King Arthur, "Only the worthy are allowed to pass". This is why there must be a master student relationship, and the student must attain a condition described by Kami-no-michi, or The

Middle Way of The Path, before they become worthy of entering The Chamber of Initiation.

The Way of The Path is that Dominion which allows us to slowly emerge from the darkness of ignorance. To transform into a condition where Virtue, Truth, and Compassion are the point, the reward, and The First Initiation. The Path of The Three Great Quests is that Dominion that allows us to emerge from the suffering of bondage. To transform into a condition where each Quest amplifies our rewards, light of awareness, and becomes The Second Initiation. The Chamber of Initiation is ascendency, a singularity of all things, a movement into a condition where the condition itself is the point, the reward, and transformative elixir of endless possibilities, all rolled into one glorious package. They reincarnate us out of the ashes of yesterday, and into The Flying Phoenix of tomorrow. The Chamber of Initiation is the Third Initiation.)

Vastness

(If the first and last thought was virtue, then the first and last principal would be Vastness.)

(In chapter one we spoke of a Force, a condition of being, a Source, a Source Field, a Power that the ancients were well aware of, but which our more recent ancestors had somehow forgotten. We said it was a "Pearl of Great Price", something so intrinsically valuable that its worth would exceed every other lifelong endeavor. We said that greed can't steal it, ignorance couldn't pilfer it, and fear wouldn't even see it if it were sitting in front of them. We said it was a Path that must be walked, a journey that must be taken, and a Quest that must be achieved. Now you know that it's Three Initiations that must be earned, achieved, bestowed, and finally, ascended guardians who might allow you to pass.

The energy we desire to harness to illuminate our world exists in a realm that is over the horizon of the human perspective, but it's most certainly not out of reach. Like gravity and inertia, light only gives its illumination in the realm of its degree of expression, but a two-way door can be opened so this special Light can shine down, and illuminate us with its radiant glory. In the same manner that assembling satellite dishes all over the world, creates an electronic web of interconnectivity, so too the more Pyramid Mandalas that are properly constructed, the more the properties of one realm will be able to transfer via the "Fuzzy Physics™" that exists between realms.

From any realm, Source Field Energy can be energetically amplified, inviscidly conditioned, and uniformly accelerated, so as to open a doorway. Because this doorway only works in one direction at a time, we either place things in its Ring of Coherence so as to move 1/64th "of that which it's composed" into a higher state of Superposition to be "treated". Or, we reverse the doorway, so as to allow all manner of properties of another realm to shine into our realm.

We know the introduction of a female torsion field moves things toward Superposition°, or in a movement toward Absolute Field Potential. We know that the introduction of agitation causes "that which is in a higher condition of Superposition°" to recollapse its expression back into its original expression. The disruption of a torsion field, via agitation, is a "closing of the door", but it's not a "reversal" of that door. So, how do we make the doorway go in both directions?

Thinking back to the inception of The Initiation Chamber, we see how the door flips both ways when a female torus field sends its energy into another realm, and that other torus field returns it back. In the second part of the same section, we see that the heart chakra conceives more torus fields within the same life form. It uses the twin torsion fields of the Cube Octahedron to point up and down, so as to energetically direct where those torus fields should collapse in this realm. Then it makes one on top, then flips energetically to make another one on the bottom, and it continues in a sequential "above" then "below", and "here$_1$" then "there$_2$" manner to make six fields in two realms (12).

In the same manner that a pyramid harnesses ambient Source Field Energy like an antenna, so too octahedrons initiate the same energetic collapse-sequence. However, rather than being a one way-door, octahedrons flip the energy back and forth. In this manner, not only do we open the door in one direction, but construct a model that allows that door to flip back and forth. With pyramids, the door is either open or shut in one direction, but with octahedrons, the door is always opened and is either flipped one way or the other. This is how the two-way door opens in both directions, and why the heart chakra must design only one other chakra field at a time in a flipping or trading manner.

Is it Poetic Irony or just the eternal nature of the universe; "As Above, So Below", that this is the exact same function of Nikola Tesla's Alternating Current Device? Could the mechanism and greater purpose of our Dolphin's "Dentem Musical Intellect" suddenly be revealed, as they squeak and communicate through the rings of torus fields? At what distances are they communicating? With whom are they communicating? In addition, what messages can return in this manner? If the student has truly comprehended and absorbed the material, then the answer can be summed up in a single word, Vastness...)

Transformative Light

(Pyramids have a counter effect on poisons, not so much because of the spinning of torsion fields, but because of the nature of The Hemisphere Effect within torus fields, torsion fields, and pyramids. If the torsion fields of poisons are said to be spinning clockwise; negatively: as we understand the two halves of The Hemisphere Effect, their classification resides in the southern hemisphere, and that they're spinning after the manner of the male torsion field. Their Field Direction is moving toward expression, collapsing their function toward a lower realm, and their dominate characteristic is Dark Light, and the expulsion or scattering of White Light.

In carbon based life forms, at our degree of expression, the scattering of all bandwidths of White Light allows ill health to enter the construct, because "things don't work as they're meant to" without the proper amounts and bandwidths of light which an entity is using to express itself with. It's not so much that the absorbing of White Light causes all manner of ill health to diminish, as much as it causes all manner of things to "work as they are meant to". This is not like "curing" the patient, as one would with an inoculation or surgery, but by manipulating the fundamental constants via natural and mechanical "conditioning", such that ill health diminishes, and good health returns.

		$Realm_1$		$Realm_2$	
Hemisphere		North	South	North	South
Dominate	»	White Light •	Dark Light =	Dark Light •	White Light
Recessive	»	Dark Light	White Light =	White Light	Dark Light

(Uncollapse) « » (Superposition) « » (Collapse)

If a poisonous product is placed in the Northern Hemisphere of a pyramid, The Hemisphere Effect of the female torsion field will begin reversing the poison's expression. The female torsion field will begin uncollapsing the poison's particle expression toward a higher degree of Superposition. As this conditioning increases with time, or energetic intensity, the dominion effect of the poison's fields will begin to break their bonds with this realm, and it will have less of an effect on anyone or anything associated with it (28 lunar days/1 lunar cycle). In the same manner that we use agitation to interrupt a torsion field, and collapse a product from a higher state of Superposition°, so too reversing The Hemisphere Effect of a product's torsion fields will impede its damaging effects, via the conditioning of the opposing torsion field, and the dominion of "The Northern Hemisphere Effect".

Because The Southern Hemisphere Effect includes the scattering of Light, the other half of this equation must include the adding of Light. So, not only does the torsion field have to spin in the correct female direction in a movement toward The Field, and bring in Amplified Energetic, Inviscidly Conditioned, Uniformly Accelerated Source Field Energy, but it must also add Conditioned White Light from The Field. In the same manner that torsion fields descend from higher degrees of expression, so too White Light is a "bandwidth product" of the Field that is conceived from the Field. It exists in greater quantities in higher realms, and it can transcend down into lower degrees of expression, if the proper doorways are opened. Or in our case, flipping back and forth, like Tesla's AC device.)

(When we set up The Triple Pentagonal Layer of our Biological Photon Pyramid Obelisk Mondala, we create 15 enhanced Female Torsion Fields. The counterclockwise spin of those Female Torsion Fields work together in a circular pattern to manifest a singular central Source Field Female torsion field in their midst. This Female Source Field torsion field is not restrained by the collapsed expression of a physical product which could impede its energetic flow. Thus, unlike those fields which created it, this free floating female torsion field can attain a greater energetic magnitude. It will "surf" "of that which it's comprised" at a more "Field Reflective" velocity and energetic condition.

Within, but not touching, the cone of the structure-less energetic female torsion field, we construct another antenna obelisk shaped after the sloping manner of the Eifel Tower in Paris. Rather than constructing a pyramidal crown, the central obelisk has an octahedral crown. In the same manner that it's the design of Tesla's Alternating Current device to energetically flip back and forth, because of the nature of polarities, so too the doorway will energetically flip back and forth, because of the nature of octahedrons, the nature of torsion fields, and the design behind our Phi (Φ) Proportionate Mandala.

The conditions of the fabric of reality within the cone of the central female torsion field, which encompasses the central obelisk, are enhanced, conditioned, or otherwise amplified. Everyone and everything within the cone or Ring is Superpositioned° into the Fuzzy Physics that exists between Realms. The two-way door of the central obelisk is flipping back and forth, and White Light from a higher realm is fully available to amplify the construct of our expression.)

Riding The Lightning

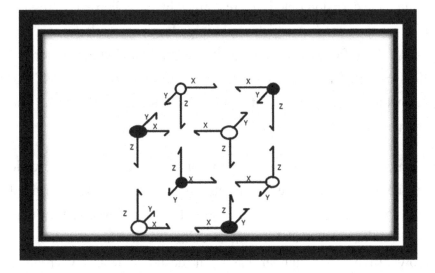

(The model represented is a triple (X, Y, Z) axis in the geometry of a cube. The (X) axis moves toward infinitesimal smallness, and represents a movement toward or away from Quantum Physics (X). The (Y) axis moves toward infinite vastness, or back and forth across the space-time continuum {(C^2) hypotenuse}, and represents Galactic Physics (Y). In addition, the (Z) axis moves back and forth between realms, and represents Field Physics (Z). With this model, we can represent different movements, relationships, Substitutions, and functions.)

(The Affinity binding energy, the conduits of a torsion field, and that which initiates the associative property of Entanglement, are those silver cords (∞) in infinite vastness that bind magnetospheres across the space-time continuum and between realms (Y) (Z), as well as those silver cords in infinitesimal smallness that connect our chakras between realms (X) (Z). In the same manner that The Architect and torus fields are universal expressions and fundamental constants of the Field, so too silver cords are universal constructs and fundamental constants of the Field. If the egg of energy came before the chicken, then the first products of the Field, White and Dark Light, which compose a silver cord, came before The Architect or torus field. However, even though we stipulate that one came before the other, this observation is the same as making an argument as to where a circle begins or ends, because the silver cord is the torus field, and the torus field is the silver cord. Both envelop The Architect, Nest Intelligence, and morph between one another in an eternal loop of expression. Like the flip function, the silver cord and the torus field are just different expressions of the same White and Dark Light. Depending on their condition of expression, they use The Hemisphere Effect, The Entanglement Function, and The Flip Function to define the behavior of their given expression.

Initiating with The Entanglement Function, White and Dark Light create the silver cord. As they collapse into an expression, the silver cord uses the Flip Function to initiate a torus field, this invokes The Hemisphere Effect. When White and Dark Light have circumnavigated their field, they invoke the Entanglement Function again between similar expressions of different hemispheres. The invocation of The Entanglement Function allows the silver cord to be created again, thus, when White and Dark light move into the central ring the flip function can once again occur. White and Dark Light, expressed as a torus field under the dominion of The Hemisphere Effect, become infinitely elastic in a movement between space-time-realms$_x$ as they move into the conditioning effects of the central ring. This infinite elasticity can be expressed as (K) or (Z). Where (K) is a Substitution in the DiRT equation for (C^2), so as to measure a given course and condition of The Architect within a torsion field. Geometrically, this can be expressed as a movement from the Hypotenuse of a triangle, to a Fibonacci Circle, or Pi circle. In addition, (Z) is representative of a movement into a higher realm, without necessarily moving in space-time. The silver cord moves toward Absolute Superposition of Field Potential, it duplicates its expression in another realm, and returns this function to the original torus field, which initiates the creation of a third field. In this model, we have the creation of our first geometric pattern, a triangle of torus fields connected by an energetically driven silver cord (180f). A step into vastness would be to think of this in terms of Platonic Solids; where each line of a Platonic Solid is represented as a silver cord, and each node of a Platonic Solid is represented as a torus field, or an (X, Y, Z) axis corner on any given Platonic Solid.)

(There is a silver cord connecting any given torus field to another torus field, which forms a plethora of geometrical patterns. In infinitesimal smallness--- this might look like eddies spinning in water, which are energetically intertwined by a silver lasso that bounces around the water like a walking Slinky creating new connections and new eddies according to The Program of The Architect («K»). It might also look like all the torus fields in your construct connecting to one another. This, whether it be on the torsion field of a double helix on your DNA, or your chakras holding onto one another with silver lassos. First, they send out a silver cord (Z) to create and link to one another in their opposing realms, and then each torus field connects to one another in the same realm via the function of Superposition. Second, the mother and father torus fields create a silver cord that entangles the "children" torus fields, which they create, to both parents (Δ). This creates our first trifecta of silver cord connectivity, expressed geometrically as a triangle (180f) among different entities. Third, those children torus fields entangle themselves after the manner of their parents, to create other "grandchildren" torus fields. Looking at this model one dimensionally, we would see a repeating grid of triangles, whose nodes were torus fields. Looking at this model three dimensionally, we would see a repeating grid of triangles, whose nodes were torus fields, whose lines were silver cords, and whose overall geometrical shape was a vast sphere. Looking at this model in Vastness, we would see the repeating grid of triangles, whose torus field nodes created a multiplicity of silver cord connected spheres that were Entangled in many realms. They would create every Platonic Solid, and they would create every Ordered Nesting of Platonic Solids. Not only would one see The Flower of Life Pattern emerge in terms of spheres and curved lines (K), but also it would be just as easy to measure it in terms of straight lines (C^2). If one were looking through Albert Einstein's eyes, and recall the ($E=MC^2$) equation, where we have all solids on one side, and all energy on the other side, then one could see how all of this connective geometrical patterning was the energetic view of solids.

Moving toward Vastness (Y) (Z)--- The Silver Cord Effect looks like hurricanes and tornados, whose silver lassos extend up or down to the magnetosphere, such that the energetic movement of the exterior torus field governs their nested behaviors without ever being in the same realm. It looks like planetary-magnetospheres creating their duplicate through the Field in an opposing realm. First, sending out an infinitely elastic silver cord to their opposing realm, and then each magnetosphere connecting to one another in the same realm via a conduit of a higher or lower realm. Second, its mother and father magnetospheres universally connecting to the constructs of their magnetosphere's "offspring". Third, like hurricanes and tornados attaching themselves to their exterior torus field, these galactic magnetospheres connect with the galaxy's magnetosphere. Fourth, those new torus fields begin "entangling" with other expressed torus fields--- depending on The Hemisphere Effect, The Nesting Effect, and Node Effects. In infinitesimal smallness or eternal vastness (X, Y, Z), the silver cord is a universal function of Field Physics, a conduit that connects torus fields in the same manner that a brain connects dendrites.

Moving toward infinitesimal smallness (X) (Z) --- The Pineal Gland is located at the central node of a torus field, where one's left or right handedness can reveal which direction one's torus field is angled, relative to their left or right eye or left or right brain hemispheres. Energized after the manner of the central ring, the Pineal Gland is the amalgamation of the body, mind and soul, as much as it's the space-time-realm hub for the Flip, Jump, Entanglement, Torus Field, and Silver Cord Functions. While in Superposition (Z), the functions of this central "hub" can be both naturally and mechanically amplified (X, Y, Z).)

(Are Silver Cords Wormholes? A better question would be, "Is a wormhole a Silver Cord?" The concept of a silver cord is at least as old as The Bible (Ecc 12:6), as ancient as the Egyptians, and even more understood by the Sumerians. Whereas, "Wormhole", as a method of travel, is a phrase or idea, which has only been recently coined. Besides, "Worm" insinuates an idiosyncratic perspective of a long degree of length between point (A) and (B); wherein with a Silver Cord, the idea of long lengths between two points separated by galactic distances is as short as the model of a torus field.

Our Light Being Teachers are not "darting" through the skies in UFO's, as much as they're creating a silver cord and "riding" it along an (X, Y, or Z) axis. To those who are observing them from this realm, their movements appear to be lightening quick, full of jerks, and incomprehensible accelerations. However, as they move toward Superposition (Z), they're removing interrelations like gravity and inertia. Thus, for those riding the lightening to or from Field Potential, it's like a gentle ride in a luxury sedan, because one does not move along the (Y) axis. However, riding a (Z) axis from Field Potential, might feel like coming out of the water onto land after swimming all day, where the buoyancy of water is replaced by the increasing pull of gravity, inertia, and other increasing interrelations. Riding a (Y) axis in either direction would feel like a surfer being driven by a wave, one would feel push, pull, yaw, roll, and pitch of every distortion and viscosity change--- a rough and tumble ride.

We use waves to dam electrons, and geometry in the form of antennas to transmit and receive those electronic waves--- waves of information or waves of electricity. Using geometry and resonance, with the function of the silver cord, we could transmit and receive information over truly vast distances instantaneously; just like Dolphins. In the same manner that Tesla Coil Technology puts electrons into the air via the radio-wave function (K»), and in the same manner that waves nest levity, so too silver cords can transmit Source Field Energy, electricity, or any other idea for fuel (photonic), which can be uncollapsed into a wave, and transmitted through the "eye" of the silver cord over infinitesimally vast distances. In this manner, vehicles would never require refueling stations. One could create a hub, where a fuel source is collected, transmit the information or utility in the form of a wave through the eye of the silver cord (Z), and inject it directly into the engine of the vehicle. As long as the product can be placed inside a silver cord, or otherwise uncollapsed, then it has a means of containment, and universal transmission. Why are UFO's so small? They're not limited in their fuel capacity. Ground vehicles, airplanes, Galaxy Class Star Ships, all means of conveyance could constantly receive "all manner of resupply" on an ongoing basis. One could then use multiple types of engines on the same vehicle to accomplish a wide variety of tasks. The Silver Cord should give the phrase, "Beam me up Scotty!" a completely new meaning.

Silver Cord Damming-tech is a means of using torus fields and silver-tubes to transmit$_F$, receive$_M$, or otherwise manipulate products of the Field. The geometry to create different torus fields, which have their own unique bandwidth function, are basic Platonic Solids, and the bandwidth of frequencies (f). Two inverted tetrahedrons create one torus field at a certain frequency, in the same manner that a cube creates a torus field at another frequency. An octahedron creates another kind of torus field at yet another frequency. This is just as true for the Icosahedron, as it is for Thoth's sacred Dodecahedron, each one resonating at particular frequencies to create their own torus field, and each model can be used like antennas to send and receive products of the Field.

So, remember the flip function? Wherein shapes can be transformed into their opposing shape in another realm? What antenna do you think sends and which antenna do you think receives across realms? In the same manner that one might block out frequencies, which interfere with the function of a machine after the manner of a Faraday Cage, so too one could nest harmonically active Platonic Solids to recreate The Realm Effect. Wherein the most internal structure is blocked from receiving any interference patterns, which might be transmitted in the air, such as a radio wave. Once the nested geometry is active, it can move its products toward Superposition in an uninhibited fashion, and travel along the (Z) axis while not moving along the (X) or (Y) axis. It can stay in the same space-time location, but move toward Superposition, along a silver cord.

In the same manner that all of our technology is based on damming, so too all of their technology is based on the silver cord, and its inverse relationship with the torus field. Our Light Being Friends are not just riding the lightening; they're using it in the same manner that we would use damming technology, by applying it to everything in their lives. Silver Cords and torus fields are a means of treating food, manipulating DNA, and improving crops. One can use them to manipulate weather patterns, as well as improve soil conditions. One could use them for thought transference, as easily as one could use them to download or upload the collective unconscious. There is virtually no application to which silver cords and torus fields do not apply.)

Morphic Field Generators

(In the 18th Century, Ernst Chladni rubbed a violin bow on a metallic plate covered in sand, such that different harmonies revealed a variety of geometric shapes. He named these shapes "Caladni Figures". In more modern times, Hans Jenny coined the name "Cymatics", which means "Wave" in Greek (κυματικς.), his claim to fame, might be thought of as taking the next step of Ernst, and modeling interference patterns. While Cymatics has become better known than Caladni Figures in our time, both descriptions fall short in fully describing the effect that both men were looking at.

In The Way of The Path and from the Creations of The Source, these effects are a continuance of The Nesting Effect of The Design of The Construct. The effects produced are not quite a wave, and they're not quite a structure, once again, it's an effect of The Nesting of The Construct along a permutation of nesting Platonic Orders in wave or fluid-particle form. The "event" falls between the collapse, wherein waves nest into solids, or the uncollapse function, wherein solids transfer back into waves. This is the exact reason why the operation works so well in water, and can be described as the "operation" of Living Water. If a "more accurate" name could be ascribed--- "Nested Harmonic Designs of The Construct" would be a good name, since they clearly reveal The Nesting Function as a universal effect of The Construct along its entire bandwidth of expression. But lo', "N.H.D.C." lacks the alluring swagger of "Cymatics".

Using the designs of the first three machines with the universal nesting operations of The Construct reveals a New Horizon as to exactly what is causing these machines to operate. In the same manner that a pyramid is a geometric antenna that picks up Source Field Energy, so too Cymatics are merely a frequency pattern that harnesses Source Field Energy. In both cases, it's The Source Field Energy they're harnessing that actually does the work, not the geometry of a pyramid or the wave of Cymatics. In the same manner that Ordered Nesting Platonic Solids carry the property of gravity, so too each nested order carry's specific functions of Source Field Energy. In the same manner that a wave carries the property of levity, so too the frequencies of Cymatics are picking up bandwidths of Source Field Energy. While one collapses the function to a wave expression, and the other collapses the function to a particle expression, this observation reveals a common function between geometry and resonance, which can be used in accord with one another, so as to amplify their common operation of harnessing Source Field Energy.

Like the wide variety of geometrically based Mandalas that are said to have a certain "ring" to them, so too a Cymascope reveals nested geometries that one could use to amalgamate the resonant and the geometric as One. In the same manner that one would use nested pentagons to attain the 1.618 to 1 ratio, which shows the precise nodal locations where one should place their obelisks, so too one could create a Cymatic pattern that reveals a new base Mandala with which to station torsion field producing structures on. Like the nested pentagons, each machine could then be "specialized" to harness a specific Source Field related function.

The Way of The Path is that Triquetra, wherein an added effect is achieved when three things are used as one. Ironically, it's the repeated design of the Triquetra in The Flower of Life Geometry that reveals our new Mandala. Placing an obelisk on the nodes of a Flower of Life Mandala with Cymatic "type" frequencies further amplifies the nature of the overall construct. The final third ingredient, of course, is consciousness with emotional content.

Our base intent is to build a two-way "Morphic Field Generator". Harnessing Source Field Energy allows consciousness to "draw out" the effects of the Field as easily as it allows one to "imprint into" the morphic field with amplified Source Field Energy. Like checking out a book, or donating a book to the library, we can add our own input to the collective unconscious, just as easily as we can retrieve things from it. By building these Morphic Field Generators, consciousness has a mechanical advantage to get out of its nested environment and in touch with the Field.

"The Romeo and Juliet Syndrome", are those human events that replay themselves in every generation, culture, and eon. It's almost as if we can't help but want to rout "The dogs of The House of Capulet", as much as we can't help but fall in love, or experience unrequited love. What if some ancient culture, such as the Atlanteans, built a hall of records, wherein they stashed all of their collective knowledge. However, rather than just building a solid structure, what if they constructed a powerful Morphic Field Generator Library? Something that comprised all of the elements of our machines, so as to mate it perfectly with the Field. The imprint that this Universal Library would have on the Field would have long-term profound effects on all those life forms within every layer of that nested environment. It could even go so far as to compel them to "replay" the events of the literature without ever actually being aware of it. It would be like a computer game, wherein the player who is represented as the machine (antagonist) is compelled to fight the same battle according to a set of preprogrammed codes imprinted into the machine itself. It would seem to the antagonist that they could never change their experience, or truly think for themselves. They would just go on year after year repeating the same patterns, and experiencing the same events cloaked with a new mask. Nevertheless, what if one day they realized how to construct one of these machines, learned how to become free of the effects of a previous code, and began adding their own code to the Field? Would that not be a genuine manner to emerge from the bondage of a predetermined fate?)

(If the salvation of one can depend upon the voice of another, then the education of one can depend on the wisdom, knowledge, and understanding of another. The function of a Morphic Field Generator is to "Thin The Veil" between realms. The purpose of a Morphic Field Generator is to communicate, program, or otherwise liberate ourselves from a repeating cycle.

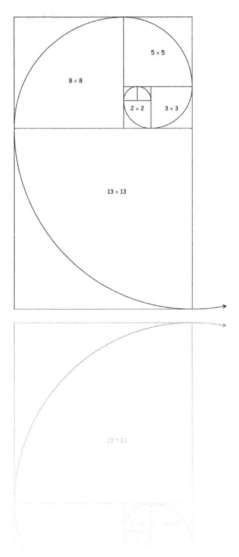

The construct of our three machines lacks a single aspect. They don't draw in Source Field Energy from distant locations$_x$. While they communicate "Torus field to Silver Cord" within their own ream, they only draw in$_F$ energy that is in the vecinity of the structure. In the same manner that our first three machines nest circles within circles, so too The Fibonicci Spiral nests circles nested within circles. In the same manner that our first three machines nest proper ratios by using pentagonal star patterns, so too the Fibonicci Spiral attains nested geometries according to The Program of The Architect. Placing torsion field producing structures along the female spiral, or at those locations where the straight male lines on the female spiral intersect with the curved female lines, will draw distant ambient Source Field Energy along the female curve to a central location. This design guides ambient Source Field Energy to the "crossroads of a circle", which has no substance of expression. Like the central circle of the torus field, this "point" has no material expression.

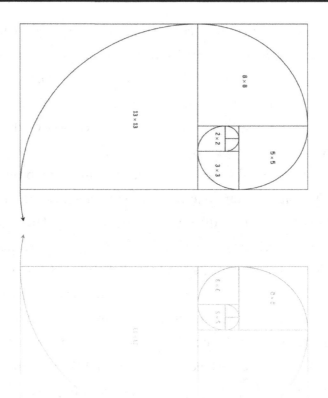

Using the male grid as a base from which to orient our formless central circle, if we rotate the spiral 90°, we will find that we can draw in Source Field Energy along another vector. Moreover, when it reaches the center this vector, it will meld with the curve of the first vector, and continue to twist the energy at the central ring.

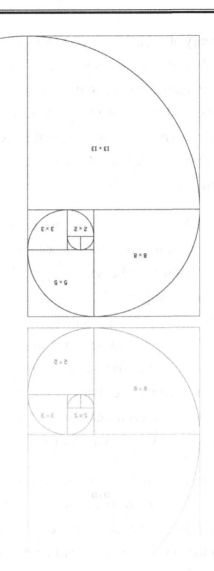

Once again, we turn the spiral another 90°. We can either use the four corners of the central square of the male grid, or we can use the same male crossed intersection as a base from which to orient our central circle. Either way, consistency is paramount to keeping the vectors praportional. Once again, we find that this design draws in

Source Field Energy along a third vector. And, once again, the center of this vector will meld with the energy from first and second vectors and continue to twist the energy into a central ring. This is done a total of four times. This model allows us to draw distant Source Field Energy from each of the four cardinal directions and create a complete central ring that is loaded with Field Potential, yet doesn't possess any form of solid structure.)

(While the sky is the limit with things we could elect do with this model, in this example we will use it in accord with the base model of The Path: The Triquetra. We will connect, think, and act, in the same manner that we employ Virtue, Truth, and Compassion--- as One. We will connect with Virtuous thoughts on our mind, while at the same time we will feel Virtuous emotions in our heart. We will think about great and noble Truths, while at the same time we feel Honor in our heart. We will act with compassion on our thoughts, while at the same time we feel the emotion of Compasion in our heart. In each step, our Heart and mind are focused as One.

Its not so much that we will pray for something to arrive, as much as we will use focus, visualization, and emotion as if the thing we desired were already present. For instance, if I stood in the central ring and prayed for rain, I would not call out to The Source and ask The Source to send rain. I wouldn't attempt to "Bring the rain", as much as I would "connect" and become "One" with The Source and the rain. I would clear my thoughts, center my emotions, and walk into the circle with a clear goal and focused intent. I begin by visualizing rain (Sight). I recall what falling rain sounds like (Sound). I recall what rain smells or tastes like (Smell/taste). I recall the texture and temprature of how mud feels squishing between my toes. I recall how the rain feels spattering on my face when I look up (Temps/Textures). While I'm doing this, I feel how virtuous it is to "bring life giving rain", feel the honor of knowing how a good rain prepares and heals the land, and I feel Compassion that the rain--- like the sun--- falls for the altruistic advantage for everyone and everything. When I am done, I don't so much claim to have created something, so much as to know that I have become One with something. In this case, that I have become One with The Source and the rain; Triquetra.

There is another aspect that can be added to the model, and while it is not necessary, it can be advantagous. By constructing a circular pool of water at the central ring, we create an element of expression that The Source Field can charge. In the vision, there are Samurai laying/floating on their backs in the circular pool of water. All of them are holding hands, concentrating on pushing Ki/Prana through one another, and into the last person. After off gassing with a deep breathing exercise, the last man releases his hand from the others, rolls face down, and "goes deeper" into his meditation. Under these conditions, their bodies are completely still, devoid of stimulation, and are therefore able to attain a deeper state of connection, thought, and action within the intent of their meditation. Similar to Sensory Deprivation Chambers, this offers a greater window "Creative Purpose" time, without the radical isolationism. In Remote Viewing, this might also be labeled as "Cascade".

After the individual has had their experience, he or she will surface, roll over on their back, and reconnect with the group by holding hands. From the last person who went under to the next person who is about to go under, each member of the group continually pushes Mana into the person next to them, so the Chi ends up in the last person who is about to go under. The design of the model allows for a maximum harnessing of Source Field Energy within the central ring. The abscence of a construct allows for a more "real velocity" of a torus field with no torsion field producing structure.

An additional advantage, of this aspect of the model, is that The Source Field can charge the water while the people are off doing other things. Like naturally existing torsion fields that push Source Field Energy into the ground, so too water that is charged with Source Field Prana can be used for a wide variety of "life force" enhancing purposes. For instance, now that we know the universal conduit of the Silver Cord is the transmitter and reciever for for virtually everything, we can look upon this model as a kind of nexus, or "control pannel" for the Matrix. We can water the garden of our minds as easily as we can water the gardens of the fields with this life force charged water. Remember, once the water has entangled with other water in the pool, it will maintain its entanglment properties while it is away from the pool. Suddenly this model becomes Vast very quickly. Can you imagine hundreds of these devices set along rivers, locked in a constant recycling process?)

(Why do we do all of this? What does it mean? When we look at random number generators (REG's), and observe extreme human events make "waves" in the collective consciousness, we realize these waves are effecting entire regions, because millions of people are experiencing the same thing. Human thought effects the "pool" of the collective consciousness, so when a few million people feel shock and awe at an event, it creates a giant wave of that kind of consciousness, which travels along the Silver Cord of ley lines to effect everyone. In other words, the collective consiousness of humanity mimics the behavior of ocean waves, time waves, and even nested Platonic

Orders. And you thought we were just talking about the outside world "As Above, So Below".

Like the model of a hurricane, one can create local storms, just as easily as one can create the central ring of absolute calm. One can inject or withdrawl their connections, thoughts, and actions into this model as easily as one can inject or withdrawl Virtue, Truth, and Compassion. Moreover, it does not require a million people to create effective waves in the collective consciousness, it only requires a mechanical advantage to a natural phenomenon. This model, this Morphic Field Generator, is the ultimate "Wave Pool Control Panel" to the Matrix. Before we can continue understanding Morphogenic Fields, we must pause here and learn about "Substitutions".)

Substitutions

Through mathematical disciplines, the soul has an organ,
Which is purified and enlightened.
An organ that is better worth saving
Than ten thousand physical eyes
Since Truth becomes visible through this alone.

Plato

(The classical meaning of "Substitution" is just "to put in place of another". While sometimes, the intent is to "repair", other times the intent is to reveal something that cannot otherwise be detected, unless one is able to compare the replaced item with the new item. This second method is intended to model our Euclidean "tertiary additive effect". "Through mathematical disciplines" the following Substitutions are designed to have a cumulative effect, which thrusts the student's intellect into hyper-drive. Not so much to take the student over many New Horizons of Understanding, but to strike their inner Phoenix with The Thunderbolt of Enlightenment, and change the course of their lives forever.)

(Worldwide methods of measuring geometry, counting music, and tabulating time trace back to the ancient Sumerians and Sexagesimal System. Their measuring systems for geometry, music, and time are based on the interrelationships of common denominators between disciplines, such as 3, 9, 12, 24, and 60. For instance, the triangle has a geometric sum of 180 degrees of its interior angles, is equivalent to 3 hours, or 180 minutes. 180 is divisible by 3, 9, 12, and 60; 180 is measured in music as an F-sharp, and 180 resonates at 180 cycles per-second in musical frequencies.

The square and circle have a geometric sum of 360 degrees of their interior angles. 360 represents one full turn of a compass, and 12 hours on a clock (360*12= 4,320 (8,640)). 360 is one perfect musical octave up from the triangle at a C-sharp, and 360 resonates at 360 cycles per second in musical frequency. Like 180, 360 is intrinsically divisible by all of the base numbers of 3, 9, and 60, which the Sumerians and Egyptians used to "circle the square, and square the circle" with. They also tabulate perfectly the 360 degree angles and 360 degree frequency sums of the square and circle in geometry, music, and time. While our base 10 numbers are what we tend to use today, that "mythos" does not carry a "System" like the Sexagesimal, which allows us to move "seamlessly" between disciplines. The base 10 method corrupts comprehension, skews the line between disciplines, and turns mathematics from a foundational observation that gives greater awareness into a foggy haze of corrupted knowledge that dilutes direction, confuses comprehension, and prevents perception.

While it is theoretically possible to create measuring systems to express geometry, music, and time that do not share common denominators, the extraordinary effort that it would take to manufacture identical measuring systems for all three disciplines begs the question, "Why go through the extra effort?" Unless there was some greater meaning to finding denominators that possessed a transitive nature, whereby those values could be used in an expression possessed of a greater purpose. The common denominators of the Sexagesimal System possess a special transitional, affinity binding, and Euclidean Entanglement function, which multiplies the principals of our new Euclidean Common Notion into vastness.)

(At the heart of particle physics is pure geometry. At the heart of energy physics is pure music. In the same manner that geometry can be expressed as "number in space" and music can be expressed as "number in time", so too particles can be measured by the "number in space" of geometry, while energy can be measured by the "number in time" of music. In the same manner that we see space as inverse to time, so too we can see "number in space" as inverse to "number in time", or geometry and music as equally inverse to one another. Thereby requireing an axis mundi of mathematical translation to reveal their inverse nature, the Sexagesimal System.

Due to their common numbering systems, common properties, and associative interchangeability, we can "Substitute" geometric and musical attributes into other formulas, and thereby arrive at a different kind of solution, which translates their initial meaning into a greater purpose. Beginning with Galileo's DiRT equation, we can substitute equations of geometry into the distance (D) variable. We can substitute the values of music into the time (T) variable. Moreover, we will find a frequency (f) variable hiding within the associative properties of geometry and music, and be able to Substitute the frequency (f) variable for Galileo's rate (R) variable.)

(When dealing with Galileo's DiRT Equation, we need to recognize that the distance, rate, and time variables are intrinsically Entangled to one another. When we do anything to the geometry of distance (D), there is a domino effect that affects the outcome to the music of time (T), and the frequency (f) of rate (R). For instance, if we replaced any number with a zero anywhere in Galileo's equation, the solution changes, and always ends up being zero. This is because all variables are intrinsically interrelated, and no matter which format of his equation that we use, anything multiplied or divided by a zero ends up being zero. Thus, we return to The Euclidean Substitution--- "In the same manner that the addition of one thing to another inevitably leads to the addition of a third thing to both, so too the absence of one thing from another inevitably leads to the absence of a third thing to all."

In the same manner that Euclid's Common Notions are translated into Science, so too The Euclidean Substitution is transitive through all disciplines. In The Way of The Path, this can be seen as Virtue (D) effecting Truth (T), and Compassion (R) effecting either Virtue or Truth, to create a greater outcome. In math, geometric expression (D) is directly related to particle expression, and particle expression is directly related to the properties of gravity (^{G}), which is directly related to the function of the rate (R) variable. In music, time expression (T) is directly related to wave expression, and wave expression is directly related to the properties of levity (^{L}), which is directly related to the function of the rate (R) variable.

$$R = \frac{(D^G)}{(T^L)}$$

Any change in one variable, demands a change in the others according to their properties and relationships with one another. Moreover, the two-way door of dominion is always flipping in both directions.)

The Fractal Substitution

(When moving along the (X) axis of Quantum Physics, there is a two-way movement of distance (D) toward infinitesimal smallness, as well as an equal and opposite movement of distance (D) along the (X) axis toward eternal vastness. This movement can be seen as a Fractal Zoom ascending or descending along the (X) axis of Quantum Physics, via the two-way door of dominion, wherein the fractals continually reveal the patterns of The Architect (K) within particle expression in infinitesimal smallness. In this manner, we realize that the mathematics of Fractals are giving us {(geometry) = (number in space)} (D), which directly relates to the duration of time (T) the program has run, as well as the rate {(R) = (f)} at which the program is running along the (X) axis of Quantum Physics. The distance (D) rate (R) and time (T) variables, as One Triquetra, are giving us the rising and falling expressions of The Program of The Architect (K) in the languages of geometry, music, and frequencies along the (X) axis. With this understanding, the program for a Fractal Zoom can be substituted in lieu of the distance (D) value, its variable of velocity can be substituted in lieu of the rate (R) variable, and the duration can be substituted in lieu of the time (T) variable in Galileo's DiRT Equation. Since fractals are a portion of The Program of The Architect, this expression also tells us where the value of (K) can be Substituted into the DiRT equation.

$$R = \frac{\text{Fractal}}{T}$$

$$R = \frac{K}{T}$$

)

The Euclidean Substitution

(The circumference (c) of a magnetosphere can be Substituted to replace the value for distance (D), because White and Dark Light travel in a circular uniform motion around the torus field along the (Y) axis of Galactic Physics. To find the circumference (c) of a torus field, one needs to know the formulas for circumference, which relate to radius (r), diameter (d), and pie ($\pi = 3.14$). Radius is a line that measures the distance halfway through a circle or sphere. Diameter is a line that measures the distance from one side to the other of a circle, and travels through the circle or sphere's center point. Two radii equal one diameter (d = r2). Pie is like The Golden Ratio, it's a number that transcends Vastness, reveals an internal wave/geometry relationship of The Architect, and takes its users over many New Horizons of Understanding. To find circumference (c), or diameter (d), depending on which values are known, we use the following mathematical relationships, and insert The Circumference Substitution into the DiRT equation.

$$d = (r2)$$

$$\{(c) = (\pi d)\}$$

$$\{(c) = (\pi r2)\}$$

$$D = \frac{c}{\pi}$$

$$r2 = \frac{c}{\pi}$$

$$R = \frac{D}{T}$$

$$R = \frac{c}{T}$$

Since anything on one side of an equal's sign is equivalent to the sum of all of the variables on the other side, the value of (c) can be substituted with its own equation. Thus, allowing The Circumference Substitution (c) for distance (D) to be Substituted with The Circumference Formula Substitution (πd) or (πr2). So long as the values of (πd) or (πr2) are not separated from one another, they retain the same value of the circumference (c) of White and Dark Light in any given torus field (Page 227, Quadratic, Pythagorean).

$$R = \frac{(\pi d)}{T}$$

$$R = \frac{(\pi r2)}{T}$$

Euclid's rules of math allow us to move Galileo's equation from (R = (D/T), to D = (RT). Thus, assigning different positions within the equation for each variable, while maintaining their relationships.

$$D = (RT)$$

$$c = (RT)$$

$$(\pi d) = (RT)$$

$$(\pi r2) = (RT)$$

Keeping in mind that we're tracking two Entangled photonic expressions of White and Dark Light in "relative uniform motion", this mathematical relationship can be expressed as, "The velocity of two objects in relative uniform motion, times the amount of time they travel, directly relate to the distance covered, while expressed as (D), (c), (πd), or (πr2)."

At this point in the expression, Euclid's rules of math allow us to move Galileo's equation back into its divisor format, but in a different order. The new value for (πr2), or (πd) can be divided by rate or time, as equally as rate or time can be inversely divided by (πr2) or (πd).

$$(\pi r2) = (RT)$$

Can change to...

$$R = \frac{T}{(\pi d)}$$

$$R = \frac{T}{(\pi r2)}$$

If we recall The Flip Function, we can see this as time being inversely related to the two object's paths (D), which are in "relative uniform motion". Or, "The distance which two objects in relative uniform motion move (πd), inversely relate to one another in time, with respect to velocity--- as well as with respect to the type of geometry of the trajectory that they follow." In the same manner that we can change the equation by dividing distance (D) and time (T), so too we can divide distance (D) by rate, and move the value for time (T) to the opposite side of the equation. In other words, geometry, music, or time can go on the top or bottom, or the left or right side of the equation, so long as their geometric (D), musical (R), and time (T), relationships are maintained.

$$T = \frac{R}{(\pi d)}$$

$$T = \frac{R}{(\pi r2)}$$

"The distance which two objects in "relative uniform motion" move {(D) = (πd)}, inversely relate to one another in space, and with respect to time--- As well as with respect to the geometry of the trajectory that they follow." This, whither they are following a linear Pythagorean hypotenuse (C^2), or a circular circumference (c).

For instance, if we compare and contrast the {Pythagorean (C^2)} of a tetrahedron to that {Pythagorean (C^2)} of a Dodecahedron, while recalling that the lines of both geometries can be represented as Silver Cords and their nodes as torus fields--- Moreover, if we recall that each one will have a different angle of trajectory, frequency {(R) = (f)}, and thus a difference in distance (D) and weight {A (D^G) and B (D^G)}, and thus velocity (R), which modifies the time (T) variable--- Then, we can plainly see that traveling through space-time distortions via a the geometry of a tetrahedron (D) along its {Pythagorean (C^2)} path will be radically different than following the Dodecahedron's (D) {Pythagorean (C^2)} path; even though they're both expressed as (C^2).)

The Architect Substitution

(Before we can find the changing value of (D), as White and Dark Light traverse all aspects of a torus field, we have to recognize some properties of Field Physics, which Entangle themselves into the machine of our Substitution Mythos. If we tracked White Light with respect to Dark Light, we would note that they come spiraling out of the male torsion field in a circular dance, Entangled with one another. Since their velocity (R) is moving so fast, and because the interrelations of collapse introduce the inertia of particle expression, their diameter (d) is compelled to widen, thus causing their value of (K) and (π) to increase. This intrinsically modifies their radius, directly effecting their geometric expression; expressed as (D^G), where (^{G}) represents the introduction of inertia from gravity. Eventually, their velocity (R @ (E) or (F)), coupled with the introduction of (^{G}), becomes greater than the Entanglement force of their affinity, and inertia, resulting from particle expression and (^{G}), shoots them off in equal and opposite directions.

White and Dark Light still possess Properties of Entanglement, as well as enough affinity to maintain a circular (c) dance of the distance (D) they travel, but now, they must do so with a new circular geometry (D), frequency (R), and music (T); in the same manner that the {Pythagorean (C^2)} changes with each Platonic Solid. In other words, when velocity, coupled with the introduction of interrelations changes the angle and direction of White and Dark Light by 90°, it intrinsically changes the nature of everything related to its expression. When geometry changes, the nature of distance (D) is changed, the nature of their frequency (R) must change, and the nature of their time (T) must modify. Thus, they not only move into a new realm (D), but a new frequency (f), as well as in a new time (T), relative to the realm (D), frequency (f), and time (T) they came from. When The Field Physics Property of Entanglement modifies the expression of Products of The Field as those products form interrelations, the properties of their expression must modify in accord with the changing relationship of the Entanglement modification.

When you change the overall nature of a given expression, via these three relationships, you automatically modify which realm it resides in. Within this relationship of the equation hides the ability of White and Dark Light to move seamlessly through the planet while they are in a state° of Field Physics (Z), while simultaneously maintaining a shielding effect when they are expressed in Galactic Physics (Y) as they move along the "bubble" portion of their path (D). White and Dark Light are constantly moving in and out of our realm, by continually modifying their geometry (D), frequency (R), and music (T) relationships, according to the interrelations between The Euclidean Substitution, The Architect Substitution, and their Entangled relationship originating from Field Physics.

Due to the interrelations that introduce inertia, and impediments of collapse that impede the movement of White and Dark Light, the diameter of their new circle (D) continually increases, while their velocity $\{(R) = (f)\}$ continually decreases. At equal and opposite sides of the torus field, the force of their affinity becomes greater than their decreasing velocity (Entanglement $\geq$ Rate). Once again, their geometry-gravity (D^G), frequency-levity (f^L), and music-time (T) must change. It is here that Field Physics Entanglement (Z) continually increases their velocity (R) passed the speed of light $\{(432^2) = (186,624)$ mps of our realm, and White and Dark Light accelerate (R@ E or F) toward one another like two fists in a head on collision.

At this point in their uniform motion, The Field Physics (Z) properties of amplified energetic, inviscidly conditioned, uniform velocity, in association with the Entanglement Property of Field Physics overcome the inertia and particle expression of Galactic Physics (Y), as well as the geometry of space and the music of time of a given realm, and the two way door of dominon changes direction. Entanglement energetically amplifies (f) White and Dark Light. Entanglement uniformly accelerates (R), White and Dark Light. Such that, their increasing uniform velocity torques space (D) and conditions time (T), which makes it appear to alter their trajectory (c) with an exponentially changing torque (K) in the space-time-velocity continuum. White and Dark Light also miss one another due to the nature of their polarity, (Entanglement = Same origin + Different expression), which keeps them from touching while in a state of expression. All of this allows them to miss one another, maintain their affinity, and continue their Dervish dance into the female torsion field toward Field Potential (Z). The Entanglement Function of Field Physics, modifies all of the relationships between our variables on both sides of The Hemisphere Effect, because it uniformly changes velocity (R @ (E) or (F)), it uniformly torques space (D), and correctly conditions the viscous nature of time (T) with two different forms of dominion.

We can use these Substitutions of math to further validate The Flip Function, as well as reiterate that space and time are inversely related to one another, by virtue of the expression of disciplines in which each Substitution is expressed. Moreover, these proofs validate that when it comes to the functions of the (X, Y, Z) axis, that all three relationships of distance rate and time, as well as their substitutions of geometry, frequency, music, are playing a critical role in finding a more genuine and meaningful solution. While we're going about this via the language of mathematics, we realize that the true cause of this Entangled relationship has more to do with The Entanglement

Function of Field Physics (Z), which is at the heart of the cause and effect relationships with products of the Field as they are expressed along any (X), (Y), or (Z) axis, than it does with a mathematical expression, which just so happens to describe events of Galactic Physics (Y). Thus, if The Properties of Field Physics alter the variables that define Galactic trajectory (D), modifies their real velocity (R), and changes their overall time (T)--- Then, this redefines the intrinsic relationships that Entangle all variables from a Property of Galactic Physics (Y), to a Property of Field Physics (Z). Thus, the Entanglement property of The Euclidian Substitution, and the following The Architect Substitution, are products of Field Physics, and can therefore be found in the Vastness of Field Physics (X, Y, Z).

$Space_x$ is bent by properties of Field Physics. $Time_x$ is conditioned by properties of Field Physics. Whenever we use properties of Field Physics to change one variable, we change Quantum and Galactic space-time continuum's functions or expressions. In other words, "In the same manner that the addition of one thing to another inevitably leads to the addition of a third thing to both, so too the absence of one thing from another inevitably leads to the absence of a third thing to all." ---even between realms. In the same manner that we applied The Euclidean Substitution to The Path of The Three Great Quests, so too it equally applies to Quantum (X), Galactic (Y), and Field Physics (Z). This transitive property of reasoning through a two-way door of three variables is at the heart of the purpose of The Substitution Mythos. Moreover, like the axis-mundi language of math, The Euclid Substitution Mythos is transitive through many disciplines of understanding.

$$\left(R = \frac{D}{T}\right) = \left(Z = \frac{X}{Y}\right)$$

)

(Within the female torsion field, the value of (K) increasingly modifies the value of White and Dark Light's path (D), the nature of their time (T), and frequency (f) of their velocity {R @ (E) or (F)} relative to the changing elasticity's of space, viscosity variances of time, increasing acceleration @ (E) or (F), and with respect to their geometry (^{G})--- and now we find--- in relationship to interrelations and Entanglement. Yes, the DiRT Equation, in association with The Euclidean Substitution, is revealing the greater idea of The Entanglement Function traversing the Quantum (X), Galactic (Y), and Field Physics (Z) axes. Moreover, as White and Dark Light move down the female torsion field toward the central ring, they move toward a condition that allows Superposition°, they increasingly break their interrelationships, and prepare to make the Jump. While this allows their velocity to continually increase, it also counter-intuitively allows the diameter of their path to become smaller. This is because, in a movement toward Field Potential, gravity and inertia, interrelation properties of Galactic Physics (Y), are continually reduced by the levity of increasing frequency (f^{L}), while The Entanglement Property of Field Physics (Z) continually increases due to their movement toward the Field. As products of the Field move toward the condition of the Field, properties of Field Physics increase {(f) = (C^{2})}, and properties of Quantum or Galactic Physics decrease. To translate this into the DiRT Equation, we would say that changing velocities {R @ (E) or (F)} are having a direct effect on the geometric nature (D) or (K) of an object, and the two way door of dominion is swinging in a counterclockwise direction, because its uncollapsing (K) the value of (D).)

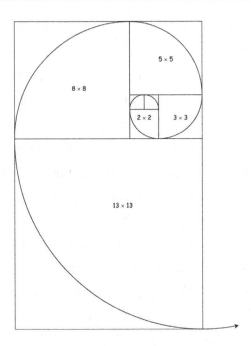

(If we look at this grid, which is representative of the ever tightening spin of the female torsion field, and imagine that a (13 by 13) grid forms 25% of a complete and balanced circle (c), and if we allow our imagination to complete that circle, then we can see that 13 equals the radius (r) of a circumference (c) at that quarter portion of the spiral. If we continue to do this for the (8 by 8) grid, the (5 by 5) grid, and the (3 by 3) grid, we can see that these values of (K) are equal to the radius (r) of their quarter portion of the spiral. Moreover, we can know that each value of (K), from (144) to (1), represent all space distortions of radii {(d) = (r2)} from the beginning of a torsion field to its opposing end. Thus, the decreasing or increasing value of The Architect (K) can be Substituted into the radius' position (πr2), to solve for the changing circumference (c) and distortion (DM), which we're using to track the distance (D) of White and Dark Light. Only this time, rather than using (c) or (D) as a relative constant, circumference (c) is now a changing variable along a changing circular path, according to the consistant changing value of The Program of The Architect (K).

$$\{d = (r2)\} = \{d = (K2)\}$$

$$\{(c) = (\pi(K2))\}$$

Or

$$(K2) = (C / \pi)$$

$$(13 * 2) = (C / 3.14)$$

$$(26) = (C / 3.14)$$

$$(26 * 3.14) = (C)$$

$$(81.64) = (C)$$

$$(81.64 * .25) = 20.41$$

$$(D) = 20.41$$

If we tracked the total distance for each changing value of (K), the final value for (c) and (D) would be 585.61, or 1,171.22 for the total of two torsion fields.

                                              226.08
                              139.73
                       86.35
                  53.38
               32.97
             20.41
           12.56
          7.85
          3.14
          1.57
          1.57
          1.57
          1.57
          3.14
          7.85
           12.56
             20.41
               32.97
                  53.38
                       86.35
                              139.73
                                       226.08

In the same manner that circumference (c) can be substituted into Galileo's DiRT Equation in lieu of the distance (D) value on the exterior of the torus field, so too the changing value of (K), within the circumference equation, can be substituted into Galileo's distance rate time equation as the distance (D) variable.

$$R = \frac{585.61}{T}$$

$$R = \frac{(585.61 * 2)M}{TN}$$

While this may initially seem to be counterintuitive, there is no immediate need to measure a distortion of space (M) in this substitution. We're not so much as talking about a movement across the galactic space-time continuum (Y), as much as we're talking about a movement along the (Z) axis of Field Physics. Within torsion fields, galactic distortions (M) are not so unequally disturbed as they are across the continuum (Y). As a default benefit, Substituting the value of (K) within the circumference equation, reveals a degree of distorted space according to The Architect while simultaneously tracking distance (D) trekked by White and Dark Light.)

The Van Tassel Substitution

$$F = \frac{1}{T}$$

(Remembering that the heart of particle physics is pure geometry, we're quickly realizing that Entangling geometric relationships with properties of Field Physics are at the heart of understanding all particle physics in a movement along the (X), (Y), or (Z) axes. Also, remembering that the heart of energy physics is pure music, we're about to realize that Entangling harmonic relationships with the properties of Field Physics, is at the heart of understanding all wave physics in a movement along the (X), (Y), or (Z) axes. Moreover, like mixing Cymatics with our three machines within The Chamber of Initiation, it's no small coincidence that we're using geometry and music as One, yet again. Quite literally, and in every since of the meaning, we're amalgamating one-half of The Bandwidth of The Construct {(space) = (D)} with its other half {(time) = (T)}, so as to create a third outcome {(f) = (C^2)}, wherein a third variable doesn't exist in the absence of the union of the other two. Bending geometry over music, folding space over time, and mixing gravity (D^G) with levity (f^L) to create a macro-synergistic outcome, which promises to create something greater than the sum of its parts, and thrust us over a New Horizon of Understanding.)

(George Van Tassel; an aeronautical engineer and creator of the Integratron in Joshua Tree California, was entrusted with an equation that caries the same Field Physics Entanglement Properties as Galileo's equation. The formula stipulates that for every "1 particular something"; or measurement of "clock or calendar time", we divide it by a function of time, such as seconds (60), minutes (60), or hours (12) (24), and thus attain a frequency (f) = (C), or velocity (C²) = (R), at which time moves forward or backward (+L-). This frequency of time is typically expressed in waves, but we will soon find it can just as easily be expressed in geometry. Thus, if we remember our section on galactic time waves, we can see this as another means of looking at those wave patterns through the lens of the (X, Y, Z) axes of perspective, as that perspective relates to the Entanglement Function between the following equations, and the relationship of their uniform motion relative to one another.

$$(R=\frac{D}{T}) = (Z=\frac{X}{Y}) = (F=\frac{1}{T})$$

These relationships, within The Euclidean Substitution, can be seen as substitutable for one another. In that (Z), represented as Field Physics, can be seen as the (R) variable, and (f) can be seen as a given expression of both (Z) or (R) variables.)

$($

$$F = \frac{1}{T}$$

$$\text{Frequency} = \frac{1 \text{ particular something}}{\text{Time}}$$

Note, The Great Year of 25,920

$$432 = \frac{25,920}{60}$$

In the same manner that we Substituted other mathematical disciplines into Galileo's equation, so too we can Substitute values of Van Tassel's formulas into Galileo's equation. To measure "the music of time", we calculate time in terms of Sexigesimal duration of time, as time relates to the number of "clock time"; seconds (1), minutes (60), and hours (24). To measure "the velocity of time", the velocity at which a given amount of "clock time" passes, we calculate it in terms of frequency of time. To do this, we substitute Van Tassel's frequency (f) variable for Galileo's rate (R) variable. "The music at which time resonates" (f), is the rate (R) at which time passes {(f) = (R)}. Or, like a film, the rate (R) at which the camera of time photographs each instant of time (T), and records the event on photons (D) (See also Remote Viewing).

$$R = \frac{D}{T}$$

$$F = \frac{1}{T}$$

Or

$$(D) = (RT)$$

$$(1) = (FT)$$

$$\text{Frequency} = \frac{D}{T}$$

$$(Distance) = (Frequency * Time)$$

$$(C^2) = (Frequency * Time)$$

(Rate @ (E) or (F)) can then be re-expressed as time changing frequency (f), and thus changing velocity (Rate @ (E) or (F)) = (frequency @ (E) or (F)). This (Rate @ (E) or (F)) change in (R) can be expressed as adding waves together, or subtracting them from one another, where two adjoining waves create a new wave that is the sum or difference of their frequencies. The interference frequency pattern on a geometric-frequency relationship of 180 and 360 would be 180 or 540. This frequency (f) based expression of numbers could be substituted into geometric particle physics as a triangle (180°) (D) plus or minus a square or circle (360°) (D), resulting in a triangle @ (180°) (D) or a pentagon @ (540°) (D). For instance, if we plugged numerical values into the DiRT Equation, and arrived at a solution of 180, we would know this value could be expressed in angels of geometry (D), notes in music (T), or even rates (R) of frequencies (f). These transitive expressions can be equally represented as the products of geometry or frequency, gravity and levity, adding or subtracting from the properties of geometry^{Gravity} (D) or frequency^{Levity} (R) in a movement through the model of a torus field.

Mathematically, this could look like---

$$(f^L + f^L)$$

$$(f^L - f^L)$$

Where two different variables of frequency (f) possess different degrees of levity (^{L}), and thus produce different outcomes in velocity (R). This is known as "The Frequency Effect (C^2)", {(C^2) +- (C^2)}.

$$(f^{2L}) = (f^L + f^L)$$

$$(f^{-L}) = (f^L - f^L)$$

$$\text{Pull } (p^{2G}) = (p^G + p^G)$$

$$\text{Push } (f^{2L}) = (f^L + f^L)$$

$$\text{Neutral} = (p^G + f^L)$$

We'll demonstrate these relationships in further detail, once we see the interference "gap" patterns within the equations. For now, it's important that we maintain conscious awareness of a wave (f) to particle (D) relationship, in the same manner that we maintain a conscious awareness of a geometry, to music, to velocity Entanglement relationship. We do this, because the properties within interference patterns can slow time (f) or speed it up, and as we know, that action modifies all other variables within a two-way door of dominion. For instance, nesting Platonic Solids, such as in the collapse function, creates an interference pattern, which changes or otherwise reduces the frequency and flow of time (-f), and increases the properties of Platonic Solids ($+^G$), such as gravity or inertia, which impede movement. When something looses or gains frequency, it looses or gains properties of frequency, such as levity (^{L}), which allows or inhibits velocity (R) within a two-way door of dominion.

$$F = \frac{1}{T}$$

$$180 = \frac{10,800}{60}$$

$$360 = \frac{21,600}{60}$$

The Van Tassel Substitution for (D) is (1), and is represented here as 10,800 and 21,600. 10,800 doubled becomes 21,600, in the same manner that 180 doubled moves to 360. Moreover, 21,600 added to 10,800 = 32,400 represented as 5 dodecahedrons (Page 227, A hundred connected pentagons, Mandala) at 6,480 for each one; an exponentially increasing return on gravity or levity; depending on whither the numbers represent a particle (D) or wave (f). Not only does this reveal a drastic return on levity or gravity, but it also represents a flip function between the (R) and (D) variables under certain conditions. Also, this is another demonstration that Van Tassel's equation, and mythos, intrinsically associates the same relationships as Galileo's equation, The Fractal Substitution, The Euclidean Substitution, and The Architect Substitution; they are all Entangled. It demonstrates the idea in such a manner that where you affect one portion, you automatically come to affect the other aspects of the formula. Where you affect geometry (D), you intrinsically effect time (T), and frequency (R). Where you affect geometry and frequency, you intrinsically affect gravity and levity, and their interrelation effects on products of the Field, as it relates to the DiRT Equation. Moreover, where you effect one equation, you effect the other two equations in the same Entangled manner.

$$\{(R=\frac{D}{T}) = (Z=\frac{X}{Y}) = (F=\frac{1}{T})\}$$

Can you see the Triquetra? Can you see three Triquetras?

Moreover, within The Chamber of Initiation of the Triquetra of all three equations, can you see why someone would set up all the disciplines that represent each variable, so as to achieve transitive common denominator variables?)

(Some examples of Van Tassel's equation, and their solution's cultural significance.

$$F = \frac{1}{T}$$

$$\text{Frequency } 180 = \frac{\text{Gaebyeok } 10,800}{\text{Time } 60}$$

This Gaebyeok number represents a sudden change in culture and human nature. This number can represent The Thunderbolt of Enlightenment within an individual. In Ancient Greece, this number is known as "The Heraclitus Cycle". Add 180 to each of the geometric angles or frequency tones, and you will see how jumping 180 (D) (f) is in itself a New Horizon.

$$\text{Frequency } 360 = \frac{21,600}{\text{Time } 60}$$

Remember, 360 relates to both the circle and square, and relates to circling the square, and squaring the circle.

$$333.333\infty = \frac{144,000}{432}$$

$$666.666 = \frac{144,000}{216}$$

144,000 days = One Maya Backtun, and a base frequency (f) for moving the Energy Serpent (∞) through the chakras (Z). The number "3" expressed in infinity is a cornerstone to Masonic Teachings.

144,000 is profoundly represented in The Bible, and was the number of casing stones of the Great Pyramid at Giza.

$$\text{Frequency } 7,200 = \frac{\text{Kali Yuga } 432,000}{\text{Time } 60}$$

A Kali Yuga is 432,000 years. This is also 3 Maya Katuns, another measure of time according to The Calendar Round. 360 and 21,600 are also numbers we find reoccurring in Hindu Tantric texts written in ancient Sanskrit, one of the oldest forms of writing known to mankind. Take note of the common denominator of 3 to all of these equations.)

Dimensional Geometry in Van Tassel's equation.

(The triangle has a sum of 180 degrees of its interior angles (D), is a musical F-sharp (T), and resonates at (180 cycles per-second = Frequency (f)). The square and circle have a sum of 360 degrees of their interior angles (D), are one perfect musical octave up from the triangle at a C-sharp (T) (Viscosity), and resonate at (360 cycles per second = Frequency (f)). The pentagon has a sum of 540 degrees of its interior angles (D), and resonates at (540 cycles per second (T) = Frequency (f)). The hexagon's interior angles equal 720 degrees (D), at F-sharp (T), and resonates at (720 cycles per second = Frequency (f)). A seven sided septagon totals 900 for its interior angles (D), an A-sharp (T), and resonates at (900 cycles per second = Frequency (f)). The octagon has a sum of 1,080 degrees of its interior angles (D), another C-sharp (T), and resonates at (1,080 cycles per second = Frequency (f)).

$$F = \frac{1}{T}$$

$$180 = \frac{10,800}{60}$$

$$360 = \frac{21,600}{60}$$

$$540 = \frac{32,400}{60}$$

$$720 = \frac{43,200}{60}$$

$$1,080 = \frac{64,800}{60}$$

)

(Like the Samarian Master Number {195,955,200,000,000}, which encompasses all galactic {(D) ((f) & (R)) (T)} cycles, The Great Year is one of those gigantic numbers, which we find encoded into ancient monuments, such as the pyramids at Giza, and the Mayan Calendar Round. It's commonality among ancient monuments is as if the ancients were silently screaming at the top of their intellectual prowess, trying to get us to pay attention to these quantities. Once again, we find that Pythagoras learned of the importance of the musical tone of 432 from Thoth. Thoth Tuning, or what we call "Pythagorean Tuning", shows the way toward a key value of 432 cycles-per-second as a cornerstone-tone to begin The Van Tassel Substitution with. When squared, the only whole number that comes to within .01% accuracy of the speed of light is $(432^2) = (186,624)$ miles per second $\{(f) = (C) = (432)\}$. Like the previous Platonic Shapes, can you see how this frequency {195,955,200,000,000} could be expressed as a nested geometry (D); who's summation of nested Platonic Orders equated to the same value in the form of (D) or (f)?)

(The (186,624) relationship to The Master Number {195,955,200,000,000} which "Encompasses 'All' galactic cycles" is 1,050,000,000.

$$1,050,000,000 = \frac{186,624}{195,955,200,000,000}$$

Comprehending that all of these numbers, when compared to the Master Number, don't come out as fractions, is a big step to embracing the significance of the Master Number, its profound Encompassing Virtues (Z), as well as the circulating nature to all of these relationships.)

This (432^2) also just so happens to be the speed of light, according to Albert Einstein. Thus, not only is $(f = 432)$ a noteworthy harmonic measurement, as it relates to George Van Tassel's equation, Thoth, Pythagoras, The Great Year, The Master Number, and ancient monuments, but its squared value directly relates to the velocity of light $(R) = (C^2)$, which is also relative to how fast a certain frequency of time $\{(f) = (432)\}$ in a given realm "surfs" $\{(R) = (432^2)\}$ light. Observing the intersection of these facts is just as profoundly significant as recognizing The Field Physics Entanglement Function within The DiRT Equation, but within The Substitution Method.)

(Remembering that the ascending, descending, and nested Orders of Platonic Solids are either assembled or disassembled by the collapse and uncollapse function in a clockwise or counterclockwise spin, we can say that all Platonic Orders are "disassembled" as they move into the female torsion field, and are "assembled" as products of the Field exit the male torsion field. Moreover, we can say that this two-way door of dominion moves with an Intelligent Order, especially where geometry and music are expressed as one in the values of geometric-frequency relationships, which are reflected in their interrelated disciplines, and transitive common denominators. While measured in terms of increasing frequencies (f) in a movement toward the field, which move up the Platonic Order ladder, and measured in terms of increasing solids (D), which also move up the Platonic Order ladder, what differentiates the two expressions are the collapse uncollapse functions. We will even see consistent anomalies within the equations, which will teach us more about their intelligent patterns.

The Platonic Solids' relation to geometric-frequencies begin with the tetrahedron's interior angle at 720 (D), an F-sharp (T), resonating at (720 cycles per second = Frequency (f)). The cube has a cumulative interior angle of 2,160 (D), is a high C-sharp (T), and resonates at (2,160 cycles per second = Frequency (f)). The octahedron has a cumulative interior angle of 1,440 (D), another F-sharp higher up the scale (T), and resonates at (1,440 cycles per second = Frequency (f)). The icosahedron has a cumulative interior angle of 3,600 (D), this is an A-sharp needed to complete another F-sharp major chord (T), and resonates at (3,600 cycles per second = Frequency (f)). Dodecahedrons have a cumulative angle (D) and frequency relationship of (6,480 cycles per second = Frequency (f)). In other words, (C^2) can be represented as (D), (T), or (f).

$$F = \frac{1}{T}$$

$$720 = \frac{43,200}{60}$$

$$2,160 = \frac{129,600}{60}$$

$$1,440 = \frac{86,400}{60}$$

$$3,600 = \frac{216,000}{60}$$

$$6,480 = \frac{388,800}{60}$$

If we look at The Van Tassel equation, after the same manner of the Galileo DiRT equation, one might say that if one wanted to travel 388,800 minutes, years, or 1 value of (D) in 60 minutes, seconds, or 1 set value of (T), then one would need to change the frequency of time

(f) to 6,480, so as to "surf" (R) products of the Field by the frequency squared (6,480²). Inserting this pattern into the DiRT equation, the frequency of (6,480) squared (R) becomes (41,990,400) miles per second, or 2,519,424,000 miles per minute, or 151,165,440,000 miles (D) per (f) hour (T). The square root of 151,165,440,000 is 388,800; as seen in the relationships above. Thus, the relationship between the velocity at which something travels, within a time-wave frequency, and the frequency at which time flows, is directly related to squaring the value or finding the square root of a value. Keep this very important fact in mind when reverse engineering each variable's solution, their entanglement to (C^2), and our final Substitutions. According to Van Tassel, according to the Entanglement property, which Entangles the DiRT Equation in the same manner that it Entangles Quantum, Galactic, and Field Physics, how do we modify space or time? By that DiRT Equation, which Entangles transitive common denominator variables of space, time, and velocities as equally as it Entangles geometry, music, and frequency.)

(If frequency (f) was one portion of The Bandwidth of The Construct, and Platonic Orders were the other portion of The Bandwidth of The Construct, then The Van Tassel Substitution could be rewritten with a (P) for which Platonic Order, nested order, or permutated order it was representing.

$$F = \frac{1}{T}$$

$$P = \frac{1}{T}$$

In other words, if we wanted to represent (f) as a particle rather than a wave, in the same manner that Einstein's equation expresses matter as particles (mass) or waves (energy), then we possess the transitive common denominators to express them within The Van Tassel equation using The Substitution Method.)

(As photons move through the torsion field, the changing value of (K) changes the geometry of, the harmonics of, interrelation expression of, and velocity of light by a factor of their frequency squared. For every ascending squared value in the velocity of light, there is an exponentially increasing return on the frequency to velocity ratio, we will find that this is upwards of 225%. This is because levity is a wave function of frequency, and thus a property of velocity (R) and (Z). The faster you go, the higher the frequency, the higher the frequency, the faster you go, and both cause more levity to be injected or otherwise nested within you. This "lightens" the load by removing inhibitions, such as gravity that causes inertia, which allows for ever more frequency and velocity, sparking an exponential return on the properties and effects of levity.

As we look at photons moving at galactic speeds, it's no wonder they behave as if gravity has almost no effect on them. As their frequency increases exponentially, photons become so "impregnated" with gaps of levity that the gaps between gravity have almost no chance to inhibit them. It takes Galactic Physics, interrelationships, and the collapse function along the (Y) axis to change their frequency, thus their speed, and thus allow for the possibility for gravity to counter effect levity. These Teeter-totter imbalances also reveal other "unseen" barriers in acceleration and deceleration, which avail themselves within the numbers expressed between the cube and octahedron of the following Van Tassel Substitution DiRT Equations.

The frequency of (432) squared (R) becomes (186,624) miles per second, or 11,197,440 miles per minute (60), or 671,846,400 miles (D) per (R) hour (T). √25,920 The Great Year, of our realm.

It is here that Samarian numbers, in terms of Sexigesimal-time, are expressed as one day passing in 24 hours, one hour passing in 60 minutes, and one minute passing in 60 seconds.

The frequency of (720) squared (R) becomes (518,400) miles per second, or 31,104,000 miles per minute (60), or 1,866,240,000 miles (D) per (R) hour (T). √43,200, The New Horizon of the expression of a New Great Year. Think of it as the same amount of time as our Great Year, but because their frequency of time flows faster, its takes a proportionally greater amount of time to reflect the same equivalency of time. Thus, all of the variables of time have been constructed around a system, whereby all variables can be used as transitive common denominators between realms, and are therefore properties of Field Physics. This is why the ancients used them, so they could translate multiple values between relatable expressions within different realms, dimensions, and "Go where no one has gone before".

While the numerical value of 720 is only 1.6 times 432, (720^2) is 2.7 times faster than (432^2). Thus, as soon as one moves into the new geometric-frequency relationship of time of (720^2), the associated variables, such as the duration of a day (T), are divided by 2.7. Thus, 24 hours becomes 8.88 hours. However, because we've been using The Van Tassel Substitution in relationship to the base number of 60, we should divide 60 by 2.7, and show that when time is moving at a frequency of (720^2), 60 minutes passes in 22.22 (432) minutes.

The frequency of (2,160) squared becomes (4,665,600) miles per second, or 279,936,000 miles per minute, or 16,796,160,000 miles (D) per (f) = (R) hour (T).

While the numerical value of 2,160 is 5 times 432, $(2,160^2)$ is 9 times faster than (720^2), and 25 times faster than (432^2). Thus, as soon as one moves into the new geometric-frequency of time of $(2,160^2)$, the associated variables, such as the duration of a day (T), is divided by 25. Thus, 24 hours becomes .96 hours, or a day passes in 58.176 minutes at a time-frequency of $(2,160^2)$. One year passes in 14.6 days.

The frequency of (1,440) squared (R) becomes (2,073,600) miles per second, or 124,416,000 miles per minute, or 7,464,960,000 miles (D) per (R) hour (T).

Anomaly, (1,440) (f) is .4444- times slower than (2,160) (f). The Platonic relationship reveals some manner of interference pattern between the cube and the octahedron. Is this a "space-time-velocity" result of the gravity, levity, and inertia relationships trying to stay in place, or being compelled to move? Perhaps it's a function of resistance within the particle to wave gravity to levity relationships? If it is a function of this resistance, perhaps it's a function of which direction the two-way door of dominion is flowing within the wave particle geometrical-frequency expression.

The frequency of (3,600) squared (R) becomes (12,960,000) miles per second, or 777,600,000 miles per minute, or 46,656,000,000 miles (D) per (f^2) hour (T).

While the numerical value of 3,600 is 8.333 times 432, $(3,600^2)$, is 69.4444 times faster than (432^2). Thus, as soon as one moves into the new geometric-frequency of time of $(3,600^2)$, the associated variables, such as the duration of a day (T) in the frequency of (432^2), is divided by 69.44. Thus, 24 hours, or 1,440 minutes passes in 20.7373 minutes.

The frequency of (6,480) squared (R) becomes (41,990,400) miles per second, or 2,519,424,000 miles per minute, or 151,165,440,000 miles (D) per (f^2) hour (T). √388,800, The Dodecahedral Great Year. Note, in each realm this number is being used as a measurement of distance (C^2), as well as time (C^2).

While the numerical value of 6,480 is 15 times greater than 432, ($6,480^2$) is 225 times faster than (432^2). Thus, as soon as one moves into the new geometric-frequency of time of ($6,480^2$), the associated variables, such as the duration of a day (T) in the frequency of (432^2), is divided by 225 times. There are 1,440 minutes in a day and 86,400 seconds. Thus, a 24 hour day passes in 384 seconds, or 6 minutes and 24 seconds. To get one hour we multiply 6.4 minutes by 9.375. 384*9.375 = 3,600... 3600/60 = 60... 60/60 =1

$$F = \frac{1}{T}$$

Taking note of the uneven acceleration relationships within the previous equations, especially between the geometric-frequencies of (1,440) and (2,160). If we hearken back to John Glenn's jet trying to go super-sonic, we remember that it almost shook itself apart when he approached the sound barrier. The accelerating velocities of a solid (D) were "squeezing" wave's together (f) in front of his jet, creating an interference pattern in front of the plane and over its wings, which threatened to rip his aircraft apart. In the same manner that he was able to "break" the barrier by overcoming the solid to wave relationships via increased acceleration (R), so too we can see here there is another kind of "barrier" holding back, or otherwise impeding, the acceleration of light at different stages of acceleration. Moreover, we can see that once a photon advances passed the gravity levity velocity barrier, its acceleration velocities are no longer inhibited, but experience an exponential acceleration relationship with the properties--- or more correctly, the direction, of levity.

John Glenn, and his compatriots, changed the (R) variable to get his craft (D) passed the wave relationship barriers. However, they could've just as easily changed the (f) variable of (D), which is directly related to the same expression of numbers within the geometric-frequency relationships. In other words, we can overcome this relationship of waves (interference) holding back particles (jets), by injecting frequencies into the particles of our craft, such that the vessel resonates at the correct frequencies related to the (R) variable that we wish to travel at, and "evaporate" the frequency wave holding back our aircraft by cooperating with it rather than trying to muscle our way through it. Can you see how this would allow The Flip Function with the (R) & (D) varaibles?

$$A + B = X$$
$$C + D = Y$$
$$A + D = Q$$
$$B + C = R$$

The Einstein Substitution

(What does Kepler's nested Platonic Order of the solar system, Dr. Moon's nested Platonic Order of particle expression, and The Einstein Rosen-Bridge all have in common? They're all based on a degree of expression of The Construct, which repeats itself in an orderly manner, according to specific geometric-frequency relationships, and it does this from one end of The Construct to the other along an (X), (Y), or (Z) axis. Dr. Moon is measuring The Fractal Substitution of collapse in infinitesimal smallness along the (X) axis of Quantum Physics and particle expression, and saying particles and protons can be expressed in nested Platonic Orders with geometric-frequency relationships within The Periodic Table of Elements. Kepler is measuring the collapse of planetary patterns in eternal vastness, along the (Y) axis of Galactic Physics, and saying planets and galactic bodies can be expressed in nested Platonic Orders with geometric-frequency relationships between one another. Both Moon and Kepler are saying that there is absolutely no touching between protons in infinitesimal smallness or the planets in eternal vastness, yet they are held in place according to particular repeating geometric-frequency relationships. This can be analogized as the relationship of nodes holding the fabric of the universe together (^{G}), or apart (^{L}), at every level of understanding, based on transitive geometric-frequency relationships--- just like The Program of The Architect constructs seashells and Galaxies after the same manner in the micro or macro. This can be related to The Flip Function between the (R) and (D) variables. Moreover, in the same manner that the DiRT equation reveals the Entanglement function of Physics (X, Y, Z), so too we will find the same Entanglement function, which Moon and Kepler are describing, within these geometric-frequency relationships between realms.

Einstein is measuring the collapse of the energy of wave on one side of his ($E=MC^2$) equation, while comparing energy to the nested Platonic Order of mass/matter on the other side of the equation, and linking both with respect to the velocity of light. Like Substituting (f) for (R), or (c) for (D), whether Einstein understood his equation in this manner or not, he was still Substituting different variables of the same expression into Galileo's DiRT Equation. Although maintaining valid relationships, he is altering the order of relationships, and saying that mass is equivalent to a certain amount of energy, so long as all variables are found in a realm which surfs light at a certain velocity (432^2) = (C^2) = (Y). The commonality between the three men? Moon, Kepler, and Einstein are all talking about the intrinsic relationships between the variables of the DiRT Equation, as well as trying to demonstrate how things "attract" (^{G}) or "repel" (^{L}) based on Entangled geometric (D)-frequency (f) orders and relationships, which are found within the Entangled nature of the DiRT equation and transitive common denominator variables of the Sexagesimal System.)

(The first Substitution of The Einstein Substitution replaces the rate (R) variable with the (C^2) variable, also expressed as the frequency (f) variable of The Van Tassel Substitution, only squared. However, rather than stipulating that (C^2) could represent a permutation of geometric-frequency variables, Einstein stipulates that (C^2) is simply the velocity of light at (432^2). Thus, Einstein's (C^2) is the (R) or (f) variables in the DiRT and Van Tassel Equations, within the function of The Substitution Method. Within the Entanglement function, this "placeholder" in the equation, also represents the (Z) axis, but we're still getting to that.

$$R = \frac{D}{T}$$

$$f = \frac{D}{T}$$

$$C^2 = \frac{D}{T}$$

$$(D) = (RT)$$

$$(D) = (fT)$$

$$(D) = ((C^2)T)$$

Einstein would've known that (R) multiplied by (T) is equivalent to (T) multiplied by (R), in the same manner that (6) multiplied times (5) is equivalent to (5) multiplied by (6). Thus, in the format below, Einstein trades the (R) and (T) placeholders of the DiRT Equation, and inserts a squared frequency (f) = (C) of time (C²).

As The Einstein Substitution relates to The Van Tassel Substitution; the function of which frequency (f) we insert is more revealing than the flipped location of the placeholder. Especially, when we consider that replacing (432^2) with $(6,480^2)$ drastically effects the expression and relationship of (f) with the other two variables of (M) and (E). We know this because $(6,480^2)$ has 225 times greater effect $(^{G,\,L})$ on the operation of (f), via the property of Entanglement, with the rest of the equation. This is especially true when it comes to the potentials of energy (E) and mass (M) at higher realms (Z), since a higher rate of return on frequency (f^n) in time insinuates a relativistic higher function of mass (M) and energy (E).

$$(D) = (TR)$$

$$(D) = (Tf)$$

$$(D) = (T(C^2))$$

In a Newtonian, equal and opposite fashion, this relationship insinuates a relativistic lower effect on functions of mass (M) and energy (E) within lower realms (f) (Z), such as (360), (216), or (180). We can express this mathematically by moving the squared (^{2}) nature of (C^2) to the other variables, taking the square root of (E) and (M). In this manner we express that mass (M) and energy (E) possess only a proportion of their potential when frequency (f) is at a lower geometric-frequency expression. Moreover, this reveals that the potentials of mass and energy are somewhat under the dominion of the conditional expression of (f), depending on its nested Platonic Order (D) (R).

$$C = \sqrt{M}$$

Or

$$C = \sqrt{E}$$

Einstein then Substitutes the (D) variable of the DiRT Equation with the mass of an object (M). The mass of an object (M) is another way of saying "The Program of The Architect" (K), as (K) relates to the expression of solids within their Platonic Orders, and geometric-frequency relationships (f). Thus, we can Substitute (K) or (M) for (D), so long as we remember that (K) is a function of the Field more than it is an expression of a product of the Field, like the mass of an object (M). Like other Substitutions, the math one would follow to find an object's mass always comes down to the singular expression of a given number within a system, whose end value is then Substituted into the DiRT equation. This is done in the same manner that we Substitute the equation $(d\pi)$ or $(\pi r2)$ for circumference (c), and then replace the (D) with the equivalent equation for (c). So too, any equation that expresses the mass of an object in a given condition can be substituted into the distance (D) variable, so long as the nature of the numerical expression possesses a geometrical-frequency relationship to the rate (D) variable; such as Fractals, The Architect (K), or other "irrational" constants such as Phi or Pi.

$$R = \frac{D}{T}$$

$$C^2 = \frac{M}{T}$$

$$C^2 = \frac{K}{T}$$

$$(D) = (RT)$$

$$(K) = (R(C^2))$$

$$(M) = (T(C^2))$$

The energy (E) variable is a Substitution expression of time (T). To understand this Substitution, and enjoy a New Horizon, think of the relation of frequency $\{(f) = (R)\}$ making a determination "in viscus time" as to how fast (R^2) an event, such as an explosion, could occur. The frequency variable $\{(f) = (R)\}$, in terms of the flow of time $\{(R^2) = (C^2)\}$, is not only a determiner of how fast the energy (T) of an event can take place, but "Potential energy" is defined by its relationships with $\{(f) = (R)\}$, when (f) or (R) are expressed as different root variables of (C^2). For instance, if we change (C^2) from (432^2) to $(6,480^2)$, this change effects the potentials of other variables in the equation by upwards of 225 times their initial potential. This can radically change energy's potential by a function of time's frequency (f) squared, or by their square root. In the same manner that we use units of time (T), to interlock their functions in relationship to geometric (D) -frequency (R) relationships, so too the energy substitution (E) for time (T) uses equivalent translations and common denominators to relate to the function of mass $\{(M) = (D)\}$ and changing frequencies $\{(f) = (C)\}$ of time (R^2) to express equivalent changes in energy, according to all variable's Entangled relationships with frequencies of time (C^2) in different realms. Remember, all three variables affect one another in a two-way door of dominion. So, the dominion of which one is affecting the other can become an expression of the direction of collapse $(^G)$ or uncollapse $(^L)$ (Two objects acting or reacting to time viscosity in the direction of acceleration or deceleration of velocities). Above this, this intrinsic relationship between all variables tells us the potentials of mass and energy in our realm (Y) are not constant potentials. In our realm, we are witnessing the functions of mass and energy's potentials while they are under the dominion of a squared $(^n)$ variable of $\{(C) = (f) = (R) = (T)\}$, which can easily change should we accelerate or decelerate the frequency (f) of the (R) variable.

$$R = \frac{D}{T}$$

$$C^2 = \frac{M}{E}$$

$$(D) = (TR)$$

$$(M) = (E(C^2))$$

Looking at the last expression of Einstein's equation, can you see The Flip Function?

The Einstein Substitution and The Van Tassel Substitution show us the relationships of The Architect {(K) = (D)} in higher realms. With the function of time changes, and Einstein's mass to energy comparison, we know geometric-frequency properties have exponential effects on the function of mass (D) and energy (T) at higher realms, as well as their squared root effect in more nested realms. Moreover, this affects the function, operation, and expression of products of The Architect in different realms, according to intelligent patterns.)

(Revealed within The Substitution Mythos, we see Newton's Second Law of Motion behaving like The Van Tassel Substitution and The Einstein Substitution. In the same manner that Einstein's equation directly relates to Galileo's equation, so too Newton's Second Law of Motion is a reproduction of The DiRT Equation Mythos (Force = Mass × Acceleration), but within The Substitution Method. Once again, we have mass (m) Substituted as the distance (D) variable, Force (F) Substituted as energy (E) or (T) variable, and Acceleration (A) Substituted as a changing variable of {(R) or (f) @ E or F)}.

$$\left(R = \frac{D}{T}\right) = \left(Z = \frac{X}{Y}\right) = \left(F = \frac{1}{T}\right)$$

After the same manner, other geometry and Pi equations are also Substituting different variables of the same triple relationship between its own equation and related equations. The equation for circumference (c) in this format (c = dπ) relates the same mathematical reasoning to the DiRT equation in this (D = RT) format. Where---

Circumference = diameter * Pi

In the same manner that---

Distance = Rate * Time

When we flip both equations into their divisor format, we observe---

(π = c/d) = (R = D/T)

The Pi (π) variable behaving like the Rate (R) variable.

The circumference (c) variable behaving like the distance (D) variable.

The diameter (d) variable behaving like the Time (T) variable.

We can see these relationships are following the same mythos of function, whether we express them as Newton's Second Law of Motion, The Van Tassel Substitution--- or a formula to find the {F (R) of (π)} = {(π = c/d) = (R = D/T)} or the (c) of (D) of White and Dark Light. Moreover, finding The Flip Function between (R) and (D) Substituted as (π) and (c). Where expressions of (π) move through the collapse function of (D^G) via the expression and function of (K), and then flips back into (R^L) in a two way door of dominion along the entire bandwidth of The Bandwidth of The Construct expressed as $\{(C^{2L}) = \{195,955,200,000,000\} = (C^{2G})\}$. We can also express them as linear or circular, this, whether we're seeking (C^2) along a linear path with Thoth's $(A^2) + (B^2) = (C^2)$ Theorem, or seeking (C^2) through the distance (D) variable of Pi (π) in a circular (c) manner. Once agin, we can also see this expressed as silver cords in Thoth's (C^2), which are epresented as a (D) variable of a Platonic Solid, or as an (R) or (f) variable of velocity (C^2) of a Platonic Order in a wave format.

$$R = \frac{D}{T}$$

$$R = \frac{\pi}{T}$$

We know that Diameter (d), Pi (π), and Circumference (c) are measurements of distance, if not applicable and directly relatable with units of distance (D); for instance units of Sexagesimal distance. Where is Pi (π) used in terms of units of Sexagesimal distance? Pi is directly related to "One full turn" of units of measurement in the Sexagesimal System. Such as, (60) and (360), are both "One full turn" of a clock in terms of hours (60) = (f) and seconds = (T), as well as one full turn of a compass in units of degrees (f). (360) can be expressed in terms of Platonic Solids as a square or circle $\{360$ (D) = 360 (f)$\}$ as well as a frequency (R) possessing levity $(^L)$ in The Van Tassel Substitution. 360 can also be represented in music (T), as a C-Sharp or two C's, (C + C) related as two 180° triangles (D) added together, and 360 resonates at 360 cycles per second (f) in musical frequency. In addition, 360 is one perfect musical octave (T) up from the triangle (D) at a C-sharp (f). This representation of multiple disciplines that are very concerned with expressing "one full turn" in direct relationship to Pi transfers the formulas of geometry from a mere base 10 number theory into properties of The Sexagesimal System. In this case, especially as it relates to concerns with geometrical units of Pi (π), diameter (d), and circumference (c) being Substituted into the DiRT equation.

Remember, no matter what units we arrive at, when we use a geometrical equation they are still only units to be found within a system that belongs to a larger system, and then plugged into another related equation within that system so as to create a greater and more meaningful outcome. In this case, "In the same manner that any solution of Pi (π) is inserted into the distance (D) variable of the Dirt equation to find a circular value, so too the (C^2) value for Thoth's Theorem can also be inserted into the DiRT equation to find a distance (D) value along a linear expression. Thus, when we see a "solution" for an equation, such as Pi or Pythagorean, we know that we must take that unit, plug it into the distance variable, and link it directly to The Sexagesimal System of numbers and mythos of reasoning.)

(Let me pause to make it clear, that what we are talking about has to do with a link between numbers, all disciplines, and our new Euclidean Notion. A Notion that is revealing its Ubiquitous Vastness through the minds of all of those who have experienced its Thunderbolt of Enlightenment. Each individual, down through the ages, has seen the same thing, and expressed it through the lens of their personal perspective. Each of them encoded it in their own manner, through their own discipline, and in a way that others could find it. "In the same manner that the addition of one thing to another inevitably leads to the addition of a third thing to both, so too the absence of one thing from another inevitably leads to the absence of a third thing to all." If mathematics creates an axis mundi to translate all disciplines through, then The Substitution Method creates an axis mundi to translate all mathematical disciplines through. As this relates to the revelation of Truth, it is genuinely Vast.)

The Common Variable Triquetra Effect:

(In the same manner that The Van Tassel equation has the common denominators of 1 and 60, which express themselves ubiquitously between realms and other Substitution equations, so too (C^2) can be used as transitive common denominator variable, by overlapping each Substitution method within the model of the Triquetra. (C^2) can be used in two different locations of the DiRT equation, because of the entangled geometric-frequency relationship between (R) and (D). Because the (R) and (f) variables are Substitutable for one another, (C^2) can be employed as a transitive common denominator variable between The Van Tassel equation, the DiRT equation, and similar equations; such as Newton's Second Law of Motion. The Common Variable Triquetra Effect between these three equations allows us to solve one equation by first solving another unknown ---but commonly expressed--- variable within another equation. In this method, we can use two other equations, which have Substitutable transitive common denominator variables between three equations, to solve for unknown variables in the third equation.

Beginning with the DiRT equation, we have one postulate value of $\{(R) = (x) = (C)\}$ with a given root relationship $(\sqrt{}) (^2)$ that we write as (C^2). As that postulate value is expressed in the DiRT equation, The Van Tassel Substitution, or The Einstein Substitution, the velocity (R) of light (C^2) is at a geometric-frequency relationship between (R) and

(D), whose value and effect on other variables within the equation are directly related to the variable's root relationships. However, (C^2) Substituted for (R) or (f) is not just related to the velocity of light in each realm, because we have a second (D) postulate value $\{(x) = (C)\}$, with a given root relationship $(\sqrt{})$ $(^2)$, which is also a representation of the type of linear distance (D) over which an item is traveling--- the hypotenuse (C^2) of an (X, Y, Z) axis. Both expressions are traveling $(R) = (C^2)$ across distorted space $\{(D) = (C^2)\}$ and through the viscous nature of time (T), both have root relationships to other variables within the equation, and both can be expressed as (C^2).

The second postulate value (D) is expressed as a linear geometric variable (C^2), whose value can only be found via its relationship with other set linear values. For instance, a straight line is a line whose value is not based on its relationship to another line's value. A straight line is possessed of a set distance, or given value, which is independent of any other line's value. However, a hypotenuse is not a line with its own "personality"; its true value can only be found via its relationship to two other known values. When a photon moves through space distortions and time viscosities, the value of its hypotenuse $\{(D) = \text{represented as } (C^2) \text{ in the Pythagorean Theorem}\}$ becomes uncertain, and can only be found in relationship to the value of other known variables. Like our time surfer, who rides a wave of space distortions and time viscosities along the hypotenuse $\{(D) = (C^2)\}$ to end up in a different space or time, the line along which he is traveling is a "Relationship line", whose ultimate value is determined via a relationship to other known values. In Vastness, this is the entire purpose of The Thoth Theorem $(A^2+B^2=C^2)$, to find an unknown "distorted" value, based on its relationship to other known values--- More importantly, The Thoth Theorem expresses this value as a transitive common denominator variable, which can be moved between multiple sets of interrelated equations or realms; making it and the other equations we are working with Properties and Equations of Field Physics.

$$R = \frac{D}{T}$$

$$A^2 + B^2 = C^2$$

$$C^2 = \frac{D}{T}$$

$$R = \frac{C^2}{T}$$

If we had two known variables for (A^2) and (B^2), we could find a value for (C^2). Since (C^2) can be represented as a frequency value $\{(f) = (R)\}$ or a distance value (D), we can Substitute the solution of The Thoth Theorem (C^2) into the DiRT equation, or Van Tassel equation, so as to take the place of (f), (R) or (D). In the same manner, The Van Tassel Substitution has a common denominator of (R), (f), and (T), wherein if we solve for the (f) or (T) in either equation, we can Substitute their value into other equations to solve for other unknown variables. In this manner, should we find ourselves beginning an equation with too many unknown variables, we can Substitute transitive common denominator variable solutions from other equations to fill in the gaps of other equations, and reach a conclusion.

When we perceive the nature of transitive common denominator variables through the perspective of the ancients creating and linking common values for geometry, music, and time through a single Sexigesimal System we begin to see their Vast purpose. When we insert any three of The Substitution Methods into the model of the Triquetra, we see a set of equations that relate to and support one another, in such a manner as to create another thing that is more synergistically Vast than any one of them on their own. "In the same manner that the addition of one thing to another inevitably leads to the addition of a third thing to both, so too the absence of one thing from another inevitably leads to the absence of a third thing to all."

$$F = \frac{1}{T}$$

$$C^2 = \frac{1}{T}$$

$$f = \frac{C^2}{60}$$

$$f = \frac{C^2}{1}$$

$$R = \frac{D}{T}$$

$$R = \frac{D}{60}$$

$$R = \frac{1}{60}$$

$$C^2 = \frac{1}{60}$$

$$f = \frac{C^2}{1}$$

$$F = \frac{K}{T}$$

$$\{F = \frac{C}{T}\} = \{F = \frac{K}{T}\} = \{F = \frac{\pi}{T}\} = \{F = \frac{\text{Fractal}}{T}\}$$

$$\{F = \frac{C^2}{T}\}$$

$$R = \frac{K}{60}$$

(C^2) can potentially be a transitive common denominator variable Substitution for (R), (D), (Z), (X), (F), (K) and (1). More importantly, it can be employed to find relationships between realms.

$$(R = \frac{D}{T}) = (Z = \frac{X}{Y}) = (F = \frac{1}{T})$$

(C^2) can also be associated with the two-way door of dominion as expressed as The Bandwidth of The Construct, when it relates to the levity $(^L)$ of frequency (f), or the gravity $(^G)$ of particle (D). Thus, creating two variations of the same expression, with an $(^L)$ $(^G)$ for identification purposes.

$$C^{2(L)} = \frac{C^{2(G)}}{T}$$

When we take in all of this information with a careful ear to the associative property of entanglement---

$$C^2 = \frac{C^2}{T}$$

---we see matching Platonic Orders {(C²) as (D)} lining up with entangled Platonic Frequencies {(C²) as (R)} within any DiRT type equation. To solve this equation, only using base formulas and still absent any real numerical expressions, all we have to recall is The Van Tassel Substitution has a transitive common denominator variable of 1 and insert it into a DiRT "type" equation. For instance, 1 hour is (60min), 1 day (24hr), and 1 minute is (60 sec)).

Thus---

$$C^2 = \frac{C^2}{1}$$

Can be mathematically reduced to---

$$C^2 = C^2$$

Or---

$$C^{2L} = C^{2G}$$

This equation becomes an expression of The Bandwidth of The Construct, which is like the Einstein equation (E=MC²): wherein we are trying to describe a flip function between mass and energy. We can take one giant leap into Vastness and realize this is a mathematical expression of the entangled flip function between the two expressions of the Silver Cord (C²ᴸ), and the torus field (C²ᴳ); in all realms, the two forms of expression of White Light (C²ᴸ) and Dark Light (C²ᴳ). Thus, it is an equation that satisfies all variables, no matter their expression, and no matter their realm.

$$C^2 = C^2$$

Thus, {(C²) = (C²)} is not only a universal expression of the most foundational expression of The Design of The Construct in our ream, it is a Vast equation that transcends all realms. Unlike Einstein's equation, that expresses a greater understanding for our realm, this equation, and these Substitutions, can be used along any (X), (Y), or (Z) axes of expression; Field Physics.)

(We say, "Mass bends the space-time continuum", because we see a star appear when and where its not suppose to, and this is explained with the Einstein Rosen-Bridge Theory as the mass of the sun bending space. Yet, mass (D); which should be more correctly expressed as (K), since the empty space around the star is being effected, is only one of at least three variables (D), (R), (T) that possess any number of permutations, and we now know all three variables are profoundly Entangled. If I changed the (R) or (f) variable by four Platonic Orders, the behavior of the (D) and (T) variables must radically change in relationship to the $(^n)$ $(^L)$ $(^G)$ variables of (C^2). If I changed the time (T) or energy (E) variable, the (D), (M) and (R) (f) variables must reflect those changes. Thus, to say that mass (D) = (M) is that thing which is responsible for bending space, is to say, "The thing that is causing the effect is only the variable that our eyes can see." It is idiosyncratic to a particular lens of perspective. However, in The Way of The Path, this notion of mass causing a reaction is expressed as having a degree of The Fruit of Awareness, and seeing a New Horizon, which points to an opportunity for a bonfire of innovation, and greater understanding of all things in vastness. Not of the cause, but one of the relationships of the cause, as being determined by the relationship of The Hemisphere Effect, and the two-way door of expression of the Field.

As a whole, The Substitution Method is a profound demonstration that any one of the three variables, or their properties, can be a cause to change an effect on any of the other two variables. That which manipulates the Quantum (X) Galactic (Y) and Field continuums are all of the variables of the DiRT Equation Model, in the same manner of that which manipulates the DiRT Equation are all those variables of Quantum, Galactic, and Field Physics. Moreover, it's the patterns they produce with their related properties, which reveals the vastness of the effects. Nested Platonic Orders of space (D), frequency variations (R), and determinations of their Entangled relationships to the functions, frequencies, and viscosities of time (T) are those things, which manipulate Quantum, Galactic, and Field Physics. This is where The Van Tassel Substitution shines so brightly, because it reveals the exponential returns on frequency patterns within (wave-levity) or (particle-gravity) expressions, and the exponential returns reveal a two-way door of interference within the gravity (^{G}) of particles or levity (^{L}) of waves. To his credit, The Einstein Substitution relates The Van Tassel Effect to mass and energy, providing a common Euclidean associative property between all of these equations. This, unity is our Thunderbolt of Enlightenment, and the opportunity to step into a new realm of Vastness.

Remembering that the numbers by which our geometric and frequency relationships are defined are intrinsically linked with identical values, whether these numbers are expressed in geometric-particles or frequency-waves, we can take their common numbering patterns, plug them into The Gravity Levity Formulas, and arrive at a mathematical expression for the pull of gravity and push of levity. When we think of a wave of water splashing against another wave of water, we get an interference pattern. The colliding waves "discombobulate" the function of the waves of energy (E) within the water, and this collision of waves lowers the frequency of the wave patterns (f), which in turn lowers (E) again. This can be expressed as two different frequency (^{n}) patterns interfering with one another, lowering their frequency, as well as the potency of their property's levity (^{L}) effects. This would move waves and levity toward zero in a collapse function where particles would begin to form, add their geometric frequency relationships together, and create increasing interference patterns in the direction of gravity, by adding nesting Platonic Orders.

If Einstein was right, and all mass can be expressed as energy, and all energy can be expressed as mass, then both gravity and levity must be able to be expressed after the manner of solids as well as waves. In other words, whether we express gravity or levity as an interference pattern in terms of particles or waves, the disruption effect of an interference pattern, within geometric-frequency relationships, must be said to create a "gap" between the relationships, wherein this "void" draws products of the Field into itself within the two-way door of dominion. This difference in geometric-frequencies can just as easily be expressed as the pull of gravity as it can be expressed as the push of levity. Adding Nesting Platonic Orders into one another creates an increasing geometric-frequency gap, which moves the interference patterns in an increasing exponential direction $(^n)$ toward gravity $(^G)$. After the same equal and opposite Newtonian manner, nesting increasingly higher wave frequencies one into another can create an exponentially increasing gap, which moves in the equal and opposite direction toward levity $(^L)$.

When we add one wave to another, it creates an interference pattern that creates a void in the direction of levity. So too, when we subtract, or interfere, one wave with another, as in collision, it creates another void in the equal and opposite direction toward gravity. This second direction can be expressed as gravity within the wave function, an expression of the collapse function of the male torsion field, and the inception of interrelationships. When we add one Platonic Solid to another, it creates an interference pattern, which creates a void in the direction of gravity. So too, when we subtract, or interfere, one

Platonic Solid from another, it creates another void in the equal and opposite direction toward levity.

Levity of Platonic waves
$$Push\ (f^{2L}) = (f^{L} + f^{L})$$

Gravity of Platonic waves
$$Pull\ (f^{-L}) = (f^{L} - f^{L})$$

Gravity of Platonic Particles
$$Pull\ (G^{2G}) = (g^{G} + g^{G})$$

Levity of Platonic Particles.
$$Push\ (g^{-G}) = (g^{G} - g^{G})$$

Note how these equations form a circular function, and apply to the two-way door of The Hemisphere Effect.

The (^{L}) or (^{G}) exponent would have to be expressed as an (^{n}) or ($^{-n}$) value, since the value of the (^{L}) or (^{G}) exponents change radically, depending on the exponentially increasing returns on frequency $\{(f) = (C^2)\}$ or nested Platonic Orders $\{(D) = (C^2)\}$. This (^{n}) variable would depend on which frequencies or solids (C^2) were interfering with one another or adding to one another. These (^{n}) variables would also have to be determined by the directional flow of The Construct, in terms of collapse or uncollapse and clockwise or counterclockwise directional flow of The Hemisphere Effect.

Both gravity and levity can be expressed as interference patterns, in relationship to the function of time, when the squared velocity of time changes by at least one geometric-frequency relationship. This can be expressed as enough of a frequency change, such that the frequency alters its geometric relationship in a two-way door of expression. For instance, this relationship variable can be as small as one geometric-frequency change of 180 (180 triangle = 180 cycles per second) moving to 360 (square or circle = 360 cycles per second). When a frequency pattern is changed along The Bandwidth of The Construct by the collapse function, such that it resonates at a new geometric-frequency relationship, it interrupts, or otherwise disturbs the even patterns in space (D) and time $\{(f) = (R)\}$, so as to cause an interference pattern. This "interference" creates a void or gap along The Bandwidth of The Construct at that space-time-velocity "location". We see this disturbance distort the "non-solid" elasticity's of space around a star (K), and say, "That star is causing 'K'!", when it is actually the direction of interruption of the (f) or (D) variable moving in a clockwise or counterclockwise direction around the DiRT equation. Moreover, part of the proof that the interruption is the cause, is that (K) is having just as much an effect on the nothingness of the elasticity's of space, as its having on the solid, liquid, or gas expression of matter and energy in the form of a star/planet, as well as a photon (^{n}), which happens to be surfed (f^2) past the interruption. In other words, "the gap" is effecting all three variables despite their condition of expression, or location within an equation.

This gap pulls or pushes along the whole of The Bandwidth of The Construct according to the given direction of the two-way door of expression. This void is a two-way door, which pulls or pushes according to the direction of expression of The Construct. The direction of expression is expressed as a counterclockwise or clockwise direction of interruption. In other words, the counterclockwise female end of the torus field creates an acceleration gap (^{L}); expressed as the cause or property of uncollapse, and potential for acceleration. In other words, the clockwise male end of the torus field creates a deceleration gap (^{G}); expressed as the cause or property of collapse. This can be expressed as, real velocity minus inhibitions of interrelations, where real velocity is the absence of inhibitive-gaps (^{G}) (John Glenn (^{L})), as opposed to a force, such as electromagnetism (D), that impregnates and levitates. However, frequency is a kind of force, thus levity, expressed as an exponentially increasing frequency, is that which removes the interference patters in the gaps that cause gravity, not by removing some mystical force impregnating matter, but by changing the direction of the flow in the interference gaps, or direction of expression of The Construct.

Increasing gravity means increasing gaps in a clockwise flow by nesting Platonic Orders. If each nest of a Platonic Solid creates another gap, which exponentially increases effects of gravity, the equal and opposite must also be true. In the same manner that nesting Platonic Orders exponentially increases gaps in the direction of gravity, we can nest frequency orders, so as to exponentially reverse the flow of gravity-gaps in a counterclockwise direction, and move the gaps toward levitation effects. Theoretically, this could look like turning on speakers at 180 cycles per second, and then adding other speakers at 360 cycles per second. Because all waves would be traveling in the same direction, like ocean waves catching up to one another, the effect would be a total of 540. We can continue to repeat this through the Platonic Order of related frequencies 720, 1,080, 2,160 1,440 3,600, and 6,480, and each time get an exponential return on levity effects in the gaps.

In other words, you know that strange hum given off by some UFO's? Yes, that is them using interference patterns for lift (T), levity (f), and propulsion (D). But, there's so much more to this, because remember, the higher the frequency, the faster you go, and the faster you go (R) or (f), the more you can move into an adjacent realm (Z). The more you move into a uniform accelerated (f) » (Z) realm, the easier it is to manipulate or potentialize energy and mass via conscious intent across the continuum. It's all Entangled... A Unified Field Theory.)

(The geometric shape, its subsequent harmony, and its duration of travel are intrinsically linked with the frequency (R), geometry (D), and time (T) at which any variable within the equation is equally effected. In other words, if we find a velocity anomaly, we will equally find anomalies within the manner at which time moves, space expresses itself, or frequency flows in the collapse uncollapse function. This can be seen as--- the paths, patterns, and programs that White and Dark Light follow are fabricated by, via the methods by which we use geometry, music, and frequency as One, so as to bend the space-time continuum, or change products of the Field so as to assail a given space-time continuum. In other words, we either geometrically bend space and alter the frequency patterns of time, so as to travel (R) along the Galactic Physics axis (Y), or we change the properties of a product of the Field, such that the product of the Field assails the space-time continuum (Y), moves toward the Field into a higher realm, or makes the jump, and travels (R) along the Silver Cord (Z) axis of Field Physics.

From here on, no longer does science "only" require the aggregation of mass of the Einstein-Rosen Bridge to define a bend in space and time. In the same manner that two Entangled particles, accelerating toward one another in uniform velocity, posses the dominion of Field

Properties that transform average photons from being surfed by space and time to manipulating space and time; due to radical changes in the $\{(R) = (f)\}$ variable. So too, when we use geometry in accord with its corresponding frequency and music, space bends, time changes viscosity, and overall velocity accelerates or decelerates, while simultaneously changing the properties of the products of the Field. Moreover, each one changes of their own accord in response to the Entanglement function of the DiRT Equation, and each portion of each Substitution Method.

At this point we have to pause, and ask ourselves if what Albert Einstein and his collogues were looking at was really the result of mass distorting space, so as to make a star appear when and where it shouldn't. We now know it could have equally been the result of the geometry of an object and its intrinsically related frequency patterns manipulating the function of space and velocity of time, so as to cause the star behind the sun, which they were looking at, to appear both "when (T) and where (D)" it was not supposed to be. Within these Substitution Methods, lies a peek into a more complete answer, "when and where", since we know all values and substitutions of the DiRT equation are intrinsically Entangled to one another, at every level of understanding, and through every language of expression.

Once again, why does it have to be all three? "In the same manner that the addition of one thing to another inevitably leads to the addition of a third thing to both, so too the absence of one thing from another inevitably leads to the absence of a third thing to all." Like The Triquetra of The DiRT Equation, or The Triquetra of The Substitution Method (X, Y, Z), this concept is universally transitive over many horizons of understanding, we cannot change one variable without effecting all the others; You cannot help but effect Love and Truth, if you leave out Virtue. Thus, not only must Einstein's observation pertain to time and space, but it must also pertain to the frequency variable by which the sun's interference patterns disrupt the velocity of time. Above this, we must evoke any Field Physics that change the overall observation, because our realm is a nested realm under the dominion of a higher realm.

We end at the beginning with our initial question... What is holding Dr. Moon's proton-particles apart from one another in infinitesimal smallness at predetermined distances, as well as adhering them together at predetermined distances? All the while, changing the weight relationships with different nested Orders of Platonic Solids or geometric frequency waves? If we look at the Platonic Order along the Quantum Physics (X) axis, as it relates to The Fractal Substitution Method, and two-way door of interference patterns $(^{L, G})$, we can see that particles are forming interruption-relationships which equally repel and attract one another in accord with their geometric-frequency relationships with the format-model of the DiRT Equation.

This is just as true for Kepler's solar system models in another direction of vastness (Y). His models are a function of collapse along the Galactic (Y) axis, which has a push-pull relationship between planets, as they relate to their geometric-frequency relationships, and their related velocities, which are Entangled in the format-model of the DiRT equation. We tie Moon and Kepler together with Einstein, wherein Einstein stipulates that all properties of mass and energy can be found in a two-way door of expression within both. This is a method by which we must be able to explain gravity and levity within the mass of a particle as well as within the energy of a wave.

Levity of Platonic Waves
$$Push\ (f^{2L}) = (f^L + f^L)$$

Gravity of Platonic Waves
$$Pull\ (f^{-L}) = (f^L - f^L)$$

Gravity of Platonic Particles
$$Pull\ (g^{2G}) = (g^G + g^G)$$

Levity of Platonic Particles
$$Push\ (g^{-G}) = (g^G - g^G)$$

We can assail a Vast New Horizon of understanding, and stipulate that in eternal vastness along the (Z) axis of nesting layers of Field Physics, this same functional relationship of geometric-frequencies of the two-way door of interruption relationships, is yet occurring in and between higher and lower realms. Moreover, we can stipulate that gravity and levity, expressed as geometric-frequency interruptions, are not products of any single realm (Y). The geometric-frequency relationships are a product of Field Physics; they are ubiquitous relationships that are holding all realms neatly in place within their nested orders, via even push-pull geometric-frequency patterns. Like so many things not listed here, suddenly we realize that The Program of The Architect, Intellect, Consciousness, and Intelligence are not properties of Galactic Physics, but are Properties of the model of Unified Field Physics™.)

(Relating all of this knowledge as One back to Morphic Field Generators; the base questions we're asking in this small excerpt are; "What is The Golden Ratio, Fibonacci Spiral, or the base Code for The Program of The Architect in any given realm? Depending which number we use as our divisor, is the solution always 1.618 or .618? Are Codes of The Program different in adjacent realms? Like the common denominator in The Van Tassel Substitution, is The Program of The Architect identical in each realm? Moreover, what is the significance of these questions? Like leap froging Faith and Knowledge, the immediate significance is to see over the next horizon.

Noting first, that we can substitute radius (r) for The Program of The Architect (K), our first clue is found on page 61, where we realize that we can divide any given value of The Program inversely against an adjacent value of The Program, and still arrive at .618 or 1.618 (« »). In other words, no matter where we are in the Code or spiral, each quarter turn value of the radius (r) can be inversely divided against its adjacent quarter turn (r). Thus, whatever the radius (r) value is for every quarter spiral of a torsion field in any nested realm, one can equally and inversely divide those numbers against one another to arrive at 1.618 or .618 respectively.

Even though the radius of a given torsion field in each realm may be larger than a nested torsion field in a nested realm, the radius (r), in relationship to their own torsion field is always proportionate. Thus, where one torsion field might have a radius of 5, at that same location in an exterior realm, the outer torsion field will have a radius (r) of 8; and The Architect (K) can be found between them. Again, at the same location in the torsion field, that field's exterior torus field will be 13 (r), and once again (K) can be found between them. Once again, this not only gives us The Program of The Architect in each realm, but like so many other things, it tells us The Program of

The Architect is not a function of Galactic Physics as much as it is a Property of Field Physics. Above this, it gives us a direct relationship of the gap of gravity and levity as directly relatatable to The Program of The Architect (K).

In the same manner that some of the properties that we experience are not properties of our realm, so too properties of Morphogenic Fields are Field Properties. In other words, Morphogenic Fields populate non-locally. In other words, Morphic Field Generators populate non-locally. When you construct a Pyramid Mandala you not only affect the Field in that area, you populate that effect into other realms non-locally. Like producing an unlimited number of "Thought balls", where an idea is nested inside a torus field, the message will multiply, resonate, and seek vastness according to the two-way door of (K) along the (Z) axis through all (X), (Y), or (Z) realms.

When you use Entanglement Theory to build these Morphic Field Generators in pluralistic locations, you unite the Field Generators and the space-time continuums of the pluralistic locations. For instance, let us say we make a Morphic Field Generator in Kansas and Washington State, and we use Entanglement Theory and Remote Viewing to unite them. Whatever ideograms or messages we encase within them will not only populate that message on the Field in that area, but it will populate that message along Ley Lines between them, and pass on that message ad infanitum around the global grid; in a method reminiscent of The Hundredth Monkey Theory. However, Vastness does not stop there. Your Morphic Field Generator begins to connect with all other torsion fields, flip through silver cords reaching out to the vastness of other torus fields. Simply put, it multiplies in a way that makes our current understanding of vastness appear quite limited.)

The Architect of Time

(To understand this section, we have to amalgamate the models of the torus field and silver cord as one singular model. To picture it, think of a silver cord flowing into the "bowel" of half of a torus field in one direction, and then think of an upside down "bowel" of half of a torus field flowing into a silver cord in the equal and opposite direction. Moreover, we have to Entangle the "torus field silver cord" relationship to the nested function of realms, as well as take into account the dual sides of the Field for each realm$_{xy}$. Now we have many bowels nested within bowels where each bowel represents a realm, and each silver cord connects one realm to the other.

Moving from the Field, the silver cord moves along the (Z) axis to connect with the torus field at its central ring. Because the central ring of a torus field is still in a degree of Superposition, we are yet moving through Field Physics along the (Z) axis. The Flip Function of the silver cord, attaching to the central ring of the torus field, turns the silver cord into its inverse expression of a torus field; this is our first silver cord moving into the bowel of a Southern Hemisphere. The torus field then goes through the dual expression of The Hemisphere Effect, moving along the (Y) axis, back to the central ring (Z) where the Flip Function occurs again, and the expression goes back to being a silver cord. This is our second upside down bowel that moves into a silver cord, which moves toward the next exterior or interior bowel.

While we might think this takes us full circle in the model, it only stipulates one round of the function of a nested model, which has at least five or more Platonic Orders. If we began this process at an exterior realm, whose torus field expresses itself at a geometrical-frequency relationship of (6,480), we could say that time flows at a $\{(f) = (6,480^2) = (C^2)\}$, its geometrical expression would be a dodecahedron at (6,480) (D), and its photonic expressions (D) would be surfed at $\{(6,480^2) = (C^2)\}$. The silver cord would move into this (6,480) dodecahedral realm from what a geometrical-frequency of (6,480) would consider its degree of Superposition°. It would move through The Flip Function, through The Hemisphere Effect, and toward the next lower realm, whose geometrical-frequency is (3,600), Icosahedron. It should be stipulated here, that the Flip Function also allows the movement of time and space to be flipped to the other side of the Field along the (Z) axis, such that the silver cord expresses itself in an inverse dodecahedral realm of (6,480), as opposed to a movement toward a more nested Icosahedra realm of (3,600).

From (6,480) to a probable geometric-frequency relationship of absolute zero, the expression goes through the geometric-frequency Platonic Order. Each one nested within the other, and each one with an equivalent push-pull relationship holding each nested realm firmly in place. However, while Inflation can move through the central ring in a two-way door of dominion, there is no possibility of distortions between nested realms, as there is between similarly expressed realms. This is because each geometric-frequency pattern holds the next geometric-frequency pattern in place with a constant push-pull relationship, such that any distortion is not probable. Distortions between realms tend to go from one side of a realm to another, which possesses the same geometrical-frequency relationship.

When we relate these functions of nested realms (D) with the movement of time (T) through those realms, we see an identical process of flow through the silver cord torus field. Our time (T) originates from what we would call "The future of a higher realm", time moves into our realm of the here (D) and now (T) from the higher realm, and time passes into a lower realm into the yesterday of our yesteryear. In this movement, time always carries the potential to return to the Field at any step along the way, or flip to an equal and opposite realm along the $\{(Z) = (C^2)\}$ axis.)

(As a product of The Field, time is expressed along The Bandwidth of The Construct, and as such, can take on any property of The Construct. Time can express itself as a solid, fluid, or gas $\{(D) = (C^2)\}$ within the models of The Construct. In other words, in the equations below, time, espressed as a varriant of (C^2), can express itself as (Q), (R), (Y), or (X) like any other product of The Field.

$$A + B = X \qquad\qquad A + B = C^2$$
$$C + D = Y \qquad\qquad C + D = C^2$$
$$A + D = Q \qquad\qquad A + D = C^2$$
$$B + C = R \qquad\qquad B + C = C^2$$

One of the first functions of The Construct is the silver cord, wherein space and time express themselves as a wave of potentials in a gas like expression of a wave. It is in this state of Superposition that White and Dark Light pass on their properties of Entanglement to the products of space (D) and time (f). Thus, not only causing an associative property of entanglement between space and time, but also between the (R) and (D) variables.

Given The Flip Function of 90°, when White and Dark Light make the jump at the central ring of a torus field, space and time express themselves within the model of the torus field. Uniform deceleration, initiated by the collapse function, and created by the interruption pattern within the male torsion field $(^G)$, introduces properties of interrelations $(^G)$, and space and time move from the wave expression of Superposition (Z) toward a fluid condition of realm expression (Y). This fluidity function can be expressed as a malleable condition of the here (D) and now (T), where the frequency of time (f) surfs ([n]) particles of the Field (D) by a factor of its frequency squared.

This is where each expression of a realm, and its time (T) are expressed as--- The frequency of time (f) (6,480) = (C) surfing products of that realm by its frequency $(6,480^2)$ = (C^2) squared. The frequency of time (f) $(3,600^2)$ surfing products of that realm by its frequency $(3,600^2)$ = (C^2) squared. The frequency of time (f) (1,440) surfing products of that realm by its frequency $(1,440^2)$ = (C^2) squared. The frequency of time (f) (2,160) surfing products of that realm by its frequency $(2,160^2)$ = (C^2) squared. The frequency of time (f) (720) surfing products of that realm by its frequency (720^2) = (C^2) squared, expressed as (T) entangled » in geometric (D) frequency (f) relationships with velocity (R). Allowing another method of solving our "$\{(C^2) = (C^2)\}$" equation, which reaches the same conclusion. However, because time has a range of solid, liquid, and gas expressions, it can carry the ([G]) or ([L]) of gravity or levity. This not only allows (T) to be expressed as (C^2), but it also allows the flip function to appear yet again.

$$C^2 = \frac{C^2}{C^2}$$

$$C^2 = \frac{C^{2L}}{C^{2G}}$$

$$C^2 = \frac{C^{2G}}{C^{2L}}$$

$$C^2 = C^2$$

(If I were some manner of space-time traveler, who carried some manner of "Tricorder device", which calculated my coordinates along any (X), (Y), or (Z) axis, then this formula---

$$C^2 = \frac{C^2}{C^2}$$

---would be the base equation of its program. The Master Number would be its numerical range of expression $\{(C^{2L}) = \{195,955,200,000,000\} = (C^{2G})\}$. Moreover, each Sexigesimal expression would be the inputs to find a common solution.)

From the outer realm to the inner most realm, the nature of time flips back and forth from a gas to a fluid. The uniform acceleration of the female torus field moves the fluidity of time back toward its wave-like state as it accelerates time into the central ring, thus allowing it to be inserted into a silver cord. This silver cord once again moves into a more nested realm, executes the 90° Flip function, expresses itself as a torus field, decelerates, interrelates, and time becomes fluid like. It then accelerates again into the female torsion field, becomes a gas like wave in a silver cord, and moves to the next nested realm. With each descending geometrical-frequency relationship, the viscosity of time (f) becomes ever more viscous, ever more stiff, and flowing at an ever-slower "thicker" pace. We can see this as a movement toward greater densities, as in the value of (K), or we can observe this as a movement toward a solid, as in interruptions $(^{G,L})$.

If we look at time in its absolute collapsed pattern at $\{$(zero (f^n)) (before one $(^G)$ = (the moment between a wave and a particle)$\}$, it would appear to us as a solid, without movement, and possessed a property of a degree of impediment of movement through it. However, according to the interference patterns (zero f) waves (^{G}) are only the beginning of nested Platonic Orders in terms of solids. While we might think of this as the removal of levity (^{L}), the direction of descending Platonic Orders was the interference pattern of gravity (^{G}) within the wave function, which was moving the whole operation through the entire bandwidth of the nested order---. "Gravity" (^{G}), or an interference pattern that moves through the whole bandwidth of the Platonic Order, is that which causes a movement into greater degrees of nested orders. Therefore, what we're talking about is more of a solidification process of time, whether expressed as a wave or solid, wherein time is increasingly turned into a solid via increasing expressions of (C^2) of interference patterns. However, in a Newtonian equal and opposite direction, the model of the torus field, and levity (^{L}), reverses the descent through the nested Platonic Order, and causes ascension through $\{(D) = (C^2) = (R)\}$ the bandwidth of The Construct. In the same manner that the two-way door is a universal expression of The Construct, so too time can reverse its flow, and move back to an increasingly inviscid state.

Gravity of Platonic waves

$$Pull\ (f^{-L}) = (f^L - f^L)$$

Gravity of Platonic Particles

$$Pull\ (G^{2G}) = (g^G + g^G)$$

Levity of Platonic Particles

$$Push\ (g^{-G}) = (g^G - g^G)$$

Levity of Platonic wave

$$Push\ (f^{2L}) = (f^L + f^L)$$

Can you see the circular nature of the equations?

Once again, not all of these equations are necessary to express, that "the gap" in the direction of collapse, or gravity (^{G}), exists within waves, so long as those waves are in a movement toward expression, interrelations, or collapse. Moreover, that "the gap" in the direction of uncollapse, or levity (^{L}), exists within solids as well as waves along the entire bandwidth of The Construct, so long as those solids or waves are in a movement toward uncollapse or Field Potential. Above this, it can be expressed as (C^2) in all locations of The Substitution Method.)

(In these nested orders, where time increasingly nests into ever more viscous states, and then increasingly solidifies in nested Platonic Orders--- space is moving right along with time. Space is also becoming "thicker" or "thinner", "elastic or rigid", in densities according to the ascending or descending value of The Program of The Architect (K)--- within the nested order of geometric (^{G}) frequency (^{L}) relationships. The Architect in a realm of (6,480) (f) is going to function with more efficiently, exceeding 255%, since that variable is only a reflection of that realm's comparison with ours. There will be less space density to distort, and less resistance of the (^{G}) interference patterns to foil the functions of (E) or (M), which are amplified by the growing (^{n}) variable of (C^2). Each realm's Architect, which represents itself in relationship with the geometric-frequency patterns that it's found in, will ascemble products of that realm in a manner consistant with their increased function. For instance, in our realm we know that we glow by looking at ourselves through thermographs and Kirlian photography. A being from a higher dimension, where light is functioning at a higher level of expression, would appear to us to "glow" more "profusely", because the light in its realm is functioning at a greater capacity. That should answer a few questions.

All realms exist in a nested pattern $\{(C^{2L}) = \{195,955,200,000,000\} = (C^{2G})\}$. Each realm is equally separated by the geometric frequency relationship, in terms of space and time. The geometric frequency controls the push-pull of levity and gravity, which holds each realm (D) in an intelligent nested order. While the (f) = (R) variable spreads all realms out in flow patterns of time, each one separated by the changing viscous nature of time (f). All realms take up the same space (D) as we do, thus the idea of nested bowels and nested silver cords that connect, but the higher frequencies exist in our future, while the more nested space times exist in our past. They all reside in the same nested location (D) within the models of the torus field and silver cord, but are uniformly "spread out" via the frequencies in time. This uniformity of being spread out in time is part of what allows Inflation Theory to function as it does.)

(The camera of time photographs our realm at (432) frames per second, in the same manner that the camera of time records other realms at (6,480) frames per second or (1,440) fps; all relative to their time (f) patterns. White and Dark Light, in the form of a torus field, in any given galactic expression, are the "devices" upon which "events" are recorded. These recorded events are moved into the Superposition of Field Potential by silver cords, and thereby are recorded onto The Field (see also; Morphic Field Generators populating nonlocally).)

(In each realm there is an (X), (Y), and (Z) axis. There is a Fractal Zoom (X) into infinitesimal smallness within the dodecahedral realms of (6,480) (f), in the same manner that there is a Fractal Zoom into infinitesimal smallness in both icosahedra realms of (3,600) (^{L}) (^{G}). There is a Galactic (Y) distance rate variable, and Flexible DiRT Equation across eternal vastness in the octahedral realm of (1,440) (f), in the same manner there is the same Galactic movement in eternal vastness in the cubed realms of (2,160) (f) (^{L})(^{G}). In each realm there is an (E=MC^2) Substitution, which modifies the expression of its realm by the two-way door of interruption patterns (^{L})(^{G}), whereby the (C^2) variable modifies the (E) and (M) variables with its particular geometric-frequency relationship. The (Z) axis is not just a movement toward Superposition or Field Potential; silver cords are consistent heartbeat links between all realms. The (Z) axis is the only axis that goes between all realms. Whereas, (D), (X), and (Y) axes can be expressed as a movement within any realm.)

(If we look at mixing The Van Tassel and Einstein Substitutions, we see a method by which we can assail all our geometric-frequency relationships by inserting The Van Tassel Substitution into The Einstein Substitution. When we use torsion fields in accord with exponentially increasing frequencies of time---

$$(C^4) = (C^2 + C^2)$$

$$(f^{2L}) = (f^L + f^L)$$

---- This (R) variable has a profound effect on the particles (M) and energy (E) of which we are composed. We move out of this realm's (C^2) (432^2) expression relationships, we make The Jump, and move along the (Z) axis of Field Physics. In this manner, we begin moving forward or backward in time in relationship to the (f) variable along the (Z) axis.)

(Time travel has to do with moving into another realm (D), via the (f) function of (R) variable along the (Z) axis, not in a higher or lower realm, but as in the flip function of an equal and opposite realm, wherein The Hemisphere Effect is flipped. If we move into a high or low enough realm, time will be seen to accelerate into the future, or drawn in reverse into the past respectively. How fast, and how far are determined by the nested order of Platonic Solids of our (f) variable and (Z) axis. When we've gone as far in time as we desire, we simply change our frequency variable and return to the realm desired.

However, to truly appear to overcome time travel challenges, we must also appear to move in space as well as time. Thus, while we are using our (f) variable to move into a higher or lower realm, we would also use other geometric substitutions such as The Hypotenuse (C^2) Substitution of the Flexible DiRT Equation, to travel in the space of a different realm$_2$ as well as surf in the time of that realm. Thus, The Substitution Method is translatable in each realm as Quantum Fractal movements into infinitesimal smallness within each nested Platonic Order of each realm. Thus, Galactic movement across space-time in a higher realm is possible along the (Y) or (D) axis within each realm. In addition, the unifying variables are the (Z) or (f) variables, which allow us to move up or down between realms as well as forward or backward in time.)

(The Field does not express products of The Field outside of nested boundaries, only within the active portions of The Field, or within torus fields, and silver cords. Thus, we can think of String Theory as an observation of infinitesimally small or eternally vast silver cords in an expression along a given (X), (Y), or (Z) axis. This answers a lot of questions, such as why products of the field "make the jump" between the strings in String Theory, as opposed to behaving as we think they should, and "move through" the space between the infinitesimally small silver cords. It is the entanglement function between the silver cord and torus field, which causes the flip and jump function to occur at every level of understanding, so of course products of The Field "skip" the space where The Field is not in a state of expression. In other words, wherein The Field is in Absolute Superposition of Absolute Inactivity, products of The Field must flip, jump, or "ride the lightning" to an expression of The Field along a (Z) axis of expression. It is at this location within the model of Field Physics that the conditional Superposition of String Theory can collapse the wave function into an expression of products of The Field along an (X), (Y), or (Z) axis. While one might think of "the flip or jump" as space, time, or dimensional travel, one might also think of this as, "Just the way things work" in Field Physics (Z).)

(If you can see this entire book as One "As above, so below" model of Vastness, then you might come to realize The Path of The Three Great Quests, and our initiation of The Thunderbolt of Enlightenment via The Chamber of Initiation leads us to the singularity of The Unified Field Theory™. In any given form or Method of Substitution, The Unified field Theory, is a base of three variables. The meaning of the Universe, in all its Vastness, could be mathematically reduced to and expressed as three, "The Triple Relationship". Therefore, The Unified Field Theory could also be reduced to the interrelationship of three. Independent of what the variables represent, The Unified Field Theory is three in one, and one in three. The new Euclidean Common Notion of one effecting two, two effecting one, and three effecting one or two. There is no effect on one, which does not affect all three.

The Unified Field means that whatever three variables you put in, they affect one another synergistically. This could be as simple as saying that love effects truth, which effects virtue. This could be as simple as saying that one effects two, effects three, causing a synergistic effect to five (K). This could be as simple as saying that distance effects rate effects time--- in a clockwise or counterclockwise circle. This could also be as complex as The Substitution Triquetra of Transitive Formulas. The Unified Field Theory is stipulated in terms of variable of three as One. This is not only the Mathematical Unified Field Theory, which expresses itself universally; it is also a diversified Unified Field Theory, which expresses itself through all forms of disciplines and expressions.)

(And here I stand on the precipice of Vastness, staring teary eyed into the magnificence of a sparkling universe, as it challenges my youth and inexperience to comprehend the immensities of such an eternal splendor. Having valiantly dove off the precipice of vastness, plunged headlong into the abyss below, and gleefully swam in the eternities of an ever diverse oceanic universe--- I embrace seeing life with new eyes, I understand the wisdom of tranquility within the throes of a violent storm, and I realize the illusive Vastness that yet goes unseen. The difference in perspectives that lies between the student and master are not as important as the journey that lies between them. Truly, there is greater vastness yet to be had.)

(As I look around our world today, it has become painfully apparent that our technology has surpassed our humanity, and we're unwittingly leaving our humanity behind in favor of that technology. But then I think of The Source Field and The Source from which it emanates, and my reasoning is rejuvenated with the hope that there will once again come an epoch for mankind when our humanity will catch up with our technology, and our technology will only be used humanely. This will be an era when The Source will be the origin of our humanity, and The Source Field will be the root of our technology. The Journey of The Path is a pilgrimage to reconnect with The Source, a banquet of a thousand horizons, which molds our perspectives toward vastness, and our connections thoughts and actions toward Virtuous Knowledge, Truthful Understanding, and Compassionate Wisdom. The Three Great Quests are the swinging hammer and sparking anvil of technology, which forges the new paradigms of tomorrow in the refining fires of The Chamber of Initiation. Three as One, they're a movement into a condition where the condition itself is the point, the reward, and transformative elixir of endless possibilities all rolled into one glorious package. They reincarnate us out of the ashes of yesterday, transform us in The Egg of Life of today, and move us over a New Horizon into the full potential of The Phoenix of tomorrow.)

Authors of Truth

(Where you begin and where you end on The Path of The Three Great Quests is not nearly as important as the journey that you've just taken. In this moment, the disciple's heart is full of fertile seeds just waiting to sprout. The mantra of the teacher, "Cultivate and Multiply The Light", has been the soil in which the student's Fruit of Awareness has taken root. But remember, even the best Master can impart only a fraction of the teaching. Thus, even though this teacher sits calmly with patience, shares The Light of Compassion with joy, and attends wisely his loan of an apprentice with the fidelity of honor--- I solemnly remind you of that flavor that we both know so well, "It's only through the devotion, practice, and virtue of the student that the dormant glory of their own blossom springs valiantly from the mire. It is only in The Middle Way of The Path that they come to bear The Light of Knowledge, step Valiantly through the Three Chambers of Initiation, and return with The Fruit of Light.)

(Hail Thoth, Architect of Truth. Give my students words of Power that when they speak the life of a man they may give his story meaning. They stand before the masters who know the histories of the dead, who decide what tails to hear again, who judge the books of lives as either full or empty. Hail Thoth! Architect of Truth! Give my students words of Power that they may complete their story and begin life anew. My disciples, who are themselves, Divine Intelligences, and Authors of Truth. And when their story is written, and the end is good, and the soul of the master is perfected, with a shout they are lifted into heaven.)

("It's not the critic who counts; not the individual who points out how the strong man stumbles, or where the doer of deeds could've done them better. The credit belongs to the one who is actually in the arena of life, whose face is marred by dust, sweat, blood, and wide streaks of tears that cut paths down his weary cheeks. It is the one who strives valiantly, the one who errs, and comes up short again and again and again that counts.

There is no effort without error, neither is their success without shortcomings. Thus, it is he who actually strives to do the deed, he who knows the great enthusiasm, and the one who understands the great devotion. It is the hero who spends himself in a worthy cause. He, who at best knows, in the end, the triumph of high achievement, and who at worst, if he should fail, at least he fails while daring greatly.

And by virtue of his Valiance, and justified by his enduring vigilance, even if he should fall into an unmarked grave, his place shall never be with those hollow and timid souls who know neither victory nor defeat, gain or loss, love or hate. And by the decree of the Gods, and declarations of the Angels, his name will be chiseled in stone forever after. From his heel to his leg, from his backbone, to his dreams crackling inside the dark cave of his skull, The Valkyries will come for him, and the cheering throngs of Valhalla will welcome him home. They will recite his story again and again, and the little children will play his game of life at his feet. He shall never die; those whom he strove so valiantly for will carry his name, sing his story, glorify his life, and honor his great accomplishments into The Vastness of Eternity.)

Let it be said that he lived in struggle, but made the jump in triumph. This labor of enduring vigilance is dedicated to Nikola Tesla. The Source Field is a Field of Intelligence. Like The Source, The Field cannot be shackled or denied to anyone. It is ours at the drop of a hat with focused arithmetic intent. Therefore, The Future is Ours!

Shine as a Light among the children of men
A Son of The Light
A Fire among men

"Multiply The Light"

≈≈≈≈≈≈≈≈≈≈≈≈≈≈≈≈≈≈≈≈≈≈≈≈≈≈≈≈≈≈≈≈≈≈≈≈≈≈≈

This is The Way of The Path

Richard Brian

Printed in the United States
By Bookmasters